SHAKESPEARE
AND ELIZABETHAN
POPULAR CULTURE

THE ARDEN SHAKESPEARE

THE ARDEN CRITICAL COMPANIONS

GENERAL EDITORS

Andrew Hadfield and Paul Hammond

ADVISORY BOARD

MacDonald P. Jackson   *Katherine Duncan-Jones*   *David Scott Kastan*
Patricia Parker   *Lois Potter*   *Phyllis Rackin*   *Bruce R. Smith*
Brian Vickers   *Blair Worden*

Shakespeare and Comedy   *Robert Maslen*
Shakespeare and Renaissance Europe   *ed. Andrew Hadfield and*
Paul Hammond
Shakespeare and Music   *David Lindley*
Shakespeare and Renaissance Politics   *Andrew Hadfield*
Shakespeare and the Victorians   *Adrian Poole*

Forthcoming

Shakespeare and His Acting Company   Tom Lockwood
Shakespeare and His Texts   Scott McMillan
Shakespeare and Language   *Jonathan Hope*
Shakespeare and the Law   *Andrew Zurcher*
Shakespeare and Religion   *Alison Shell*

THE ARDEN CRITICAL COMPANIONS

SHAKESPEARE
AND ELIZABETHAN
POPULAR CULTURE

Edited by
STUART GILLESPIE and NEIL RHODES

The general editors of the Arden Shakespeare have been
W.J Craig and R.H. Case (first series 1899-1944)
Una Ellis-Fermor, Harold F. Brooks, Harold Jenkins and
Brian Morris (second series 1946-82)

Present general editors (third series)
Richard Proudfoot, Ann Thompson, David Scott Kastan and H.R. Woudhuysen

This edition of *Shakespeare and Elizabethan Popular Culture*, first published 2006 by
the Arden Shakespeare

Introduction © 2006 Stuart Gillespie and Neil Rhodes,
remainder © 2006 Cengage Learning

Visit the Arden website at **www.ardenshakespeare.com.**
For your lifelong learning solutions, visit **www.cengage.co.uk**

Printed by TJI Digital, Padstow, UK

Arden Shakespeare is an imprint of Cengage Learning

Cengage Learning, High Holborn House, 50-51 Bedford Row, London WC1R 4LR

Cengage Learning products are represented in Canada by Nelson Education, Ltd.

For product information and technology assistance, contact
emea.info@cengage.com.

For permission to use material from this text or product, and for
permission queries, email Clsuk.permissions@cengage.com

ISBN 978-1-90427-168-0 (hbk)
NPN 3 4 5 6 7 8 9 10 – 10 09 08

CONTENTS

NOTES ON CONTRIBUTORS   vii
LIST OF ABBREVIATIONS   ix
LIST OF ILLUSTRATIONS   xi

Introduction
Shakespeare and Elizabethan Popular Culture   1
Stuart Gillespie and Neil Rhodes

Chapter One
Shakespeare and the Mystery Plays   18
Helen Cooper

Chapter Two
Shakespeare and Popular Festivity   42
Leah S. Marcus

Chapter Three
Shakespeare's Clowns   67
Alex Davis

Chapter Four
Shakespeare and Popular Romance   92
Helen Moore

Chapter Five
Shakespeare and Elizabethan Popular Fiction   112
David Margolies

Chapter Six
Shakespeare, Ghosts and Popular Folklore   136
Diane Purkiss

Chapter Seven
Shakespeare's Sayings   155
Neil Rhodes

Chapter Eight
Shakespeare and Popular Song   174
Stuart Gillespie

Chapter Nine
Shakespeare's Residuals:
The Circulation of Ballads in Cultural Memory   193
Bruce R. Smith

NOTES   219
SELECT BIBLIOGRAPHY   247
INDEX   251

NOTES ON CONTRIBUTORS

Helen Cooper is Professor of Medieval and Renaissance English at Cambridge University. In addition to books on Chaucer and late medieval literature, she is the author of *Pastoral: Mediaeval into Renaissance* (1977) and most recently *The English Romance in Time: Transforming Motifs from Geoffrey of Monmouth to the Death of Shakespeare* (2004).

Alex Davis is a lecturer in the School of English at the University of St Andrews. He is the author of *Chivalry and Romance in the English Renaissance* (2003).

Stuart Gillespie is Reader in English Literature at the University of Glasgow. He is the author of *Shakespeare's Books: A Dictionary of Shakespeare Sources* (2001), editor of the journal *Translation and Literature*, joint general editor of *The Oxford History of Literary Translation in English* (2005–) and co-editor of *The Cambridge Companion to Lucretius* (forthcoming).

Leah S. Marcus teaches English at Vanderbilt University. Her books include *Childhood and Cultural Despair* (1978), *The Politics of Mirth* (1986), *Puzzling Shakespeare* (1988), *Unediting the Renaissance* (1996) and (co-edited with Janel Mueller and Mary Beth Rose) a two-volume edition of the writings of Elizabeth I. She has just completed a Norton Critical Edition of *The Merchant of Venice*, and is currently working on an Arden edition of Webster's *Duchess of Malfi*.

David Margolies is Reader in English at Goldsmiths College, London. As well as essays on Shakespeare and Elizabethan fiction, his publications include *Novel and Society in Elizabethan England* (1985) *Monsters of the Deep: Social Dissolution in Shakespeare's Tragedies* (1992) and, as editor, *Writing the Revolution: Cultural Criticism from 'Left Review'* (1998).

Helen Moore is Fellow and University Lecturer in English at Corpus Christi College, Oxford. Her published work includes articles on Elizabethan fiction and drama and on the romance tradition, and an edition of Antony Munday's translation of *Amadis de Gaule* (2004).

Diane Purkiss is Fellow and Tutor in English at Keble College, Oxford. Her books include *The Witch in History* (1996), *Troublesome Things: A History of Fairies and Fairy Stories* (2000), *Politics, Gender and Literature in the English Civil War* (2005) and *The English Civil War: A People's History* (2005).

Neil Rhodes is Professor of English Literature and Cultural History at the University of St Andrews. His books include *Shakespeare and the Origins of English* (2004) and *The Power of Eloquence and English Renaissance Literature* (1992). He has also edited (with Jennifer Richards and Joseph Marshall) *King James VI and I: Selected Writings* (2003) and (with Jonathan Sawday) *The Renaissance Computer: Knowledge Technology in the First Age of Print* (2000).

Bruce R. Smith, College Distinguished Professor of English at the University of Southern California, is the author of *Homosexual Desire in Shakespeare's England* (1991), *The Acoustic World of Early Modern England* (1999) and *Shakespeare and Masculinity* (2000). His current work, a book on the colour green, contrasts early modern valuations of passion and imagination with post-modern suspicions.

LIST OF ABBREVIATIONS

References to Shakespeare plays are to the most recent Arden editions unless otherwise stated. The following abbreviations are used for individual works:

AC	Antony and Cleopatra
AW	All's Well That Ends Well
AYL	As You Like It
CE	Comedy of Errors
Cor	Coriolanus
Cym	Cymbeline
Ham	Hamlet
1H4	King Henry the IV, Part 1
2H4	King Henry the IV, Part 2
H5	King Henry V
1H6	King Henry the VI, Part 1
2H6	King Henry the VI, Part 2
3H6	King Henry the VI, Part 3
H8	King Henry VIII
JC	Julius Caesar
KJ	King John
KL	King Lear
LLL	Love's Labour's Lost
Luc	The Rape of Lucrece
MA	Much Ado about Nothing
Mac	Macbeth
MM	Measure for Measure
MND	A Midsummer Night's Dream
MV	The Merchant of Venice
MW	The Merry Wives of Windsor
Oth	Othello

Per   Pericles
R2   King Richard II
R3   King Richard III
RJ   Romeo and Juliet
TC   Troilus and Cressida
Tem   Tempest
TGV   The Two Gentlemen of Verona
Tim   Timon of Athens
Tit   Titus Andronicus
TN   Twelfth Night
TNK   The Two Noble Kinsmen
TS   The Taming of the Shrew
WT   The Winter's Tale

LIST OF ILLUSTRATIONS

1. The Mummers of St George, from *The Life and Death of the Famous Champion of England, St George* (1660). BY PERMISSION OF THE PEPYS LIBRARY, MAGDALENE COLLEGE, CAMBRIDGE 8

2. Pedlar, from Hartmann Schopper, *De Omnibvs Illiberalibvs* (1574). BY PERMISSION OF GLASGOW UNIVERSITY LIBRARY, DEPARTMENT OF SPECIAL COLLECTIONS 13

3. Skimmington, from *Halfe a dozen of good Wives: All for a Penny* (1634), in *The Roxburghe Ballads*. BY PERMISSION OF THE BRITISH LIBRARY 44

4. Further versions of the Skimmington, from *The Roxburghe Ballads*. BY PERMISSION OF THE SYNDICS OF CAMBRIDGE UNIVERSITY LIBRARY 44

5. Tollet's Window, designed for Betley Hall, Staffordshire. BY PERMISSION OF THE VICTORIA AND ALBERT MUSEUM 58

6. Richard Tarlton, from *Tarltons Jests* (1638). BY PERMISSION OF THE BODLEIAN LIBRARY, UNIVERSITY OF OXFORD 71

7. Will Kemp as morris dancer, from *Kemps nine daies wonder* (1600). BY PERMISSION OF THE BODLEIAN LIBRARY, UNIVERSITY OF OXFORD 73

8. Guy, Earl of Warwick, from Samuel Rowlands, *The Famous Historie of Guy Earl of Warwick* (1625). BY PERMISSION OF HOUGHTON LIBRARY, HARVARD UNIVERSITY, AND PROQUEST INFORMATION AND LEARNING COMPANY 96

9. Tom a Lincoln, from Richard Johnson, *The Most Pleasant History of Tom a Lincoln* (1682). BY PERMISSION OF THE BODLEIAN LIBRARY, UNIVERSITY OF OXFORD 123

10. Pieter Bruegel, *The Blind Leading the Blind*. BY PERMISSION OF THE GALLERIE NAZIONALI DI CAPODIMONTE, NAPLES 158

11.   Pieter Bruegel, 'Pissing at the Moon', from *Twelve Flemish Proverbs*.
      BY PERMISSION OF MUSEUM MAYER VAN DEN BERGH, ANTWERPEN
      © COLLECTIEBELEID   165

12.   A ballad singer, by Inigo Jones. © THE DEVONSHIRE COLLECTION,
      CHATSWORTH. THE CHATSWORTH SETTLEMENT TRUSTEES/
      PHOTOGRAPH: PHOTOGRAPHIC SURVEY, COURTAULD INSTITUTE OF
      ART. REPRODUCED BY PERMISSION OF HIS GRACE THE DUKE OF
      DEVONSHIRE   176

13.   A courtier and a rustic, from Robert Greene, *A Quip for an Upstart
      Courtier* (1592). BY PERMISSION OF THE FOLGER SHAKESPEARE
      LIBRARY   179

14.   Title page from Thomas Percy, *Reliques of Ancient English Poetry* (1765).
      BY PERMISSION OF THE PEPYS LIBRARY, MAGDALENE COLLEGE,
      CAMBRIDGE   201

15.   *A new Song, shewing the crueltie of Gernutus a Iew* (1620). BY PERMISSION
      OF THE PEPYS LIBRARY, MAGDALENE COLLEGE, CAMBRIDGE   210

16.   *The Ballad of Gernutus, part two* (1620). BY PERMISSION OF THE PEPYS
      LIBRARY, MAGDALENE COLLEGE, CAMBRIDGE   212

Introduction

SHAKESPEARE AND ELIZABETHAN POPULAR CULTURE

Stuart Gillespie and Neil Rhodes

The term 'popular culture' is likely nowadays to suggest Hollywood and the TV soap, games shows and fast food outlets – commercialized leisure activities designed for mass consumption. These are indeed cultural products created *for* the people, but they are not *of* the people, which is an older meaning of the term 'popular'. Older forms of popular culture were for the most part not specifically commercial activities, and may be understood as the cultural expressions of the people themselves. They include the dramatic enactment of Bible stories, the festive rituals associated with holidays, clowning, old romances told around a winter's fire and other products of oral tradition such as proverbs, ballads and songs. These older forms of popular culture still retained considerable power in the sixteenth century and were very much part of the social fabric with which Shakespeare grew up. The media he worked in – the playhouse and the printing house – were of course commercial ventures, and they represent what is perhaps the earliest stage in the transformation of popular culture by the dynamics of the marketplace. But we should not underestimate the extent to which Shakespeare's writing itself was created from materials that might genuinely be described as being 'of the people'.

We may define the popular in relation to the process of commercialization, but also, and more crucially, in relation to education. In the context of the sixteenth century this meant a culture that was, if not unscripted, then certainly innocent of any close acquaintance with the classical values of antiquity to which education was entirely dedicated. Shakespeare had some education, and this shows in his plays, but this did not strongly colour early perceptions of his work. On the contrary, Shakespeare was for a century and a half after his death reputed to be 'barbarous', 'vulgar', 'Gothic'. He was, of course, brilliant at some things – such as his representation of the passions – but his work as a whole was spoiled by lowness and spectacular failures of taste. From a neoclassical point of view Shakespeare's problem was that he remained too mired in the popular culture of his own age. There were certainly Shakespeare enthusiasts in the early eighteenth century (Charles Gildon is one example), but even the comparisons with Homer that were already being made did not affect Shakespeare's status in other respects. As late as 1746 Mark Akenside could produce a league table of great writers (for the magazine *The Museum*) which ranked Shakespeare equal first with Homer but awarded him 10 out of 20 for 'Taste' and zero for 'Critical Ordonnance'.[1] But in the second half of the eighteenth century all this changed. Popular culture itself was revalued in terms of the genius of the folk, both Homer and Shakespeare were viewed as authentically bardic, and, assisted by theories of the sublime then current, Shakespeare too was propelled into the elite.[2] When he became an established part of the academic curriculum in the nineteenth century, his translation from 'low' to 'high' culture was complete.

For us, in the twenty-first century, he has been a classic for so long that our sense of his being part of popular culture has been largely obscured. That is why it is possible for a critic now to write that modern multiculturalism has promoted 'a cultural imperialism more arrogant than humanism ever was and underpinned by popular rather than high culture – Hollywood and McDonald's rather than Shakespeare and Claridge's'.[3] There is much to agree with in this polemic, but it is nevertheless quite misleading to link Shakespeare's name only with Claridge's, that well-known resort of the upper classes. McDonald's does not, as yet, have a franchise at the Globe, but Hollywood has embraced Shakespeare, and from the early 1990s film has helped to secure him a place within the media of modern popular culture.

This is not, however, a book about modern popular culture and the modern media. It is about the popular culture of the sixteenth century and the influences that shaped Shakespeare's drama then, and we use the term 'Elizabethan' rather than 'Renaissance' or 'early modern' in order to identify more precisely the England of his childhood and earlier career. Nevertheless, the book does also suggest, implicitly, that the grounding of so much of Shakespeare's work in the popular cultural forms of his own age has been an important factor in his continued popularity down to the twenty-first century. Furthermore, it aims to show that, while the association of Shakespeare with Claridge's gives a strangely skewed picture of him as an elitist writer, we need to be aware of the complex negotiations between high and low culture and between classical and popular literary forms which make Shakespeare what he is.

Modern study of Shakespeare's debt to Elizabethan popular culture might be said to begin in 1959 with C.L. Barber's highly influential account of the relationship between festive custom and Shakespeare's dramatic forms.[4] But the subject really came of age, intellectually speaking, in the late 1970s, with the publication of Peter Burke's panoramic survey of European popular culture, Robert Weimann's account of Shakespeare and popular theatrical traditions (both 1978), and articles in the journal *Past and Present* presenting history 'from below'.[5] The study of popular culture offered a meeting place for historians and literary scholars at a time when the terms 'cultural history' and 'cultural studies' were almost unknown, and the New Historicism was still quietly germinating in the California sun. One work that had an enormous impact on literary scholars at this time was Bakhtin's book on Rabelais, which had originally appeared in English in 1968 but did not become widely influential until the 1980s.[6] Bakhtin's models of carnivalesque subversion and his concept of heteroglossia became one of the most powerful strands of cultural theory in what was, above all, a theory-driven decade for literary studies. Since then there has been notable work focused specifically on Shakespeare, of a more traditional kind by François Laroque (1991), and with a New Historicist slant by Annabel Patterson (1989), while more recently there have been some useful short surveys of the relationship between popular culture and literary/dramatic practice in the early modern period.[7] What has not emerged is any single work that attempts to address the full range of popular cultural and literary forms available to Shakespeare, and the impact they had on him. This is what the present book aims to supply.

First it is worth pausing for a moment to consider what have probably been the two most influential works for the study of early modern popular culture over the last twenty-five years, those by Burke and Bakhtin. Burke's much-cited argument is that in the sixteenth century popular culture was a shared culture in which the nobility and gentry as well as the lower social orders participated, but evolving concepts of civility, propriety and good taste led to the withdrawal of the nobility from popular culture in the eighteenth century. Removed to a suitable distance from the sweaty multitude, the more refined classes could now indulge in a cult of the primitive. A broad, general proposition such as this is obviously subject to many local variations, and Burke points out (though this is much less frequently cited) that in England 'the withdrawal of the upper classes came relatively early'.[8] By way of illustration he quotes Sidney on the 'rude style' of *Chevy Chase* and Puttenham on the difference between 'vulgar poesie' and 'artificial poesie'. Since Sidney was otherwise praising the old ballad and Puttenham was writing specifically for would-be courtiers, these examples have their limitations, but one is struck, mainly, by their date (*c*.1580). If the withdrawal of the upper classes from English popular culture had started even before the literary renaissance of the late sixteenth century, then when was the golden age of participation, and what does this tell us about Shakespeare? And what does one make of the fact that such a withdrawal is 'relatively early' in England, given that sixteenth-century Englishmen regarded themselves as relatively backward, culturally speaking, by comparison with their European neighbours?

Burke goes on to suggest that 'by the early seventeenth century' private theatres had superseded the public theatres in which Shakespeare had been performed, and that the jig (a brief entertainment following the main performance) had become 'a pejorative term referring to a "low" form of art'.[9] But private theatres were in operation before

Shakespeare had begun his career, and the play which is usually regarded as the first major work of the Elizabethan professional theatre, Marlowe's *Tamburlaine*, 1586, opens with a derisory reference to the jig. This is not to say that the jig was no longer a possible element in a performance by the time Shakespeare started writing for the theatre, of course, but it had already been identified as a 'low' one. It is understandable that a study spanning three centuries, as Burke's does, may not be altogether reliable about the cultural chronology of one country over three decades. The point here is not that Burke's overall argument is incorrect, but that it seems not to account for one of the most significant of all local variations, the age of Shakespeare in England.

The other most influential work in the field of early modern popular culture, Bakhtin's *Rabelais*, also needs to be treated cautiously with regard to Shakespeare, though in a different way. Where Burke's study has been seminal for historians, Bakhtin's ideas were appropriated by literary critics, particularly during the 1980s. The Russian Bakhtin, like the (East) German Weimann, was writing from a Marxist perspective. This produced a proletarianized and some might say sentimentalized view of popular culture as an entirely positive, liberating, body-focused phenomenon, which finds its apotheosis in the communal virtues of laughter. Bakhtin's work opened up fruitful theoretical perspectives on both language and literature, but its social model might seem rather unsophisticated, particularly from the point of view of the historian. (Burke does not mention Bakhtin, though the English version of his book had appeared ten years earlier.) The other objection, in this case from a Shakespearean perspective, is that Bakhtin's theories of carnival derive – not surprisingly, in a book about Rabelais – from continental, Catholic contexts which have a limited application to Shakespeare. Put simply, there is very much more material of this kind in French and Italian than there is in English. The 'Battle between Carnival and Lent', for example, has been much discussed, but it is a theme which is difficult to illustrate extensively from English documentary sources.[10]

If there are some problems in applying these different models of popular culture to the age of Shakespeare and to Shakespeare's dramatic practice, how then should we define the 'popular' in this context? While the term 'class' might be somewhat anachronistic for the sixteenth century, Elizabethan commentators do identify three, or perhaps four, social orders. William Harrison, writing in 1577, described a hierarchy of gentleman (including nobility, knights and esquires), citizens and burgesses, yeomen, and finally those who had 'neither voice nor authority in the commonwealth, but are to be ruled and not to rule other'.[11] This is very similar to the scheme outlined earlier by Sir Thomas Smith, who compares the English to the Roman social structure. He divides the rank of gentlemen into two, 'Nobilitas major' and 'Nobilitas minor'; then describes citizens and burgesses who 'serve the common wealth' and may be elected to parliament 'to have voices in it'; then treats yeomen 'whom our lawes doe call *Legalem hominem*'; and finally 'those which the olde Romans called *capite censij proletarij* or *operae*, or day labourers, poore husbandmen, yea marchantes or retailers which have no free lande: copyholders, all artificers, as Taylers, Shoomakers, Carpenters, Brickemakers, Bricklayers, Masons, &c'.[12] There is no doubt as to which category the fathers of Marlowe, Shakespeare and Jonson would have been placed in: a shoemaker, glover and bricklayer, respectively. But it is much less clear what might be meant by 'the people' and hence by the term 'popular'. Citizens and yeomen were frequently classed together as 'the middling sort of people', divided between town and country, and it is these groups, rather than those who 'have no voice nor authority in our commonwealth', as Smith puts it, who would usually have been referred to as 'the people'.[13] The term 'popular' itself appears only six times in Shakespeare, four of these references occurring in *Coriolanus*, a play which undoubtedly splices the 'old Romans' with contemporary English matter.[14] It is significant that the popular voice in this play is represented by characters called 'citizens', who are eligible to vote, rather than by an inarticulate mob. Quite how we would then wish to distinguish this popular voice from that in other Shakespeare plays is a delicate *critical* question, but this should alert us to the fact that the terms 'popular' and 'the people' are both more broadly based and more socially fluid than the Bakhtinian model would suggest. When Shakespeare himself applied successfully for a coat of arms he was translated, at least nominally, from the lowest to the highest social class.[15]

The concept of the popular can at least be referred to the social ranks recognized by sixteenth-century people. The concept of culture cannot, since the word first appeared in English in the late eighteenth century when it was imported from the German.[16] Where the historian might want to attempt a fairly broad definition of this elusive term, from a literary perspective it is probably more useful to start with a simple distinction between practice and text. Popular culture as practice would encompass holiday customs, seasonal rituals and other forms of communal activity which might be gathered under the label of 'folk tradition'. These are the concerns of Bakhtin and Laroque, and are what many would understand by the term 'popular culture' in a historical rather than a modern context. There are other aspects of practice that would define culture as entertainment, and it is at this point that popular culture starts to shift from being a ritual to a commercial activity. The entertainment provided by clowns would be one example, though its commercial status is marginal since it comes in amateur as well as professional form; the popular Elizabethan spectacle of bear-baiting, on the other hand, was a purely commercial enterprise. The form of entertainment which most clearly acts as a bridge between ritual and commerce is of course the drama. The origins of drama in ancient Greek ritual – in particular, the festival of Dionysus – were studied long ago by anthropologists, and England has its own ritualistic drama, closely linked to holiday customs, which is represented by such things as the Revesby Play (featuring morris dancers and a fool), the Mummers Play (featuring St George; see Figure 1) and the Robin Hood plays.[17] This primitive folk drama may yield relatively little in the way of profound symbolic meanings, and its influence on the later professional theatre was minimal. But the same could not be said of another type of ritualistic drama, the Corpus Christi or mystery plays, which were being performed right up to the opening of the commercial theatres in the second half of Elizabeth's reign. The present volume contains chapters on popular festivity and on clowning, but begins with a treatment of the mystery plays and their legacy for Shakespeare and his contemporaries.

These aspects of popular culture, whether designed principally as forms of entertainment or not, can be understood in terms of activity or

FIGURE 1   The Mummers of St George, from *The Life and Death of the Famous Champion of England, St George* (1660).

performance or, as we have already put it, 'practice'. This is to distin-guish them from those other forms of cultural expression which can be classed as popular literature, or, more broadly speaking, as texts. Shakespeare grew up in the first age of print. Print was responsible for many learned volumes which aimed to preserve and transmit the knowl-edge of classical antiquity, but it also produced a vast amount of lower matter. This would include jest books, such as *A Hundred Merry Tales* or *Scoggin's Jests*, which recorded practical jokes rather than jokes of the Christmas cracker variety; rogue literature, which could excite the curious reader with a (suitably moralistic) view into the criminal under-world; and the humble almanac, which would eventually, by the late sev-enteenth century, become the most frequently owned type of printed book after the Bible.[18] The paradigm of popular literature in the six-teenth century, however, is romance and allied forms of fiction. 'Few forms of literature have been thumbed to pieces more completely than these slender quartos', wrote H.S. Bennett of the romances published in the first half of the century.[19] They were also routinely condemned as worthless and immoral, promoters of sex and violence. Queen Elizabeth's former tutor, Roger Ascham, was severe on the 'open mans slaughter, and bold bawdrye' to be found in Malory; others thought that romance served not just 'to busie the minds of the vulgar sorte' but also to threaten the vulnerable, uneducated reader with 'the poison of Impietie' and 'the poyson of revendge'.[20] Romance as a genre, however, enjoyed something of a revival in late Jacobean England, and this is certainly evident in Shakespeare's work. To reflect this we have devoted two essays in the present volume to popular fiction and popular romance, though it is perhaps worth pointing out here that it is extremely difficult to draw a clear line between the 'popular' and the more mainstream examples of prose fiction by writers such as Lodge and Greene.[21]

The simple distinction between practice and text may be useful as a starting point, but it will only take us so far, since it elides the oral character of Elizabethan popular culture. The sixteenth century may have been the first age of print in England, but it was also a time when the majority of people were unable to read.[22] Stories, jokes, knowledge of the seasons and the land, and the oak-aged wisdom of proverb lore, often structured by mnemonic devices such as rhyme and alliteration, were handed down over generations in local communities.[23] The first age of print was also the last age of the saying. The ballad is another aspect of this oral world. It intersects with drama because the jig which rounded off performances in the theatres was essentially a ballad, and it also intersects with other forms of popular music.[24]

The oral or acoustic dimension of Elizabethan popular culture occupies intermediate territory between practice and text. Speech act theory might describe the oral world as performative and consign it to the sphere of practice, but sayings and ballads existed both as speech or song and as printed texts. Jokes were available in printed form, but were also copied down into table-books by gentlemen attending stage performances. Nor is it possible any longer to imagine a clear divide between oral and literate cultures in the early modern period. Rather, there was access and reciprocity between the two. There was much communal reading aloud; printed ballads were pasted on the walls of inns and the homes of the poor; in towns, meeting places such as barbers' shops acted as conduits of information between the literate and the illiterate.[25] Some of the most important recent contributions to our understanding of early modern popular culture, by Adam Fox and Bruce Smith, for example, are concerned precisely with orality and literacy and with the relations between speech, sound and text. So we have essays in this volume on sayings or proverbs and on popular music, and we conclude with a chapter on ballads which tracks that aspect of Elizabethan popular culture into the eighteenth century.

Another way of putting all this, from the point of view of Renaissance literary studies, is that in the present climate – post-theory, post-New Historicism – the most significant contribution to the understanding of popular culture has been provided by media studies. We use the term here not in its narrow sense, which restricts it mainly to television, but in one that releases it into broader historical meanings. At the same time, the term may act as a useful bridge between 'popular culture' as it is generally understood today, and the forms it took in early modern literature. The most significant of those forms is drama, which might certainly be approached in terms of media studies if we understand that to refer here to speech, performance, text and print, and to the overlapping relations between them. We introduced the mystery plays under 'practice', and it is true that they may have been devised, and by the sixteenth century were certainly thought of, principally as spectacle.[26] But there are also texts of the plays from Shakespeare's day, in manuscript though not in print. Clowning we also presented in terms of practice, but, as we have just seen, the clown's repartee circulated through different media. In fact, Barry Reay has usefully pointed out that 'it is vital to be aware of what could be termed the orality of popular print'.[27] In the professional theatre the process of composition, rehearsal, performance and commercial afterlife would be likely to include most of the following stages: access to printed sources and folk memory, writing, communal reading (for both literate and non-literate actors), oral delivery (memorized and improvised), and finally the journey into printed play-text – a much-debated stage which would have been made by different routes. The transmission of popular culture into the Elizabethan theatre, and the relationship between practice and text, is clearly a highly complex process.

To think about the relations between the different media in the sixteenth century is also to become aware of certain cultural hierarchies.

Allowing for the considerable amount of traffic beteen the two, we can still think of the relationship between oral and literate cultures in hierarchical terms, and this might be signalled by print itself. Ballads and chapbooks containing popular tales often combined black letter (or 'Gothic') type, used for lowbrow material, with the more elite Roman form. This mixture of high and low, with its appeal to different audiences, is reflected in the fact that, as Barry Reay describes it, 'these books are crammed with gentry values, gentry heroes and heroines, woodcut representations of gentry demeanour and dress, and allusions to the classics which were the staple of a grammar-school and university education'.[28] It is also reflected in the Elizabethan theatre in ways that hardly need to be explained here. So any discussion of Shakespeare's relationship with popular culture must necessarily recognize that outside as well as within his plays themselves, the popular interacts with the elite in terms of audience, genre, and value systems or beliefs. This is something we have tried to recognize in this volume by dealing with what is perhaps the most unclassifiable aspect of popular culture – belief and superstition – in the context of Shakespeare's most highbrow play and his most consciously intellectual character: Hamlet. And while this play, this character, may be an extreme case, there is throughout Shakespeare's work an interweaving of high and low cultural forms which ultimately defines the nature of his drama and of his distinctive achievement as a writer. The case of Shakespeare is a challenge to Burke's model of an eighteenth-century withdrawal of the nobility from popular culture. One might even say that many of Shakespeare's plays actually debate Burke's model. Certainly, the popular element in Shakespeare can hardly ever be viewed in a stand-alone way, as it once was, as something inserted to please the groundlings; there is, constantly, a creative and critical dialogue between the popular and the sophisticated.

In discussing the impact of popular culture on the drama of Shakespeare and his contemporaries we can, in purely materialistic terms, describe a process of commodification.[29] But we can also talk about a literary refashioning of popular culture in the later sixteenth century as it is absorbed and transformed by the new media of print and the theatre, since it is this that creates the dialogue between the popular and sophisticated in Shakespeare. Shakespeare's own literary and dramatic adaptations of the forms of popular culture available to him in the Elizabethan era are the subject of this book.

* * *

Here it may be useful to press a little further on this point about the dialogue between popular and sophisticated, domestic and exotic, homespun and 'literary' in Shakespeare. Perhaps all readers have at some level noticed this, and felt the evocative power Shakespeare can generate from it – even, for example, at the micro level of Cleopatra's description as 'a lass unparalleled' (AC 5.2.318). It can be said that this is not only a distinctive but an extremely pronounced feature of his work; that, in fact, Shakespeare can be at his most unexpectedly 'literary' when dealing with most ostensibly 'popular' material, and vice versa.

In some ways, of course, we are already familiar with the Shakespearean mix of exotic and domestic, classical and demotic. As Sarah Brown has recently put it, 'within the complex historical and geographical matrix of educated reading practice there is a corner of a classical Athenian wood which will be forever Elizabethan England'.[30] This outpost of England in Athens, of the Elizabethan in the classical, is a matter of cultural intersections at all levels. Titania's speech may tell of a ploughman, a 'murrion flock' and a 'nine-men's-morris' (MND 2.1.94–8), but its expressive force derives from Ovid's Metamorphoses as much as from anywhere else.[31] As Patricia Parker has recently explained, that most English-sounding of carpenters, Peter Quince, may derive his name – and more – from a web of literary sources stretching back to Seneca and Plutarch.[32] Overall, though, the inter-marrying of the English and the Athenian in Midsummer Night's Dream, as Robin Goodfellow meets Pluto and Proserpina, Jack and Jill the Minotaur, is perhaps sufficiently familiar. A more arresting instance may be the similarly exotic genealogy attaching to what looks very like one of Shakespeare's most thoroughgoing demotic creations, Autolycus in The Winter's Tale (Figure 2 shows an engraving regularly

FIGURE 2   Pedlar, from Hartmann Schopper, *De Omnibvs Illiberalibvs* (1574).

used nowadays to suggest Autolycus' visual appearance as a realistic figure of common life). If Shakespeare owes a debt to a classical source for this character, one may feel, can any corner of his work be entirely innocent of ancient Greek or Latin associations? The first bearer of the name of Autolycus was Odysseus' grandfather in Homer's *Odyssey*,

Book 19 (described by Homer as the most accomplished thief and per-
jurer in the world). Shakespeare's knowledge of him would have come
from Ovid's tale of Mercury and Chione (his parents) in the *Metamorphoses*.
There has never been any doubting that the name was Homeric and the
immediate source probably Ovidian, but commentators have in the past
contented themselves with the assumption that Shakespeare was in
need solely of a name, and took little or nothing more from the classical
sources. Although Autolycus' first speech in *The Winter's Tale* contains
a correct self-description of him as 'littered under Mercury' (4.3.24),
even those critics who investigated the subject felt that 'Ovid's allusions to
him and Homer's, when all are taken together, can hardly have been more
than the starting point of Shakspere's interest in him'.[33] More recently,
however, the prospect has been very seriously canvassed that Autolycus is
a specifically Ovidian artist-figure.[34] Against Paulina's artist-as-moralist,
Autolycus' artist-as-wit stands as one half of a traditional duality that, for
Shakespeare's time, was felt as particularly pointed in relation to Ovid –
and was specially pertinent to a play with other strong links to the poet of
the *Metamorphoses*, and one that seems implicated in contemporary debate
about the morality of the theatre. Autolycus, in a word, has begun to seem
about as 'literary' as any other Shakespearean material.

   What of the converse we have posited – that behind Shakespeare's most
apparently 'literary' creations may be discovered the structures of popular
culture? One example must suffice here. *Timon of Athens* is hardly the first
Shakespeare play in which one would look for strongly popular elements.
It is set in ancient Greece, it has no countrymen or peasants, no songs or
ballads, and it is, as is well known, heavily indebted to Plutarch's lives of
Alcibiades and Marcus Antonius, as well as Lucian's *Dialogue of Timon*. Yet
in none of these sources, nor in any of the other analogues known to
Geoffrey Bullough, is Timon said to take up residence in the woods after his
ruin.[35] In Plutarch he remains in Athens until the time of his death
approaches, at which point he removes to the town of Hales so as to be
buried near the ocean. In Lucian he becomes a farm labourer and tills the
earth under Mount Hymettus. Only in Shakespeare does he wish to live in
the forest: where does this variation spring from? In this part of Timon's
story Shakespeare is parting company with the classical sources to draw

on the 'wodewose' or 'wild man in the forest' tradition, ultimately related to the ancient 'green man' phenomenon, somewhere within which areas lie also the figure of Robin Hood and several characters in Spenser's *Faerie Queene*. The tradition had found recent expression in a couple of plays known to Shakespeare, *Mucedorus* and Greene's *James IV*. The terms in which Timon expresses himself as wishing to withdraw from human company mark him out as, quite literally, a wild man:

> Nothing I'll bear from thee
> But nakedness, thou detestable town!
> Take thou that too, with multiplying bans!
> Timon will to the woods, where he shall find
> Th' unkindest beast more kinder than mankind.
>
> (4.1.32–6)

And Timon, as Anne Barton writes, 'although probably his most extended investigation of the subject . . . was neither Shakespeare's first nor his last wild man'.[36]

We have suggested that Shakespeare's work shows a deep intermingling of ingredients from high and low cultural traditions. The range of several of the essays in this volume shows him drawing again and again on the same kind of popular elements throughout his career, in different contexts and for often different purposes (his interest in wild men takes in Oliver, Timon, the dancers in Bohemia, Caliban, Cardenio, and Herne the Hunter). But if 'popular culture' is to be so commonly found in Shakespeare's work, perhaps this merely means we are defining it too broadly. We might accept the Forest of Arden in *As You Like It* as a site of folk or pagan ritual (as Leah Marcus would see it), but should we be happy to extend the claim as far as Laroque in suggesting its relevance to Bohemia and Belmont? Laroque has written:

The forest of Arden in *As You Like It*, the pastoral 'shores' of Bohemia in *The Winter's Tale*, and Portia's enchanted place at Belmont in *The Merchant of Venice* were all Shakespearean versions of the pagan, ritualized vision of a traditional green world with its hunting rites and grounds, chance or sporting games, and its

> utopian or topsy-turvy scenarios . . . The green world is not just
> limited to forest and green pastures.[37]

We would argue that, while it is indeed in the nature of popular culture
that its forms are manifold, it is also in the nature of Shakespeare's work
that it tries a new mix each time: Belmont, Bohemia and Arden are
importantly different places, in which 'traditional green world' elements
are differently arranged, differently contextualized, and differently related
to others. 'All Shakespearean versions', yes – and all the versions offer
different emphases and permutations.

But if this makes Shakespeare sound too much like a Lévi-Straussean
bricoleur, another way of insisting on the meaningfulness of the admittedly
broad concept of popular culture in Shakespeare would be to show that it
is possible to make valid generalizations about it, about what is at stake in
his use of it, and that his use of it varies from that of other writers. It is, for
example, easy enough to see how very differently Jonson deploys his
knowledge of popular culture. One need only quote the titles of the ballads
sold by Nightingale in *Bartholomew Fair*, and ask whether Shakespeare
could be imagined presenting so reductive a dismissal of such material:

> Ballads, ballads! fine new ballads:
> Hear for your love, and buy for your money!
> A delicate ballad o' *The Ferret and the Coney*!
> *A Preservative again' the Punks' Evil*!
> Another of *Goose-green Starch, and the Devil*!
> *A dozen of Divine Points*, and *The Godly Garters*!
> *The Fairing of Good Counsel*, of an ell and three quarters!
> What is't you buy?
> *The Windmill blown down by the witch's fart*!
> *Or Saint George, that O! did break the dragon's heart*![38]

Or take Spenser, just mentioned in connection with wild men. Mary
Ellen Lamb has recently written suggestively of the Red Cross Knight as
'a hybrid figure, existing in tension between the world of literate, even
hyperliterate, readers, and a once common culture in the process of
becoming increasingly . . . distinct'. Lamb adds to this very plausible

picture an account of what Spenser does with this creative tension: 'Book I [of *The Faerie Queene*] forms a particularly productive site of contest as it engages the often complex and unstable cultural alliances of readers during a period of increasing social stratification in the late sixteenth century.'[39] Whatever exactly this means, words like 'contest' and 'stratification' imply a way of using popular culture entirely unlike Shakespeare's. What then is Shakespeare's way?

If the answer to that question could be summed up in a paragraph, the rest of this book would not need to follow, and we do not propose to attempt to reduce the matter to one or two simple propositions. Nevertheless, we believe that answers to that question are possible, and will emerge; and an initial suggestion is worth offering here. Diane Purkiss has written in the following terms of belief in fairies in the early modern period:

> Tellers frequently knew – as well as we do – that they were telling stories. The early modern populace did not 'believe' in fairies and they did not disbelieve. Fairies both are and are not; they exceed the terms of what is likely or acceptable or sayable in the everyday . . . The way fairies hover between belief and disbelief is what makes them natural symbols for other things that cannot be said, or cannot be acknowledged, or cannot be believed.[40]

The question as to whether people believed in romances, or in the stories old ballads tell, could be answered in a similar fashion. One feature of popular culture's texts and practices is that they do not compel belief and disbelief. It would be in itself naive to imagine a populace naively credulous of legends and romances. Rather we may say that popular cultural forms are characterized by a 'what if?' quality. What if fairies really do interfere in human life? Or, let's suppose God is malicious, or that men can do magic, or that ghosts revisit us, or that corpses can reveal murderers, or that we can read our future in portents, or that an ancient folk hero is still among us. Perhaps it is no surprise after all that a writer like Shakespeare finds so much he can do with the popular culture of his time: each of these scenarios is to be found in one (or more) of his plays.

Chapter One

SHAKESPEARE AND
THE MYSTERY PLAYS

Helen Cooper

The year is 1644, almost thirty years after Shakespeare's death, and
the Civil War is well under way. The place is Cartmel in
Westmorland, on the edge of the fell country far from the London of the
theatres. An old man is being interrogated by a visiting Calvinist cleric
named John Shaw, who has come to instruct the local people in knowledge of the Bible, in which, he has been told, they are sadly lacking, and
therefore potentially on the fast track to Hell. Salvation through Jesus
Christ, which is the topic of the interrogation, means singularly little to
the old man; but when Shaw presses him on the subject, he does manage
to come up with a recollection: 'I think I heard of that man you speake
of, once in a play at Kendall, called Corpus-Christi play, where there was
a man on a tree, and blood ran downe.'[1]

The 'Corpus Christi play' was the contemporary term for what are
now generally known either as the mystery plays (by analogy with the
comparable French *mystères*, though the term does not seem to have
been used in this dramatic sense in English before the eighteenth century),
or the cycle plays: a series of dramatic pageants encompassing the history
of the world from the Fall of Lucifer to the Last Judgement.[2] Shaw's
story constitutes a forceful reminder of a number of things that are very
easy to overlook, but which made a decisive difference, not just to
Shakespeare's own plays, but to the whole early modern experience of
theatre. As the old man's recollection indicates, the mysteries are as
much an early modern as a medieval phenomenon. Furthermore,
although they were sponsored by the civic guilds, and may have been

written by clerics (there is no evidence either way, beyond the knowledge of the Bible and Church doctrine contained in the texts themselves), they were a genuinely popular theatre in that they involved a large number of ordinary townsfolk in their production, and in that they were accessible to everyone, regardless of class, social or religious affiliation, wealth, or even their degree of literacy. For the old man in Cartmel, they were almost certainly the only kind of drama he knew. And third, they were extraordinarily powerful: powerful enough to remain in an old man's memory many decades after he had seen them, and to have made an impression on him that any number of the church services he was supposed to have attended and the sermons he ought to have heard had failed to do. There was, moreover, one particular reason for that power, and that was that these plays *acted out their action*. The Crucifixion was not reported, but staged. The cycle plays do not just tell, they show; and their effects come from that – from the staging more than from the words. What the old man remembers is a visual, a theatrical image; enactment, not description. Other accounts of the Passion, in treatises and sermons and lyrics, urge their readers to imagine Christ's wounds, to conjure up his sufferings in their imagination. The spectators of the plays *see* the processes of torture, the crown of thorns and the wounds: the blood running down.

That might seem so evident as scarcely to need saying; but it is also so evident that it is easy to miss. For it is that element of enactment – of subordinating the word to the deed, supplementing speech with embodiment – that the plays written for the sixteenth-century public theatres carry over from the cycle plays, and which mark both sorts as a distinctive kind, not just of text, but of theatre. Acting their action decisively separates them from humanist or classical drama, which works within a tradition that has been defined as 'play as rhetorical event'.[3] Plays of that kind locate their action offstage, and so privilege the spoken word to the exclusion of almost everything else. There is still a debate over whether Seneca wrote his plays to be staged or declaimed, and it has to be said that it makes very little difference which is done. The staging of Latin comedy requires little more than a series of entrances and exits. Greek drama was not given much attention in England outside the universities (and even that seems to have declined in the later part of the sixteenth century), but Aristotle insisted that Attic tragedy did not need to be performed in order to make its effects.[4] Yet the Corpus Christi plays take a subject, salvation history, that is on the very limits of what was possible to stage – most periods would say, beyond them – and embody it, in a kind of literalization of the Incarnation that lies at the core of that history. And Elizabethan drama takes its cue from them.

Modern playgoers and scholars alike are so familiar with the idea of a drama that acts its action that it is easy to take it for granted: *of course* that is what plays do. It is, after all, what Shakespeare does, and it is his work that has set our assumptions as to what constitutes drama ever since. His treatment of the stage has come to be regarded as normative, for all the post-Restoration discontent with his ignoring of every classical (or supposedly classical) rule of dramatic composition. But drama that acts its action is not the automatic default position, as classical and humanist drama shows. Rather, it is a medieval invention, and one that the sixteenth-century public theatre adopted and built on. The basic conception of such drama is not play as rhetorical event, however magnificent the language, and however much the university-trained Marlowe may have conceived his Tamburlaine in such terms; it is rather of drama as following what has been called an 'incarnational aesthetic',[5] action embodied.

It is no coincidence, moreover, that 'incarnation', literally 'enfleshment', the embodiment of God as Man, is inseparable from the plays that take their name from the feast of Corpus Christi, of the body of Christ. The broken body remembered by the old man at Cartmel is the most direct expression of that principle. One reason why the connection of the cycles with the sixteenth-century public stage has been so extensively overlooked may be that their religious focus seems to set them apart from the great surge in secular theatre in the wake of the Reformation. The links between the public theatres and morality plays and interludes have been given much more attention, even though the allegorical qualities of many of those plays set them apart from both the cycle plays and most of what appeared on the Elizabethan stage. The Puritan opposition to the whole theatrical enterprise should, however, serve as a warning against assuming a discontinuity between the two kinds of incarnation. The resistance was not based on any inherent objection to drama. The Protestants of the earlier sixteenth century happily wrote plays to promote the reformed cause; John Bale's works included a cycle on the life of Christ.[6] The objections to the biblical plays were not grounded on their promulgation of Catholicism, since the texts were put through some fairly rigorous screening in the sixteenth century to weed out false doctrine. The minister John Northbrooke, writing in 1577, expressed little disapproval of the reading of classical dramatists, so long as one read them for a good Christian moral; or even to acting them, so long as it was done privately and in Latin, and for the sake of improving learning.[7] But the Reformation was a movement that substituted the word for the flesh, the Bible for transubstantiation.[8] Incarnation, other than Christ's own – enacted, embodied drama, text incarnate – seems increasingly to have terrified the reformers, quite apart from the issue of whether it was God or man that was being represented. Northbrooke was horrified by the claim that as much could be learned from dramatized 'histories out of the scriptures' as out of sermons on God's word, but he condemned all staged performance along with those. In 1603, Henry Crosse (rather a shadowy figure biographically, but his views are clear enough), objected to drama precisely on the grounds of its visual power supplementary to the text, even though he acknowledged that plays are not forbidden in the Bible 'in expresse words' ('expresse' being a reformist term for the plain meaning of the Bible, dating back to the Lollards, the proto-Protestants of the late fourteenth and early fifteenth centuries who likewise set themselves against the Corpus Christi cycles):

> Is not this the way to make men ripe in all kinds of villanie, and corrupt the manners of the whole world? . . . For are not their Dialogues . . . made more forcible by gesture and outward action: Surely this must needes attract the minde to imitate such vices [as] are portrayed out, whereby the soule is tainted with impietie: for it cannot be, but that the internall powers must be moued at such visible and liuely obiects.

We might assume from this that his objections were to the secular theatre; but in fact he makes no such distinction, continuing to write as if he were still watching the cycle plays:

> Must the holy Prophets and Patriarkes be set vpon a Stage, to be derided, hist, and laught at? or is it fit that the infirmities of holy men should be acted on a Stage, whereby others may be inharted to rush carelesly forward into vnbrideled libertie? doubtlesse the iudgement of God is not farre off from such abusers of diuine mysteries.[9]

God's mysteries should stay just that – mysteries; and Crosse, like Northbrooke, makes no distinction between the acting of divine mysteries, and stage performance of any kind.[10] Their polemics run straight on from one to other. Had they, like Shaw's old man forty years later, seen the mystery plays? First-hand experience would go some way to explaining the ease with which they run the two kinds of drama together in their minds. Northbrooke indeed was writing just after the construction of the first custom-built playhouse, and while a number of cycles were still being acted; Crosse was writing well within the time-band for having been brought up on them. The old man of Cartmel would presumably have been a child in Northbrooke's days; his words were recorded two years after the public theatres had been closed, when their plays too threatened to appear an anachronism left over from an irreligious past. His lifetime encompassed the whole history of high Renaissance drama in England, from widespread living experience of the Corpus Christi plays to late memory, as if the whole of post-Reformation theatre were no more than an interlude. It is quite possible that all the great flowering of English drama had simply passed him by.

Northbrooke, Crosse and Shaw demonstrate how deeply unhistorical is our habit of thinking of the cycle plays as medieval, and of Elizabethan drama as early modern. The Corpus Christi plays, like other institutions that began in the Middle Ages – the law courts, or Parliament and its meetings – were simply carried forward from the Middle Ages into the sixteenth century; Parliament and the law courts happened to continue, while the mystery cycles did not, but that does not make the cycles any less of an early modern as well as a medieval phenomenon. The Chester plays were given a thorough rewriting in the same decade as Wyatt was composing his poetry; all six of their surviving manuscripts were copied after 1590, when the drama of the public theatres was at its height.[11] The texts of all the cycles were given an active vetting at the Reformation, to make them fit the new doctrinal standards. The surviving records of performances are often patchy, but it is clear that they did not cease the moment the Reformation appeared on the horizon. There was indeed considerable resistance to their suppression. The first decade of Elizabeth's reign saw Corpus Christi plays (either full cycles or shorter series of the same kind) acted at New Romney, Norwich, Worcester and Chelmsford, with Lincoln hoping for a revival that never in fact happened. Many more, including some of the greatest, lasted longer. York saw the last performance of its cycle in 1569, though the city was still hoping to mount it again in 1580. Chester's at last succumbed to Puritan opposition in 1575. Durham and Doncaster saw their cycles acted until 1576, but hoped for their revival for longer; Newcastle's seems to have been acted intermittently until 1589. Coventry's (which may have been just a New Testament series) lasted until 1579, and came very close to being revived in 1591; one of the guilds held on to its pageant wagon until the 1630s, just in case. Cornish biblical plays were still being played in 1602; and at Kendal, and perhaps Preston as well, they lasted into James's reign, until c.1605.[12] It was the Kendal cycle that Shaw's old man remembered in 1644; but he would only have needed to be in his mid-seventies to have been able to recall other of those Northern or Midland cycles. And in addition to these urban centres of drama, there is an abundance of records of individual plays of similar type, especially Passion plays, such as indicates a much more widespread but analogous form of drama in a host of smaller towns and villages. There are no comparable records for late sixteenth-century London, though privately sponsored Passion plays were performed there both in the reign of Mary and on one Good Friday in the reign of James I, the latter reputedly attracting a vast audience.[13] A capital city in any case has plenty of connections with the country it heads, enhanced in the later years of the sixteenth century by a huge influx of immigrants from the provinces,

Shakespeare among them; and many of those incomers would have been brought up on this kind of theatrical experience. The educated members of the audiences at the public theatres may have learned their Seneca and Plautus in grammar school or university; they may even have acted in them, since that was held to be an appropriate element of humanist education. But the dominant living theatrical experience of the childhood and youth of a large number of the playgoers would have been the cycle plays. These were seen by far greater numbers than could ever have seen indoor interlude performances. The Corpus Christi audiences may well have numbered thousands for each performance, rather than the dozens of members of the household and invitees who could cram into a hall. So their expectations of drama derived from these plays, not as something learned, but as something taken for granted – so engrained as to be instinctive, in an 'unthinking effortless familiarity'.[14]

'Expectations of drama' is a very unparticularized phrase, in the sense that it is very hard to demonstrate by way of annotation. Early modern plays have been largely mediated to modern readers by way of annotated editions, a text with accompanying commentary or gloss, just as humanist scholars and schoolboys read their Seneca or Plautus on the page as an annotated text. Such editions therefore massively privilege the words over the action. The similarities between the mysteries and the later stage plays, however, are not something that lend themselves to line-by-line annotation. Verbal parallels between the two are rare – indeed, few editions acknowledge that there might be any at all, and demonstrable allusions, such as Hamlet's complaint about actors who out-Herod Herod (*Ham* 3.2.14), are often treated as if they were merely proverbial. But what is at issue is not there in the words on the page, or in specific sources for specific lines, just as what the old man in Cartmel remembered is *supplementary* to the text. Expectations of drama relate not to the particular words that are spoken, but to the way plays represent reality, and to what the stage can do.

An argument that such expectations were carried over from the pageants to the theatre may seem a lost cause, as the critical silence on the subject might be taken to imply a massive rejection of any such idea. In fact, the silence represents oversight rather than rejection. Emrys Jones was expressing his amazement at the lack of studies in the field in 1977, and things have not moved on much since then despite the massive increase in research on the cycle plays as a phenomenon in themselves.[15] The lack of interest in them shown by Renaissance critics is as much a fact of life as the proliferation of scholarly interest in theory, and the two would seem to be connected. Scholars have a tendency to think that if something does not have a theory, it does not exist. The notion that drama could and should be theorized appears only with the rediscovery of Aristotle's *Poetics*, around 1500; and with that came the belief that his ideas should be imposed on dramatic practice. The cycle plays, however, developed entirely outside Aristotelean, or indeed Horatian or Ciceronian, theories, and never produced a theorist of their own, so it was easy for humanist academics to assume they had no theory, and were therefore a kind of primeval chaos waiting to be reduced to order by regulation. The sixteenth-century debate over Aristotle, however, was most concerned with the morality and structure of a play rather than with the basic idea of enacted drama, drama incarnate, the whole conception of what theatre is up to. The classical genres have enabled an abundance of theory about the tragic and the comic, even (rarely and ambiguously) about the dramatic, but there is no equivalent adjectival noun from the native term 'play'. The absence of a critical theory for the Corpus Christi plays tended for many years to be filled by a doctrinal theory, but the Reformation abhorrence of Catholicism and its long legacy served them ill: to Protestant commentators, they appeared both superstitious and damnable; to the Victorians, they appeared at best childlike and at worst barbaric.[16] Secular New Historicists have varied the pattern only so far as to interpret them in terms of being the product of an urban rather than a religious elite, with the emphasis falling almost entirely on the plays as an expression of social control.[17] Their anonymity also seems to put them outside the bounds of any discussion of conceptions of authorship, and ideas of the death of the author only serve to confirm how central such conceptions are. This lack of named playwrights encourages their consignment to the margins of academic study as mere low culture (ironically, in view of New Historicist charges of elitism), while Shakespeare and the other named dramatists represent high culture. Relocate the cycle plays in their full popular context, however – as a social practice, not as an academic theory, or an elitist plot, or some mindless expression of a collective folk – and the sheer power of their existence, their forcefulness on stage that could survive in the memory for decades, dominates over their absence of theory or their anonymity: indeed, their lack of informing theory itself witnesses to their origins outside the academic worlds of the Church or the universities.

Elizabethan drama came to claim a different theoretical basis from the cycle plays despite their common incarnational emphasis; and their most characteristic forms of staging, the pageant wagon and the public theatres, seem to separate them still further. Here too, however, the forms of drama are closely linked. Both were performed in the open air, with the spectators gathered around a raised thrust stage. The less well-off would stand; the better-off paid more for better seats ranged vertically in the body of the encompassing walls behind the standing audience, in the upper rooms of houses along the play routes, or in the 'upper rooms' (the terminology was preserved) of the playhouses.[18] Even the clustering of the groundlings around the stage replicated the pattern created by the favoured sites for pageant performance at corners or crossroads, where audience numbers could be maximized. It has been something of a puzzle for modern theatre historians as to just what the model was for the public playhouses; the Vitruvian Roman models that have been suggested do not bear much resemblance to the Rose or the Globe. For the many spectators of Elizabethan drama who had seen the cycle plays, however, an Elizabethan theatre would have seemed far more familiar than any time-travelling Roman would have found it.[19]

The playhouse stage was of course much bigger than that of a pageant wagon, but its configuration was not so different. William Dugdale, writing in the mid-seventeenth century, described the pageant wagons as 'theatres . . . very large and high'.[20] The balcony too was a feature of many mobile pageant stages, where it was typically used for God. The roof of the Globe was painted with the signs of the zodiac, and other theatres may have had the same decoration – hence its description as 'the heavens'; and that too, both the painting and the descriptive term, was a feature of some of the pageant wagons.[21] A spectator used to the

Corpus Christi plays would recognize its symbolism: it is a reminder that all the world is, not so much a theatre (which would be a classical idea, and would put the emphasis more on the audience), but a stage, with him- or herself as part of the action. The Elizabethan plays were written, like the cycle plays, with mass audiences in mind. Acted beneath the heavens, that meant they were designed not just for the broadest dramatic appeal, but with an acknowledgement that the spectators were part of the cast list within the larger drama of humankind. The players, the characters they act and the spectators are alike positioned between the Fall and the Last Judgement, between birth in original sin and ultimate salvation or damnation.

Elizabethan drama did not attempt to match the ambition of range of the cycles, but it did make the most of the high expectations of drama that they raised. The Corpus Christi performances represented the high point of the civic and ritual year for the towns that staged them, which included many of the leading cities of the country; they thus had more in common with the dramatic festivals of ancient Athens than with village folk plays. The cycle plays, moreover, were of massive scope: they covered the entire history of the world, of time itself. They lasted an entire long summer's day – at Chester, three days. Only in the 1590s did it become possible to see again something more like that larger scope the cycles had offered, through two series of plays that offered a single overarching story of fall and recovery, even though they were conceived in terms of secular rather than divine history: Shakespeare's two tetralogies, each about the working out of a historical curse through to a culminating national recovery.[22]

More immediately striking even than this ambition of subject is the fact that neither form of drama sets limits to itself. Neither cares anything for the unities of time or place, or for any rule-bound generic shaping such as requires that lords and shepherds, or gravediggers and princes, never appear in the same play, or that forbids jokes in plays about suffering.[23] If all the world is a stage, then kings and peasants necessarily share it, just as they share the drama of salvation. *Totus mundus agit histrionem*, 'everyone plays a role', was the motto of the Globe. The cast lists of the plays in the public theatres, as of the cycle plays, comprehend all of humanity. They therefore comprehend the spectators too, since the actors so easily enlist them as participants in the plot, by direct appeals to them as present at the Crucifixion, or at the crowd-manipulating machinations of Richard III.[24] Those plots can also cover the whole range of human happiness and grief, just as the utter bliss of the saved and the utter despair of the damned coexist in the Last Judgement, or, on a more human scale, as adjacent pageants juxtapose the intimate, delighted scene of the Magi paying homage to the infant Christ with the slaughter of the other babies and the laments of their mothers.

It necessarily follows, as Sir Philip Sidney famously complained of contemporary dramatists, that 'all their plays be neither right tragedies, nor right comedies',[25] and his complaint applies to the biblical plays as much as to the public theatres. His formulation implies that while an affiliation to classical genre is 'right', being a mere 'play' is wrong. The English dramatic resistance to generic regulation was however a princi-pled one. It was precisely its quality as play, as something not to be taken seriously, and therefore, when it dealt with religious matters, potentially blasphemous, that most offended many of the early reformers.[26] The dis-tance of play from the regulations governing the classical genres was, however, central to its conception. The cycles *require* the mixing of social classes in the same play, and a flexibility of language and style to match (though the greatest contrast is not between king and clown, but between Creator and creature, whether human or devil). They likewise require that what may appear as tragic may yet be an episode in a divine comedy analogous to Dante's. And 'comedy' in that sense is not the clas-sical definition, Cicero's or Sidney's definition, of ridiculing the common errors of our life (though that may come into it too), but of comedy as the happy ending. In that, the cycle playwrights and Shakespeare see eye to eye. The cycles find common ground with comedy in the happy end-ing characteristic of romance, and it is probably no coincidence that the great age of romance was also the great age of faith. Romance does not, generically speaking, need to be funny; it is indeed likely to include loss, hardship and even apparent death, just as the divine pattern of human history traces the course of a circle from Paradise through the Fall and the Passion to resurrection and salvation. The comedies of the early modern English stage, not least Shakespeare's, often present a similar movement, with suffering and trial along the way but with the ending defined by a return from death, by reconciliation and forgiveness. Like the mysteries, these plays tend to present a providential ordering in their final plot shaping, even though such an ordering is far from being apparent to the characters along the way.

The stage representation of space is as flexible as its attitude to genre. Tamburlaine's world conquests present no problem to spectators accustomed to seeing heaven and hell on the same stage. A play consisting substantially of a series of voyages to and fro across the Mediterranean was being staged in the early sixteenth century in the Digby *Mary Magdalen* long before Shakespeare repeated it in *Pericles*.[27] Movement within a scene is no problem for a playgoer who has seen the shepherds travel from the fields to the stable by crossing the pageant wagon. It is even less of a problem for those familiar with the alternative method of staging, used for the *Magdalen* and for the *N-Town Cycle*, where scaffolds or other designated *loci* indicate specific places but where the main acting area in front of them consists of an open space that represents wherever the characters are. Staging of this kind allows for concurrent scenes involving different characters in different places to be intercut – a form of simultaneous representation that incurred Sidney's scorn ('you shall have Asia of the one side, and Afric of the other').[28] Whichever way they were performed, the mystery plays typically change scene by taking characters across from one time or place to another in front of the audience's eyes: it is the stage equivalent of what in film is a dissolve or a fade. Early spectators may indeed have been initially disconcerted by the new convention of the cleared stage, just as film audiences could be disconcerted by the appearance of the jump-cut. Neither the cleared stage nor the jump-cut explains itself, or gives the spectator time to adapt; one way acts out the move from one scene to the next, the other way it just happens.[29] The early dramatic conventions became problematic only with the introduction of scene divisions in the printed texts of plays at the very end of the sixteenth century, and those were magnified by later editors working from naturalistic assumptions about stage place – assumptions that at their worst led to the uncontrolled proliferation of scene divisions (typically headed 'Another part of the field') for the run-ning battles of the *Henry VI* plays or *Troilus and Cressida*. It is largely, but not entirely, a problem peculiar to print rather than to performance; but the new style did make life harder for the dramatists, since they could no longer follow one scene by another that used the same characters, and had to invent some intermediate action. George Peele uses the old-style dissolve method explicitly in the 1580s, in his *Old Wives Tale*, the title carrying the implication that this is a form of staging that is on its way out; but it was not, as is evident from Shakespeare's continuing use of it in 1608 in *Pericles*. *Pericles* too stresses its quality as an 'old tale', but its narration is performed according to dramaturgical conventions that were evidently still comprehensible to its audience.

Time in this dramatic model is as fluid as space. Romance-style plays that cover the life of the hero or heroine from birth to maturity and sometimes beyond – plays such as Gosson and Sidney were objecting to in the 1580s but which Shakespeare was still happily writing almost three decades later – are easy to accept compared to a cycle that encom-passes the entirety of time: a cycle that typically starts, 'I am alpha et O, God withouten bigynnyng.'[30] And if a cycle or a play can compress time, so can individual pageants or scenes. Plays of the childhood of Jesus often start with the presentation of him as a baby in the temple, and carry straight on with his dispute with the doctors; it was universal prac-tice to present the building of the ark, the Flood and the restoration of the earth with no break in continuity. Apparent impossibilities of timing in early modern drama were similarly part of the conventions that were taken for granted. There was no bafflement at being invited to live through Faustus's long career in the course of his opening soliloquy; nor at the double time-scheme in *Othello* (i.e. the fact that the stated chronol-ogy of the scenes does not allow any time at all for Desdemona to have an affair with anybody between her marriage and her calumniation); nor at the temporally sequential scenes in *Richard II* (1.4, 2.1) that open with everyone coming back from seeing Bolingbroke off into exile, and end with the first reports of his return. In the first Folio and in modern editions, those scenes are separated by an act division that gives the illu-sion of time passing, but in the early quartos, as in performance, the action flows easily and immediately from one to the other. In the first act of *Titus Andronicus*, conversely, there is an implied passage of time between the burial of Mutius and the entry of the married couples at 1.1.396, but since Titus and his sons have not left the stage, a scene break cannot be marked in a printed text – once again, the effect is the fade, of the same characters across one time or place and another, rather than the cleared stage or the jump-cut. The supposition that Peele may have been responsible for this act is of a piece with his dramaturgy in *The Old Wives Tale*, though here there is no question of *faux-naiveté*.[31] If there is no prior assumption of a parallel between stage time and real time (and no one brought up on the cycle plays would assume anything of the kind), then scenes of this kind are not problematic; they appear so only as a consequence of later assumptions of temporal literalism, and of the conventions of print. Aristotelean rules of temporal and spatial consistency are as artificial as if we were to expect the cinema screen to show only one place, or one time.

Neither the Elizabethan secular drama nor the cycles were illusionist; but neither form exactly invites a suspension of disbelief. Rather, all those stage conventions cue the audience imagination so that they *make believe* that the unstageable is being staged – and for an audience that had grown up with the cycle plays, that would have appeared both normal and normative. It is those that make the staging of *anything* possible. An 'incarnational aesthetic' invites the representation not just of the human but of the supernatural or even the invisible. John Bale, reformer that he was, is prepared to stage God, but only given the saving grace of an opening declaration of invisibility: 'I am Deus pater, a substaunce inuysyble.'[32] It is normal practice for the God of the mysteries to open the first play with a great 'I am' speech declaring his power, insisting on the difference between the actor as signifier and the signified beyond imagination; Bale's line insists not just on difference but on an absolute otherness, a denial of theatrical incarnation even while he presents it on stage. That denial has as its consequence the elimination of further possibilities of shifting between the visible and the notionally invisible that other dramatists exploit. So in the *N-town Cycle*, an onstage God becomes invisible to Adam from the moment he falls.[33] Fairies or ghosts who are supposedly invisible to other characters are similarly no problem on the secular stage. 'I am invisible', declares Oberon, without bewildering either the other figures on stage or his real spectators (*MND* 2.1.186). The real spectators share Hamlet's and Macbeth's experience of their respective ghosts despite their invisibility to Gertrude and the dinner guests, just as it is a premise of plays of Balaam and the ass that the angel should be visible only to the spectators and the ass. Supernatural figures that could take visible form, notably angels and devils, regularly appeared on the early modern stage as on the medieval. Angels such as those in *Guy of Warwick* (?1593)[34] and Katherine of Aragon's vision in *Henry VIII*, or devils such as figure in *Dr Faustus* and Jonson's *The Devil is an Ass*, were presumably costumed and acted in keeping with audience expectations inherited from both biblical and morality plays. Playgoers who came from anywhere near Coventry would know at first hand of one particularly famous devil who served as the porter at the gates of hell,[35] and who did so, no doubt, as was customary for devils, in a style that came closer to what the humanists would call the low style of comedy than the high style of tragedy; so they would have a distinct advantage when it came to recognizing the porter of *Macbeth*. Such playgoers might have a running start too in recognizing the ancestry of a character called Lightborne, the murderer of Marlowe's *Edward II*, for the name is not just a near-anglicization of Lucifer, but was already familiar as the name of a devil.[36]

Violence took illusionism a large step further, for when the blood ran down in front of the spectators' eyes, they scarcely even needed to make believe. The Slaughter of the Innocents and the Crucifixion mutate easily into Bajazeth beating his brains out, and the technology for such things, the bloodbags or collapsing swords, would have been held in common. Judas regularly hanged himself on stage, and the expertise required to enable him to do so was worth fourpence in Coventry in 1573.[37] The hanging of Horatio and Pedringano in the *Spanish Tragedy* in the next decade no doubt used the same techniques, and (since the key point is that the spectators know that it is not for real) it may well have been that kind of theatrical experience, not the executions at Tyburn, that Kyd's episode recalled.

Incarnation was backed by other, more symbolic means of implying meaning. The cycle plays enhanced both God and grief through music. Music figures everywhere in the cycles as an expression of the divine. The mothers of the slaughtered innocents at Coventry sing the lament known to us as the Coventry Carol. Theophanies and laments on the early modern stage were likely to take musical form: the appearance of Hymen in *As You Like It*, or the music of the spirit-filled island of *The Tempest*, or the willow song of *Othello*. So far as God or the gods are concerned, the music is not just emotive in effect, but intellectual: it invokes the harmony of the divine order.

A comparable process of analogy is at work in the relationship between different narratives within a larger dramatic structure. Audiences of the cycle plays would be trained to recognize such theatrical analogy, in a way that would come in very handy for understanding subplots (there are no subplots in classical or humanist drama, or in morality plays). There is a sense in which every individual pageant is a subplot in the greater drama of salvation. Each one is related to it, not just as a chronological step in the sequence, but by typology, by likeness within difference. The patterns are repeated even while the overt subject matter changes: the ark offers a model of salvation, Isaac's carrying the wood is re-enacted in Christ's carrying the Cross. The first recognizable subplot in the Elizabethan sense in English drama (perhaps even the first in Western drama) – a subplot, that is, that provides a supplementary parody of the main action – comes from the cycle plays, in the episode of Mak the sheep-stealer and the visit to the wrong baby in the Towneley *Second Shepherds Play*. That particular play had its last known performance in the 1550s, but all the habits of thinking by analogy that the cycles required would have given later popular audiences a finer dramatic training than the academic education that made the humanists regard subplots as a mere distraction from the main business of a play or an infringement of Aristotelean rules of unity of action.

It is undeniable that many of the playgoers of the 1580s to 1600s would have seen the cycle plays. It is much harder to prove in the case of any single individual, whether playgoer or playwright. We do know that Ferdinando, Lord Strange, the future patron of the company that probably first performed *Titus Andronicus* and other Shakespeare plays, saw the Chester Shepherds' Play in 1577, together with his recusant father.[38] Shakespeare himself had the most obvious opportunities of all the major Elizabethan dramatists to see one of the civic mystery cycles, since the magnificent dramatic spectacle of the Coventry plays was taking place just a few miles down the road from Stratford until he was in his mid-teens. Proximity alone does not prove he knew about raging Herods and devilish porters at first hand (though it makes it likely that he did);[39] but what is clear is that he and his contemporary playwrights shared the same understanding and conventions of drama as the cycle playwrights – conventions being 'things agreed', the assumptions shared with those audiences familiar with either or both kinds of drama. Those assumptions covered time and place and how they were staged; working without genres and rules; the inclusiveness of characters and events; and not least, embodiment – that action, however violent, is acted out before your eyes.

* * *

Shakespeare opened his career with evident humanist ambitions. *The Comedy of Errors* is more classical than anything Ben Jonson ever produced; *Titus Andronicus* draws extensively on Ovid and Seneca. Neither of those plays, however, can be adequately explained in terms of their Latin influences alone, and both show how Shakespeare found classical dramatic and dramaturgical models inadequate to generate the kind of theatre he wanted to produce. *The Comedy of Errors* frames Plautus' source within an overarching story of family loss and reunion borrowed in from the archetypal romance *Apollonius of Tyre*,[40] the same romance that he was later, and with a blithe rejection of any kind of formal unity, to dramatize as *Pericles*. *Titus*, as has been noted, insists on a thoroughly unclassical freedom of time and space. And both plays break free in the direction of what the cycle plays were doing, or being – enacted, embodied drama. There is no messenger speech about what happens to Lavinia; indeed, being tongueless, she threatens to disappear from the printed page altogether in many scenes. But we *see* her, and despite her silence, she seizes audience attention whenever she is onstage – like Christ in the Passion sequences, who in some plays (the Towneley *Buffeting* is a notable instance) never speaks at all. The onstage, enacted violence of *Titus* is accompanied too by a thoroughly non-classical grotesque or black humour, very close to that exploited in the Passion sequences. It may well be that *Titus* represents not the classicizing Shakespeare, but the Shakespeare for whom (as Emrys Jones has it), 'before he became aware of more neoclassical ways of writing tragedy', the popular Passion plays took 'a position of absolute priority in his mind, seeming to him more moving, more fundamental, forms of tragic drama'.[41]

Along with embodiment goes a readiness to imitate iconography, the visual representation of Christian belief. It is easy to assume that Shakespeare's models were artistic, but some highly recognizable configurations of staging were not in fact given any artistic representation. For anyone who had seen Lucifer seating himself in God's throne, the staged seizing of a secular throne carries all the more of a *frisson*. The Massacre of the Innocents was not a common subject in church art, but it figures in all the surviving cycles, and it seems to be that representation rather than the biblical account which is recalled in the scene of the slaughter of Macduff's children, or verbally in Henry V's invocation of 'the mad mothers with their howls confused' at 'Herod's bloody-hunting slaughtermen'.[42] Furthermore, religious art in England had effectively been wiped out a generation earlier than the cycle plays. We have had to substitute the Italian term *Pietà* for the English 'Pity' or 'Our Lady of Pity', since what was one of the most beloved iconographic representations in England, of the Virgin cradling her dead son, has disappeared almost without trace. Of surviving plays, it was staged in the *N-Town Cycle*, the non-cyclical Digby *Burial of Christ* and probably much more widely,[43] and it is echoed in the father-and-daughter tableau of Lear's entry with the dead Cordelia in his arms; but here there is no resurrection. The plays could overgo pictures by *enacting* their iconography,[44] but they rarely re-enact it in straightforward ways. As in the case of Cordelia, it is at least as likely to be used obliquely, to reject any simple allegorical equation. In *Richard II*, the play that for the first time in Elizabethan tragedy questions its own rhetoric, Richard describes himself as Christ betrayed by his followers, a description that could be drawn direct from the Bible; but appropriately for Richard, he is a very voluble Christ, calling attention to his own sufferings, in a way that carries full impact only if the comparison figure is the dramatized Christ who suffers both silently and visibly. The iconography of the deposition thus works to ironize the very parallel the king is so keen to invoke. These configurations of staging most often provide suggestive analogies as to how to respond to the scenes, sometimes perhaps even at a subliminal level for the spectators. So Richard Duke of York, in *3 Henry VI*, set on a hillock and mocked by cruel bystanders before they murder him, comes straight out of an earlier dramatic tradition,[45] without Shakespeare's ever committing himself or the audience as to whether his cause is right or wrong. The torchlight arrest of Othello, with Iago acting as the Judas who has told his enemies where to find him, and Othello's echo of Christ's 'Put up thy sword', does not turn Othello into Christ;[46] it does, however, reconfigure the balance of good and evil in the play, and imply a very different reading of the characters from the one Iago has been at pains to put over in the opening scene.

By the time Shakespeare is writing his later tragedies, another change has happened that pushes him still further away from humanist 'drama as rhetorical event' towards embodied drama, theatre incarnate. In *Titus*, the spectacle of violence is still backed by rhetoric, as in Marcus' speech describing the newly mutilated Lavinia:

> Alas, a crimson river of warm blood,
> Like to a bubbling fountain stirred with wind,
> Doth rise and fall between thy rosed lips
>
> (2.3[2.4].22–4)

This is the equivalent of the description of Christ's wounds such as is found in the Passion lyrics and sermon; but on the stage it is superfluous (and indeed is often cut in production), for the horror of what is happening is already visible to the audience. Shakespeare rapidly came to realize that he did not need language when spectacle could do the work, and that spectacle may well be more important. So Gertrude describes at length the death of Ophelia, because it happens offstage; the Player King describes at even greater length the death of Priam, in a quintessential Senecan messenger speech. The staged murders, by contrast, such as the death of Polonius, are *enacted*, with no rhetoric whatever. Hamlet's notorious reputation for procrastination, for being a man of thought rather than action, is based partly on the fact that when he does act the words are so few and the stage directions tucked so far to the side of the page or so safely sealed off in brackets, that the reading critic scarcely notices when the prince's own murder count starts steadily going up. Take, for instance, the moment of the first of these murders, when he believes he has indeed killed the king:

> How now? A rat! Dead, for a ducat, dead.
> [*Thrusts his rapier through the arras.*]
>
> (3.4.22)

As the square brackets indicate, the stage direction (here in Harold Jenkins' Arden 2 edition) is editorial; the Second Quarto gives the dialogue alone, leaving the murder implicit in the spoken line, and the Folio provides a bare '*Killes Polonius*'. Within half-a-dozen lines the action has moved on to Hamlet's confrontation of his mother, the corpse ignored by the characters and invisible on the page. To the spectators, however, it remains a constant presence, drawing their eyes, a compelling and embodied distraction from the spoken word.

The contrast between the various kinds of drama is played out in *Hamlet* in the difference between the Senecan report of the death of Priam and the enacted death of Polonius. The distinctiveness of what Shakespeare and the dramatic tradition he represents are doing becomes even more evident when it is set against Seneca's works themselves. The Tudor translator of Seneca's *Oedipus*, Alexander Neville, devoted huge rhetorical resources to describing his protagonist's self-blinding:

Out with thine Eyes (he sayd:) and then with fury fierce enflam'de,
Like to a bloudy raging Feend and monstrous beast untam'de,
With fiery flaming spotted Cheekes his breast he often beates,
And scratch, and teare his Face hee doth and Skin a sunder treats,
That scarse his eyes in head could stand so sore he them besets . . .

When sodenly all franticklike himselfe from ground hee teares,
And rooteth out his wretched Eyes, and sight a sunder teares.
Then gnasheth hee his bloudy Teeth, and bites, and gnawes, and
    champs,
His Eyes all bathd and brude in bloud, for fury fierce he stamps.
And raging more than needes (alas,) his Eyes quight rooted out:
The very holes in vayne hee scrapes so sore the wretch doth dout.[47]

This kind of speech, intensified in style when spoken by a tyrant rather
than a mere messenger, also serves as a useful reminder that the taste for
bombast was one shared by the humanists and the Herod playwrights,
and their audiences. If those who had seen the biblical plays ever got to
hear any Senecan translation – and hearing, not seeing, is what matters
here – they would find a tyrannical style, alliteration and all, close to
what they were used to. But in *King Lear*, there is no need for anything of
this kind to describe the blinding of Gloucester; we just see it. Instead of
these inflated descriptions of gruesome sights, we are given the casual,
mocking commentary of those who are inflicting the torture, just as in
the Crucifixion plays we hear, not Christ, nor any description of the
blood or the pain, but the perpetrators' mockery as they get on with the
job of stretching Christ with ropes to fit the holes bored in the cross:

III *Miles* Nowe are feste faste both his hende.
IV.   Go we all foure thanne to his feete,
    So schall oure space be spedely spende.
II.   Latte see what bourde his bale myght beete,
    Tharto my bakke nowe wolde I bende.[48]

Here for comparison is the blinding of Gloucester:

CORNWALL   Fellows, hold the chair;
    Upon these eyes of thine I'll set my foot . . .
REGAN   One side will mock another – th'other too.

(3.7.66–7, 70)

The action in both episodes is similar, of a man enduring appalling torture: for Christ, while he is stretched with ropes to fit the wooden frame of

the Cross as it lies on the ground; for Gloucester, bound to the chair as it is tipped backwards in preparation for Cornwall's descending boot – and what is the chair doing there? Why not just bind and blind Gloucester, if not to recall an iconographic moment already familiar from the stage? The dialogue in both consists not of a rhetoric to equal or to convey the magnitude of the event, but of stage direction, instruction to the actors. The terribleness of what is happening is conveyed by the *in*adequacy of the language, and by what we see: blood running down.

Shakespeare, at first glance, seems to offer as little explicit theory of drama, of plays, as do the Corpus Christi cycles; but this does not mean he just warbled his native woodnotes wild without ever thinking about it.[49] The array of different kinds of theatre in *Hamlet* punningly stages, enacts, that process of thinking about enactment, with its embodied main action, its reported actions, its dumbshow, its play-within-a-play, its Senecan set pieces modelling the play-as-rhetorical-event, its comments on the children's companies and on acting styles, and so to its remark about out-Heroding Herod. And just occasionally, Shakespeare does come closer to saying something more explicit. The opening chorus of *Henry V* is so familiar that it becomes quite hard to think about what it is actually saying; but one of the things it says most emphatically is that humanist theories of drama are quite inadequate to account for his own practice. Here, Shakespeare seizes the initiative from the academic objectors to this all-encompassing kind of theatre to assert dramatic freedom on a positively medieval scale:

> O for a muse of fire, that would ascend
> The brightest heaven of invention,
> A kingdom for a stage, princes to act,
> And monarchs to behold the swelling scene! . . .
> Can this cockpit hold
> The vasty fields of France? Or may we cram
> Within this wooden O the very casques
> That did affright the air at Agincourt? . . .
> Piece out our imperfections with your thoughts . . .
> For 'tis your thoughts that now must deck our kings,

> Carry them here and there, jumping o'er times,
> Turning th'accomplishment of many years
> Into an hour-glass.
>
> (Prologue 1–4, 11–14, 23, 28–31)

This is a kind of drama that encompasses as much space and time as the dramatist wills. 'O for a muse of fire!' sounds as if such a muse is absent, but Shakespeare goes ahead and does everything he wants to do all the same. The Coventry Doomsday play included the burning of the world;[50] Shakespeare's fiery muse can create worlds.

The 'wooden O' is also a wooden nought. Shakespeare was working just at that moment of transition from roman numerals to arabic numerals as the norm, and therefore when the O, the circle, goes from being a symbol of infinity, of everything, to being nothing; yet, as the Chorus goes on to point out, even ciphers can make a single figure into a million (15–17). Donne picks up the same process of transition in his image of the mapmaker who can take a round ball and 'quickly make that which was nothing, all' ('A Valediction: Of Weeping'). The theatre is both everything and nothing. It is whatever happens between that alpha and omega, the beginning and the end; yet the whole world will, as Prospero puts it in *The Tempest*, fade like an insubstantial pageant, and leave not a wrack behind.

The Tempest was not quite Shakespeare's last play, and that speech of Prospero's customarily known as Shakespeare's farewell to the stage is not the character's last speech either. That comes as the epilogue, and is still more interesting. It is a plea for audience approval, cast, very strongly, in terms of a plea for approval from God, for mercy at the Last Judgement.

> my ending is despair,
> Unless I be reliev'd by prayer,
> Which pierces so, that it assaults
> Mercy itself, and frees all faults.
>> As you from crimes would pardon'd be,
>> Let your indulgence set me free.
>
> (Epilogue 15–20)

Shakespeare ends this play of farewells not just by saying goodbye to the stage, but foreshadowing the ending of the world; and with that, the Last Judgement that will be passed on each person. That is the point where this stage-play life – this cycle-play life – ends. 'All the world's a stage'; but it is the stage of the mystery cycles, which encompasses all of humankind, all times, all places, and which ends the cycle of each life with judgement. And it is this that goes a long way towards explaining the sheer excitement of drama in the wake of the Reformation. It is a drama of infinite possibility, as infinite as heaven and hell; but it was playing with fire. That might be the Muse of Fire for Shakespeare, but it was everlasting fire in the eyes of the Puritans; and if the Puritans were right, then actors, dramatists and playgoers alike were acting out a drama not of salvation, but of damnation.

In 1642 the godly won out, and the theatres were closed. Popular access to the drama of the cycle plays had ended with their suppression in the wake of the Reformation; popular access to secular drama largely ceased with the suppression of the playhouses by a Puritan Parliament. When the new theatres opened after the Restoration, they were to present a different kind of dramatic experience: one that kept itself reserved from the public at large, and kept even its elite audience at a distance from the action by the intervention of the proscenium arch; an urbane drama for the polite classes, that bound itself by the rules of generic decorum and time and space. It did not altogether forget its incarnational roots, but it was no longer in any sense a popular theatre.

Chapter Two

SHAKESPEARE AND
POPULAR FESTIVITY

Leah S. Marcus

'Then are we in order when we are most out of order'

(Jack Cade, 2H6)

Arguably more than most other plays of the period, Shakespeare's are full of evocations of popular festivity which, depending on the dramatic context, can be menacing, neutral, or benevolent. At one end of a wide spectrum, there is the rebellion of peasants and artisans led by Jack Cade in *2 Henry VI*, which carries overtones of the holiday 'liberty' associated with May Day and other festivals. The Duke of York, who claims to have seduced Cade into stirring up 'commotion', compares his fighting to traditional morris dancing: 'I have seen / Him caper upright like a wild Morisco, / Shaking the bloody darts as he his bells' (3.1.364–6). At the other end of the spectrum, there is Sir Toby Belch's comic 'rebellion' in *Twelfth Night*. When Malvolio reproves him and his drunken crew for staying up drinking into the wee hours during the Christmas season, Sir Toby retorts, 'Dost thou think because thou art virtuous, there shall be no more cakes and ale?' and the fool Feste, whose very name suggests holiday feasting, adds 'Yes, by Saint Anne, and ginger shall be hot i' th' mouth too' (2.3.114–17). Both examples of festivity are branded as disorderly by at least some elements in their respective plays, but Cade is killed and his followers dispersed, while Sir Toby and his companions are allowed to triumph over Malvolio. Over and over again, Shakespeare stages confrontations between proponents of order and forms of disorder that are specifically associated with elements of popular festivity. What is at stake in this recurring confrontation?

'Popular festivity' is a phrase that can cover many different activities. I will use it here to refer to popular pastimes connected with religious holidays or secular community functions and carrying a significant element of ritual repetition that has to be included in order for the festivity to be performed correctly. Many popular festivals in the early modern era were at least loosely tied to Christian observances: Christmas mummings, dances, games, carolling, gift-giving, and feasting; Whitsuntide, May, and Midsummer bonfires; Whitsun ales; dancing around Maypoles; sprinkling the crops with May dew; May games; and folk-plays of Robin Hood and Maid Marion. I would also include agricultural observances less closely tied to holidays of the Church but still retaining some connections with religious observance, such as 'beating the bounds' of the parish on Rogation Sunday to affirm property boundaries and bless the crops, sheep-shearing festivals, hock tide bindings, and harvest homes. Many of these festivities involved communal eating and drinking, and were at least in theory designed to affirm or create harmony among those who lived in close proximity with one another – what Shakespeare's contemporaries liked to call 'good neighbourhood'.[1] More often than not, they were not exclusively 'popular' in that elements of the gentry and aristocracy could also take part or host the events in the interests of 'good neighbourhood'. Sometimes these observances overflowed into rioting, as in the case of 'Evil May Day', 1517, when London apprentices engaged in large and bloody battles against alien residents and had to be subdued by military force.

Often, popular festivities involved formal elements of inversion that turned the usual social order topsy-turvy for the duration of the holiday, as in the custom of electing 'Lords of Misrule' to preside over Christmas or spring holiday observances, or in holiday pastimes that allowed servants brief 'liberty' from the authority of masters, and women from the authority of men. But there were other popular festivals not tied to the ecclesiastical calendar that also involved elements of topsy-turvydom, such as the 'rough music' or Skimmington by which local communities enforced their standards against members considered to be deviant (scolds, fornicators, adulterers, encroachers upon land held in common) through public shaming rituals that involved dunking the offending parties, hauling them around on a donkey backwards, peppering them with verbal abuse, or sometimes imitating them through the antics of mocking cross-dressed surrogates (see Figures 3 and 4). Unlike some of the other topics treated in the present volume, popular festivity in Shakespeare has attracted a significant amount of critical attention and

FIGURE 3   Skimmington, from *Halfe a dozen of good Wives: All for a Penny* (1634), in *The Roxburghe Ballads*.

FIGURE 4   Further versions of the Skimmington, from *The Roxburghe Ballads*.

controversy – as popular pastimes themselves did in Elizabethan and Jacobean England.[2] How we interpret their dramatic functioning from play to play will depend to a significant degree on the explanatory model we invoke.

MODELLING POPULAR FESTIVITY

A traditional and uncritical account of Shakespeare's evocations of popular festivity presented them simply as reflections of the 'Merry old England' in which he lived. On this view, which is close kin to Milton's depiction of the Bard of Avon in *L'Allegro* as a native rural genius warbling his 'native Wood-notes wild', Shakespeare revelled in the sweet liberty of traditional holiday pastimes – particularly rural sports – because they were as much a part of his native environment as the fields of Stratford or the streets of London. This view tends to interpret Shakespeare's times and writings through the rosy glow of an ideal of 'good neighbourhood' which elements of contemporary culture sought to promote. It is a perspective that seriously underestimates elements of conflict and disjunction in Elizabethan society. For example, the 'naive' view of Stratford-upon-Avon – still widely disseminated even in our own sceptical times through mass media evocations of 'Merry Old England' – is of a timeless, achingly beautiful river community linked in fecund harmony with the land and the seasons. We need to remind ourselves that Stratford was marked by serious rifts between a town population that was largely Catholic and a local rural gentry that was strongly Puritan, and that it was highly litigious: Shakespeare and his family were involved in almost perennial lawsuits, and may also have been subjected to public shaming rituals on one or more occasions.[3] So the traditional view of Shakespeare as a dramatist whose plays do not comment upon popular festivity, but simply mirror the common festival practices of his own culture, is by now seriously outmoded.

The traditional view can, of course, be advanced to explain some depictions of festivity within the plays, such as, perhaps, the spring sheep-shearing scene in *The Winter's Tale* (4.4), which occurs after three wintry acts of apparent tragedy in which the jealous Leontes loses his wife and children. As the old shepherd explains early in the scene, the spring festival is celebrated to ensure the fecundity of the flocks: 'Come on, / And bid us welcome to your sheep-shearing, / As your good flock shall prosper' (4.4.68–70). If his logic is extended to the action of the play as a whole, the scene would herald the restoration of 'good neighbourhood' and harmony in Bohemia and Sicily, and indeed the final two acts of the play give back much of what Leontes has lost, reunite his long-sequestered queen Hermione with her exiled daughter, and resolve the long feud between Leontes and Polixenes by uniting their children in marriage. But the pivotal scene in *Winter's Tale* is a bit more complex than that. Florizel takes advantage of the 'freedom' of the holiday to woo the seeming shepherdess Perdita without his father's consent. The simple festival which the shepherd expects is given uneasy undertones and finally broken off in a most unmerry fashion by the presence of hostile nobles in disguise, especially Polixenes, the king himself, who views his son's holiday 'freedom' as traitorous. The traditional model cannot account for elements of conflict within the scene, or for its complex interactions among different social groups. *The Winter's Tale* requires much more than an artless rural festival to mend the ancient wounds of Sicily and bring about a final reconciliation. And more generally, the 'Merry England' model of popular festivity fails altogether to explain modulations of holiday 'liberty' into actual violence in the plays, such as Jack Cade's alliance with Maying customs in *2 Henry VI*.

A more sophisticated anthropological argument was offered in 1959 by C.L. Barber, who argued in *Shakespeare's Festive Comedy* that Shakespeare was poised historically between a past in which the festive 'misrule' of popular customs had functioned as an escape valve for tensions that might otherwise have threatened the community, and a present in which this release was no longer available because the rituals had fallen into disuse as a result of urbanization and commercialization. In Barber's view, Shakespeare's 'festive comedies' recaptured the energy of popular festivity in order to enact a version of its movement 'through release to clarification', but without ever losing sight of its fragile status as art rather than life:

> Shakespeare's plays are full of pageantry and of action patterned in a ritualistic way. But the pageants are regularly interrupted; the

rituals are abortive or perverted; or if they succeed, they succeed against odds or in an unexpected fashion. The people in the plays try to organize their lives by pageant and ritual, but the plays are dramatic precisely because the effort fails.[4]

One of Barber's most influential examples of drama's assimilation of dying ritual is his discussion of parallels between Falstaff in the *Henry IV* plays and the traditional holiday 'Lord of Misrule', specifically, the carnival figure of Shrove Tuesday or Mardi Gras (literally 'Fat Tuesday') – an enormous, waddling bag of guts who embodied the spirit of carnival excess that was to be aired and celebrated for a while, then banished as the corpulent figure of Shrove Tuesday was customarily sacrificed to make way for the abstinence of Ash Wednesday and the beginning of Lent. As Barber points out, the fat knight is occasionally linked with Shrove Tuesday in the plays: in *Part 1* Falstaff is all beef, guts and tallow; Prince Hal, who ends Falstaff's disorderly 'misrule' when he takes the crown at the end of *Part 2*, is associated, by contrast, with eels, stock-fish and the leanness of Lent. *2 Henry IV*, in which Falstaff loses some of his girth and Prince Hal gathers strength, explicitly takes place during the Lenten season, when 'suffering flesh to be eaten' is 'contrary to the law' (2.4.341–2). In Barber's view, understanding the Carnival-to-Lent pattern underlying the Henry IV plays allows their audience to make sense of Prince Hal's sacrifice of Falstaff at the end of *2 Henry IV*, at least insofar as Shakespeare succeeds in transforming ritual into drama. By first consorting with Falstaff and then casting him off, Prince Hal is able to master the misrule that Falstaff represents: what would have taken place earlier as quasi-magical ritual observance is rationalized as historical and psychological development.[5]

Shakespeare's Festive Comedy has been enormously influential among Shakespeareans, and did much to create the preoccupation with traditional festivity that has been a prominent feature of more recent scholarship. But this is not to say that more recent scholars have accepted Barber's work uncritically. One of the ways in which his modelling of festivity has been challenged is in terms of its lack of historical precision. Barber's model of a carnival season giving way to Lent, for example, is based on continental examples. Popular carnival as he describes it was as a rule not celebrated in Britain, though Shrove Tuesday itself was

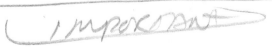

sometimes the occasion for feasting, drinking and rioting by apprentices.[6] For us now, basic motifs from the carnival season as practised in predominantly Catholic countries are familiar through widespread media coverage and also tourism to Venice, New Orleans or Rio. Ironically, Barber's festive model for the plot development of the Henry IV plays may resonate more for us than it did for audiences in Shakespeare's England. The imprecision of Barber's model has been redressed through more recent historical work that studies popular festivity in terms of the specific forms it took in the late sixteenth and early seventeenth century, and the specific issues it linked up with in contemporary commentary.[7] In particular, though he does mention it, Barber underplays the religious and political significance of popular festivity in a culture which was predominantly Protestant and for which many of the old customs smacked of the 'old religion' of Catholicism.

Much of our information about the 'disorders' of Maying and Christmas festivity come from hostile accounts by contemporary Puritans like Philip Stubbes who rejected almost all of the traditional holiday pastimes as unacceptable because of their pagan or Catholic origins. In his enormously popular *Anatomie of Abuses*, which went through four editions and two reissues between 1583 and 1595, Stubbes lambasted village and parish 'wakes and feastes' as gluttonous, whorish relics of 'Pagans and Heathen people, who when they were assembled together, and had offered sacrifices to their false goddes and blockish Idols, made feasts and banquets togither before them'.[8] Anticipating the confrontation between Feste and Malvolio in *Twelfth Night*, Stubbes inveighed against Christmas masquing, mumming and drunkenness on the part of people who 'thinke they haue a Commission & prerogatiue that time, to do what they list, & to follow what vanity they will . . . What will they say? Is it not Christmas? must we not be merry?' (p.239). Stubbes called the holiday Lord of Misrule a 'filthy Idol' and May games 'diuillish exercises' to promote a 'stinking Idoll'. The 'Idoll' in question could be either the Lord of Misrule presiding over the May games or the Maypole itself, but was in either case a focus for disorders and sexual promiscuity: 'of fourtie, threescore, or a hundred Maides going to the wood ouernight, there haue scarcely the third part of them returned home againe vndefiled' (pp.208–10).

Modern historians agree that Stubbes's lurid accounts exaggerated the prominence of 'disorders' practised along with popular festivity. But his blanket condemnation of holiday pastimes, whether dating from pagan or Roman Catholic times, was an attitude widely held by his contemporaries, particularly in London and other towns. In *Society and Puritanism*, Christopher Hill has suggested a correlation between proto-capitalist ideas among 'the industrious sort of people' and an opposition to traditional pastimes, which wasted much time and energy that could more profitably be spent on work and religious worship. As is suggested by Shakespeare's title *Twelfth Night*, Christmas festivities had traditionally lasted twelve days or more. The Protestant Church stripped down the number of holidays in England by about seventy-five per cent, to twenty-seven days plus Sundays,[9] but that was still too much sin and idleness in the view of many of the 'hotter Protestants'. Especially after the 1603 accession of James I, who had already argued for the harmlessness of 'public spectacles of all honest games' in his *Basilikon Doron*,[10] the issue of popular festivity became increasingly polarized and politicized, culminating in what came to be known as the *Book of Sports* issued in 1618 and again by Charles I in 1633. The *Book of Sports* was originally published for King James under the title *The King's Maiesties Declaration to His Subjects, concerning lawfull Sports to be vsed*. It is not listed among James I's official proclamations, but appears to have carried some of the legal weight of a proclamation. In it, James (or someone writing in his name) argued that popular festivity should be encouraged for the familiar, traditional reason that it increased 'good neighbourhood', but also for the more innovative reason that the traditional pastimes, in the Stuart view at least, firmed up popular loyalty to the English Church and Crown. By the 1620s and 1630s, promotion of popular festivity became a kind of religio-political litmus paper, at least in some prominent circles. To argue for the 'freedom to be merry' was to adhere to royal policy; to attempt to suppress the traditional sports or legislate against them was to risk being branded as overly Puritanical, 'precise', even seditious.

From 1604 onward, Shakespeare wore royal livery as a member of the King's Men; he could not possibly have been unaware of the brewing controversy over traditional pastimes. But he had been dead for two years by the time the *Book of Sports* was published in 1618, and had been retired from the stage for several years before that. And in any case, his most obviously 'festive' plays are Elizabethan rather than Jacobean. Nevertheless, Shakespeare was arguably more prone than contemporary dramatists such as, for example, Christopher Marlowe or Ben Jonson to introduce scenes of popular festivity into his plays.[11] How are we to read the functioning of traditional pastimes in Shakespearean drama? Hill would probably see Shakespeare as aligned with those who sought to preserve the old customs against ultra-Protestant opposition. If only because of his vocation, he had a vested interest in defending popular festivity in the face of disapproval by Puritans and London authorities: Philip Stubbes and other controversialists condemned the London stage with the same language that they used for mummers' plays and May games. All were suspect, particularly on Sundays, because they encouraged idleness, drunkenness and idolatry, and involved falsifications of identity and the particular 'abomination' of cross-dressing.[12] And more than Shakespeare's theatrical vocation may have been involved: if, as some recent biographers have contended, Shakespeare was either Catholic himself or a strong Catholic sympathizer, then it is reasonable to speculate that he may have felt some personal attachment to forms of popular festivity that in Catholic times had been closely associated with official holidays of the Church.[13]

But the dramatic and ideological impact of evocations of festival 'liberty' in Shakespeare's plays is by no means clear-cut. Other competing interpretations of the ideological functioning of popular festivity can be fruitfully invoked alongside Hill's, and can yield altered readings of the political and religious implications of popular festivity in the plays. Bakhtin, for example, has emphasized carnival's independence from government control, interpreting it as largely separate from the official culture, 'outside of and contrary to all existing forms of the coercive socioeconomic and political organization, which is suspended for the time of the festivity'.[14] If popular festivity is studied from the bottom up rather than from the top down, we may develop rather a different understanding of its functioning from that sanctioned by orthodox opinion in its own time.

In *Carnival and Theater* (1985) Michael Bristol has taken a Bakhtinian view, suggesting that critical work on theatre and popular festivity needs to put 'struggle, social difference and cultural antagonism at the centre of critical analysis, rather than consensus, harmony and accommodation'.[15] For Bristol, it is the anti-theatrical faction in Shakespeare's England that speaks for authority, while the drama, in its carnivalesque insouciance towards all forms of coercive restraint, is more fundamentally allied with the popular. Bristol's work addressed an important moment in Shakespeare studies in which critical attention had arguably come to centre too exclusively on cultural and political authority. But at present we tend not to see the functioning of popular festivity in the drama in terms of stark dichotomies. Perhaps the most useful interpretive work for the present critical scene has been that of Natalie Zemon Davis, who has studied particular episodes of popular 'misrule' in France and shown that their effects can be various, depending on time and place, ranging from reaffirmation of the *status quo* (which would be akin to the Stuart position), to subversion of it (which would approximate the position of early modern Puritans), but also including the potential for effecting minor adjustments in the pre-existing order of things, and for generating new cultural forms.[16] Order and disorder are notoriously slippery ideas. By now, our earlier dependence on the order–disorder binary for analysing popular festivity has been largely discredited as an outgrowth of 'subversion–containment' Cold War thinking. But we cannot discard the binary entirely, because, as my epigraph from Jack Cade suggests, it was also an element of Elizabethan and Jacobean thinking. London authorities and members of the Privy Council who were interested in shutting down the theatres habitually branded them 'disorders'.

Then, too, more than one critical model can be invoked simultaneously to explain a single cultural practice or response. What looked like unacceptable licence to an unsympathetic authority could perhaps feel like patterned ritual to one of its celebrants; what looked like artless and harmless popular mirth to a sympathetic authority could perhaps feel like unbridled rebellion to one of its participants. And Shakespearean audiences – both in the early modern era and more recently – are sufficiently diverse that many responses to the same theatrical production could swirl about simultaneously. The best recent critical work on popular festivity in Shakespeare has assimilated all of the models I have surveyed briefly above and invokes them flexibly, eclectically, and with careful attention to the shifting circumstances of performance.

STAGING CHRISTMAS FESTIVITY

Shakespeare scholars and directors have long recognized his tendency to structure plays in terms of polar opposites, both of which contain elements of vibrancy and truth, and both of which, paradoxically, are capable of arousing the audience's empathic identification. This characteristic helps to account for the great profundity of the plays: we sense ourselves in the presence of an interpretive network that becomes more intricate as we explore it more deeply because we are continually forced to qualify and complicate the ideas by which we seek to interpret it. For a dramatist writing in an era of controversy about the moral value of the drama itself, there was an obvious pay-off to be gained by building an enemy of plays and pastimes into the action of a play: the audience could be confronted with a range of possible onstage attitudes towards popular festivity, and the balance between them could easily be adjusted to fit the needs of a specific performance. In a setting that was receptive to traditional ideas about the 'freedom to be merry', the onstage antagonist of plays and pastimes could be made a comic butt or scapegoat whose elimination was cause for celebration; in a setting that was more ambivalent, the onstage antagonist could be rendered more credible, even noble, and serve to deflect negative feelings about the drama as an institution by articulating them from within it.

As already suggested, *Twelfth Night* stages a confrontation between holiday celebrants and an upwardly mobile household steward who attempts to suppress them in the interests of order and sobriety. There can be little question that for early audiences, the play, which was probably first performed in 1600 or 1601, carried echoes of contemporary controversy over holiday 'liberty'. To the extent that it was staged during the holidays – as it was for Candlemas at the Inns of Court on 2 February 1601, and more than once during the Christmas holidays at the Stuart court later in the century – the echoes would have intensified. Twelfth Night was the night before the Feast of the Epiphany (6 January), and marked the official end of the Christmas season – a final chance to cram in one last bit of drinking and jollity before the holiday was over. Malvolio's disdain for Christmas gambols and drinking mirrors that of many contemporary 'Puritans or precise people'; in fact, Maria identifies the style of his anti-festive rhetoric quite directly: 'Marry sir, sometimes he is a kind of Puritan.' Sir Andrew responds with instant hostility, 'O, if I thought that, I'd beat him like a dog' (2.3.140–1). And the name Malvolio suggests ill will towards everyone, implying that Puritan attitudes are essentially misanthropic and self-serving. But the case is muddled by the fact that in Maria's view, Malvolio only affects Puritanism because he believes it is in his interest to do so: 'The devil a Puritan that he is, or anything constantly, but a time-pleaser, an affectioned ass' (2.3.146–8).

The audience is given a choice: is Malvolio despicable because he is a Puritan, or because he is a hypocrite who only pretends Puritan principles, which would leave open the possibility that genuine Puritan sentiment against Christmas feasting and 'liberty' could be acceptable? And in fact, Malvolio's mistress Olivia and even Maria herself share many of his misgivings about the disorderly 'misrule' of Sir Toby and his drunken cohort. The play works quite well on stage if the audience is encouraged to share Sir Toby's view of the proper keeping of Christmas and join in the feasting and fun, but it is perhaps more interesting if Sir Toby's holiday excess is presented as problematic. As the action moves along, Malvolio's Puritan sentiments are shown to be only skin deep. He displays his foolish vanity by appearing yellow-stockinged and cross-gartered to win the heart of his mistress, and by apparently affecting the very levity he had previously condemned in the revellers once he thinks it will win her favour: 'To be Count Malvolio!' (2.5.35). Feste, the embodiment of festival, and the other revellers scourge him by literalizing his Puritan rhetoric. If, as Stubbes and other controversialists argued, Christmas pastimes were the creation of the devil, then Malvolio, who laments that he is surrounded by demonic madmen 'without any mitigation' (2.3.91–2), must be in hell. The revellers mock him by turning his Puritan invective back upon him: 'Lo, how hollow the fiend speaks within him!' 'La you, and you speak ill of the devil, how he takes it at heart!' 'What, man, 'tis not for gravity to play at cherry-pit with Satan!' (3.4.92–118). Not content with mere baiting, Feste imprisons the hapless steward in a dark, hell-like pit and visits him in the disguise of Sir Topas, the Parson, to convince him he is lunatic, so that the Puritan and the fool trade places and the holiday inversion is complete.

What makes the holiday baiting of Malvolio most thought provoking is that it is carried too far. If *Twelfth Night, or What You Will* enacts the 'liberty' of Christmas festivity, it also shows how easily that liberty can take on a logic of its own and spin out of control. At some point during the torturing of Malvolio, if not earlier, audience sympathy is likely to shift to his side, but at what point this happens and how strongly the audience responds will depend significantly on performance – the particular ways in which festivity and its enemy are balanced against each other, and the degree of credibility afforded to each. Malvolio can be performed as a complete hypocrite with few redeeming features who deserves most of the punishment he receives, or as a weak but basically decent man who is more wronged than those he contemns. In modern performances, his agitated refusal to participate in the general merriment at the end of the play usually casts a shadow on its mirth. It is easy to see how Shakespeare's play-loving contemporaries could have reacted to Malvolio's self-exile in a spirit of relief and good riddance. For them, the play on stage would perform a wish-fulfilling expulsion of dissident elements that were harder to extirpate in reality. Did *Twelfth Night* as performed in 1600–1 carry the message that all Puritans are Malvolios, spouting righteous invective but interested only in supplanting their betters? Or did it instead cause its audience to reflect on the confrontation between popular festivity and its enemies and come to new and possibly diverse conclusions about the value and purpose of holiday? We cannot be sure, but we can be certain that the confrontation between Feste and Malvolio was important in terms of at least some early response. Some thirty years later, in his copy of Shakespeare's Second Folio (1632), Charles I titled the play 'Malvolio'.

Popular festivity can also be found in tragedy, as Naomi Liebler has argued in *Shakespeare's Festive Tragedy* (1995), a companion study to Barber's *Shakespeare's Festive Comedy*. There are important links in terms of Christmas revelry between *Twelfth Night* and *King Lear*, which was performed at court, according to the title page of the First Quarto (1608) *'before the Kings Maiestie at Whitehall vpon S. Stephen's Night in [the] Christmas Hollidayes'* – that is, on 26 December 1606. Feste ends *Twelfth Night* with a plaintive song of holiday levelling that carries the play from the snugness of ale and hot ginger out into winter weather. Lear's Fool sings a verse of the same song during the storm scene at the middle of *King Lear*.

> He that has and a little tiny wit,
> With heigh-ho, the wind and the rain,
> Must make content with his fortunes fit,
> Though the rain it raineth every day.
>
> (3.2.74–7)

Feste's fuller version is especially appropriate for *King Lear* because its second verse describes a circumstance that is enacted in the tragedy:

> But when I came to man's estate,
> With hey, ho, the wind and the rain,
> 'Gainst knaves and thieves men shut their gate,
> For the rain it raineth every day.
>
> (5.1.392–5)

There is a significant difference between the gate shutting in the song and in the play. In *King Lear*, according to the laws of holiday inversion, it is not 'knaves and thieves' against whom the householders bar entry, but a king.

King Lear as performed at court on St Stephen's Day, 26 December 1606, provides a vivid illustration of the resonances that popular festivity elements of Shakespearean drama can take on as a result of a defined holiday context.[17] St Stephens Day, more recently known as Boxing Day, was the traditional holiday most associated with hospitality towards the poor, as echoed in the more recent carol of King Wenceslaus and his charity 'on the Feast of Stephen'. On St Stephen's Day, the day after Christmas, parish poor boxes were broken open and the money distributed to those in need. In addition, in many areas of England, poor people were 'licensed' to proceed in groups from house to house requesting Christmas charity that could be denied only at the peril of those within. If the householders tried to evade their responsibility to offer holiday hospitality, the suppliants in some areas of England felt justified in breaking into the pantry and raiding the food. So compelling was the day's injunction for the rich to show hospitality towards the poor that the idea even appeared in a popular proverb: 'Blessed be St Stephen / There's no fast upon his even.' *King Lear* performed on St Stephen's Night depicted the unthinkable. By the storm scenes in Act 3, Lear is reduced to just such a suppliant, lacking even a roof over his head. The storm resembles a holiday inversion writ large, in that the elements, at least in the king's own interpretation, seem bent on erasing distinctions between high and low. He commands, like some cosmic Lord of Misrule, 'Strike flat the thick rotundity o'the world' and 'Take physic, pomp, / Expose thyself to feel what wretches feel, / That thou mayst shake the superflux to them / And show the heavens more just' (3.2.7; 3.4.33–6).

Within the context of St Stephen's Day observances, the play's language resonates strongly with the holiday 'licence' afforded needy beggars. Suppliants called a house that refused hospitality a 'hard house'. Kent uses just that phrase for Gloucester's 'hard house', from which Goneril and Regan have allowed their father to wander out into the storm, and which has also denied Kent shelter. Kent condemns it as a house 'More harder than the stones whereof 'tis raised, / Which even but now, demanding after you, / Denied me to come in'. In keeping with the holiday prerogative of the poor to seize the hospitality that has been unjustly refused, Kent vows to 'return and force / Their scanted courtesy' (3.2.63–7). On the feast day itself, and especially in performance before a monarch who was known for his support for popular holiday pastimes, an audience's sense of the moral reprobation of Goneril and Regan would probably have intensified: in denying their father they were breaking not only filial bonds but also the 'laws' of holiday observance. And further, by refusing to participate in the spirit of the holiday on grounds of thrift and prudence, they were, at least fleetingly, allying themselves with contemporary rhetoric about the financial and moral profligacy of traditional festivity. Even at court, however, not everyone shared James's support for traditional pastimes; to the extent that they did not, they might have viewed the Act 3 confrontation between Lear, his 'disorderly' followers, and his daughters rather differently. Indeed, as I have argued elsewhere, the play as performed at court may well have appeared especially savage in its treatment of some of King James's other cherished ideas, such as the project for the union of England and

Scotland.[18] How much of the play's resonance with ideas from the Christmas season would have been available to audiences attending performances at other times? Perhaps little or none. The example of *King Lear* shows how evocations of popular festivity in Shakespeare can wax and wane depending on the context of performance.

MAY AND MIDSUMMER MADNESS

Thus far, my discussion has been conducted as though the drama functions rationally and members of the audience are free to accept or reject its evocations of popular festivity on the basis of consciously held systems of belief. But what if, rather than being mere imitations of earlier ritual patterns, plays can be viewed as ritual enactments in their own right and therefore as extensions of pre-Reformation rituals by means other than the Church? In such a case, the magical efficacy of popular festivity that is sometimes alleged within the plays – such as the Shepherd's recommendation of the sheep-shearing festival in *The Winter's Tale* to anyone who wanted his or her flocks to prosper (4.4.69–70) – would articulate the functioning of the drama itself, and that efficacy might operate on an audience regardless of their conscious beliefs. Arguably, a fear of this potential efficacy lay behind the vehemence of Puritan enemies of the stage and popular pastimes: if such debased, popular forms had the power to transform participants willy-nilly, then they were dangerous indeed. Few people, whether or not they numbered themselves among the godly, would willingly surrender to a work of art knowing that it had the power to destroy their souls!

Although they are not interested in reproducing the Puritan fear of the effects of dramatic performance, some recent anthropologically inclined critics have contended that Shakespeare's plays, or at least a few of them, do indeed operate on a deep cultural level to address communal problems. This is essentially Naomi Liebler's position in *Shakespeare's Festive Tragedy*, though she, with other like-minded critics, is careful to differentiate between dramatic intent and achievement:

> Ritual and theater do not share similar efficacies, but they do
> share similar intents. In tragedy, as in 'real life', ritual action is an

FIGURE 5   Tollet's Window, designed for Betley Hall, Staffordshire.

effort at containment; it is controlled, dispassionate, ordered, and impersonal. It is the community's, not the subject's, well being, its organizational pattern, that is at stake in the drama.[19]

What interests me here is less the objective validity of such a contention than its correlation with a thematics of communal redemption through ritual enactment that occurs in some of Shakespeare's plays. Whether or not he believed in its efficacy, Shakespeare was at times interested in claiming such a function for his art through the vehicle of popular festivity – perhaps as a way of pre-empting opposition sentiment by conceding the ritual efficacy of plays and pastimes but claiming that it operated for good rather than evil.

Let us consider the case of *A Midsummer Night's Dream*, which probably dates from 1594 or 1595. Like *Twelfth Night*, it refers to a holiday in its title, and thereby arouses certain expectations about its content. The popular festivities attached to Midsummer Day (St John's Day, 24 June) varied from place to place, but sometimes involved bonfires 'to bless the apples'; floral garlands; morris dancing; pageants, processions of giants, devils and dragons; and night watches of various kinds. The festival was timed to coincide with the Summer Solstice, and its bonfires, which had fallen into disuse in many parts of the country, had clear roots in pagan solar rituals. In addition, the May Day practices decried by Philip Stubbes were also sometimes observed on Midsummer Eve as part of a long spring season of 'Idolatry':

> Against Maie day, Whitsunday, or some other time of the yeare, euery Parish, Towne, and village, assemble themselues together, both men, women and children, olde and young, euen all indifferently: and either going all togither, or diuiding themselues into companies, they goe some to the woods, and groues, some to the hils and mountaines, some to one place, some to another, where they spende all the night in pleasant pastimes, and in the morning they returne bringing with them Birch boughes, and branches of trees, to deck their assemblies withall. And no maruell, for there is a great Lord present amongst them, as Superintendent and Lord ouer their pastimes and sportes: namely, **Sathan** Prince of **Hell**.[20]

A Midsummer Night's Dream conflates Midsummer Eve and May Day, exhibiting the traditional ritual pattern of young couples going into the woods overnight with predictably 'disorderly' results: when Lysander and Hermia plan their flight to the woods to escape the repressive marriage laws of Athens, they choose a place where they had earlier met 'To do observance to a morn of May' (1.1.167). But the play also offers up a Maying or Midsummer game of Bottom transformed to an ass (which somewhat resembles the devils and monsters of the Midsummer pageants that were, by Shakespeare's time, in decay), and a more decorous Maying encounter in the forest by Duke Theseus and Hippolyta during which they encounter the wayward lovers. The duke remarks, 'No doubt they rose up early, to observe / The rite of May' (4.1.131–2).

Shakespeare made frequent dramatic use of what we can call a 'Maying' pattern: a dramatic replication of the traditional May Day practice of heading off into the forest or hills for disorderly conduct, renewal and clarification. He uses it in several 'festive comedies' – most notably the *Dream* and *As You Like It*, and also occasionally in tragedies, especially, in terms of the specific use of Maying customs, the tragedy of *Macbeth* (as we shall see shortly). Part of the attraction of the pattern was no doubt its easy accommodation of motifs from pastoralism, a sophisticated literary form disguised as the antics of simple shepherds. What makes the Maying-Midsummer festivities particularly interesting in *A Midsummer Night's Dream* is their specific ties to elements of popular magical belief. The love-in-idleness Puck dispenses to transform the lovers' affections seems to concretize a claim that is made within the play itself about the transformative power of its Maying rituals. In Shakespeare's time, May dew was still believed in some rural areas to have special curative properties, like holy water come down from heaven: girls washed in it to beautify their faces, and farmers sprinkled it on their crops to ensure fertility.[21] In the play, similarly, the dew that decks the flowers and grass 'with liquid pearl' (1.1.211) has magical efficacy. At the end of the play, the vegetative spirits and Titania's fairies bless the chambers of the lovers with 'field-dew consecrate' to ensure their continuing fidelity and the health of their offspring (5.1.401).

But that resolution comes later. For most of the action, the forest has succumbed to 'misrule'. The magic of the Athenian woods is writ large in the persons of Titania and Oberon, vegetative spirits whose harmonious union is necessary if crops, gardens and people are to prosper and reproduce. According to Titania's long explanatory speech (2.1.81–117), she and Oberon have lived apart since 'middle summer's spring' – whatever season that is! Titania's speech writes Maying observance into elements of the landscape. Oberon's 'brawls' have disturbed her fairies' customary dances in 'ringlets', the winds have piped 'in vain' since there were no dancers to respond to their piping, and have retaliated for this neglect by sucking up fogs from the sea. As a result the crops are spoiled by foul weather and the places in which Maying festivities were traditionally set are disused:

> the green corn
> Hath rotted ere his youth attain'd a beard;
> The fold stands empty in the drowned field,
> And crows are fatted with the murrion flock;
> The nine-men's-morris is fill'd up with mud,
> And the quaint mazes in the wanton green
> For lack of tread are undistinguishable.
>
> (2.1.94–100)

Similarly, and as a result of Oberon and Titania's feud, human beings have abandoned popular festivity: 'No night is now with hymn or carol blest' (2.1.102), and the natural world, deprived of its usual human offerings, has retaliated by destroying the harmonious progression of the seasons. Shakespeare is constructing a model – or dream – of a world run by the power of ritual observance. Divine benevolence, supernatural ritual and human popular festivity are aligned in their effects. The 'disorder' of popular pastimes is required for the 'order' of natural fecundity. The play's construction of a universe under the control of ritual practices capable of warding off hungry lions, wolves, ghosts, witches and other evils mentioned by Puck in the final scene of blessing, helped to inaugurate an argument about the beneficent effects of popular festivity that would be articulated by Stuart monarchs over the next several decades. But in Shakespeare, it presented as fantasy – or dream.

Unlike the other comedies considered thus far, *A Midsummer Night's Dream* is not structured around an internal enemy of festival like

Malvolio, whose antipathy to holiday pastimes helps to rally other members of the play's imagined community in their defence, or at least helps to defuse negative opinion by articulating it within the play. *As You Like It* is more diffuse in its evocation of Maying customs, but more akin to the pattern of the other 'festive comedies' in that it too has a misfit – the melancholy Jaques – who refuses to surrender to the prevailing 'holiday humour' of Arden Forest and ends up abandoning the 'country copulatives' for the ascetic life of a 'convertite'. Jaques, however, is purely misanthropic rather than ideologically Puritan. He offends only against the 'good fellowship' of holiday observance, and in so doing, cuts himself off from the divine beneficence that this play, like *Midsummer Night's Dream*, associates with popular festivity. The Senior Duke and his merry band of men are specifically associated with Robin Hood, who was a staple of May Day pageants. Of course they have escaped to the green world for an extended period, not a single night, but there are many ways in which the 'liberty' of the forest correlates with traditional elements of holiday misrule: Rosalind's cross-dressing, her status as a figure of festival inversion – a 'woman on top' who orchestrates the action, the general environment of sexual license and freedom from ordinary social constraints. The echoes of Maying custom become stronger as the play draws to its conclusion. The Page's song of the 'lover and his lass, / With a hey and a ho and a hey nonino' describes a village Maying: the lovers pass over the green cornfield and lie between 'acres of the rye' as early modern country people sometimes coupled in the fields during the Maying season to help ensure the fertility of the crops. The carol they sing has survived, and is explicitly associated with May Day:

> This carol they began that hour,
> With a hey and a ho and a hey nonino,
> How that a life was but a flower,
> In springtime, the only pretty ring-time . . .
> And therefore take the present time,
> With a hey and a ho and a hey nonino,
> For love is crowned with the prime

(5.3.26–34)

Not only that, but the *carpe diem* sentiment of this pleasant ditty comes directly out of Ecclesiastes and James, the lessons and epistles proper for May Day, the Feast of Saints Philip and James the Less:

> Go thy way, eat thy bread with joy, and drink thy wine with merry heart . . . Whatsoever thy hand findeth to do, do it with thy might; for there is no work, nor device, nor knowledge, nor wisdom, in the grave, whither thou goest.
>
> (Ecclesiastes 9: 7–9)

> Let the brother of low degree rejoice in that he is exalted: But the rich, in that he is made low: because as the flower of the grass he shall pass away. For the sun is no sooner risen with a burning heat, but it withereth the grass, and the flower thereof falleth.
>
> (I James 9–11)[22]

In *As You Like It*, as in *A Midsummer Night's Dream*, the antics in the forest are directly linked with the possibility of divine beneficence. The marriage goddess Hymen arrives to the sound of music and blesses the couples, saying 'Then is there mirth in heaven / When earthly things made even / Atone together' (5.4.107–9). 'Made even' in the sense of 'brought into accord', but also in the sense of 'socially levelled', at least for the duration of their time amidst the liberty of the forest; 'atone' in the sense of 'make amends', but also in the sense of forming a community 'at one' in good neighbourhood.

Macbeth offers a provocative variation upon the Maying pattern in that its witches, more 'women on top' who attempt to control the destiny of Scotland through supernatural means, can also be interpreted as orderly by means of their disorders. They tempt Macbeth into the bloody murders that gradually drain the country of well-being, but they also engineer, or at least successfully predict, the 'Maying' mechanism that helps to restore Scotland. The witches show Macbeth the spectral image of a child carrying a tree who assures Macbeth that he need not fear 'until / Great Birnam wood to high Dunsinane hill / Shall come against him' (4.1.92–4). Macbeth in the final act of the play has reached a personal and political impasse which he expresses through images of winter: 'my

way of life / Is fall'n into the sere, the yellow leaf' (5.3.22–3). But when
Malcolm and his army cut down trees from the forest and bring them to
Dunsinane, they are in essence performing a Maying ritual that infuses
the nation and the play with the vigour of spring renewal. The tragic hero
has so embroiled himself in blood that he has himself become the dissident element that has to be cast out in order to restore the community. Like
early modern villagers who brought huge boughs from the forest on May
Day to decorate the town, in effect making it an extension of the forest in
order to do proper observance to the holiday, Malcolm brings the green
world to Macbeth's stronghold and thereby kindles an aura of new quick-
ening and life that is unusual at the end of Shakespearean tragedy. The
sight of the moving forest offers the prematurely aged king his first intimation of defeat, and, given the scene's allusion to May Day ritual, that
defeat takes on some of the quality of holiday levelling. The 'disorder' of
popular festivity helps to drive out Macbeth's misrule.

ROUGH MUSIC AND SKIMMINGTON

Not all Shakespearean popular festivity is tied to calendar customs. The
plays also invoke material from the 'rough music' or Skimmington – local
community rituals that existed in various forms in disparate parts of the
country, but generally functioned to drive out dissident elements. These
rituals were usually not attached even indirectly to ecclesiastical observances or government policy, and were therefore largely independent – or
even critical – of centralized authority. They were usually quite impro-
visatory, and could be as simple as a public scolding by village wives or
as elaborate as a procession by the whole community, accompanied by
banging pots and pans, with effigies of its disorderly members seated
backwards on an ass, and culminating in a mock trial and punishment.[23]
The Merry Wives of Windsor depicts Windsor as the setting for a ritualized
expulsion of a type familiar to Shakespeare's contemporaries, if not to us.
The play carries fleeting references to Shrovetide and Halloween folk
customs – when Falstaff is punished in the guise of Herne the Hunter in
Act 5, he refers to himself as 'Jack-a-Lent', which suggests Barber's link-
age between Falstaff and carnival (5.5.127).[24] But the local situation is

ripe for a ritual shaming. When the visiting court hanger-on Falstaff threatens to ruin Mistress Page and Mistress Ford's reputations by attempting a conspicuous seduction of both of them simultaneously, the wives retaliate with a series of punishments that recall traditional elements of Skimmington or 'rough music'. Many such rituals culminated in the ducking of an adulterer in a nearby pond, which is similar to Falstaff's dumping into the Thames along with the dirty laundry in the great 'buck-basket' in which he has been hidden to escape the suspicions of jealous Mr Ford (3.3). Often, men participating in Skimmington were cross-dressed, and if the target of the ritual was a man, he could be carried or carted about the village dressed as a woman and beaten or flouted by passers-by. That is akin to Falstaff's second trial, when he is forced to dress in a gown belonging to the 'fat woman of Brentford' and soundly beaten before being allowed to slink off in disgrace (4.2.71–2). Horns were also a prominent element of Skimmington, as in *As You Like It* where the 'horn music' of the middle of the play evokes traditional shaming rituals. Villagers would affix horns to the gate of a cuckold or dress a symbolic victim in horns and punish him as a message to sexually deviant neighbours. Falstaff's third and most heinous punishment is to be ritually shamed in the Forest of Windsor as Herne, the horn-wearing hunter. The women of Windsor have adapted popular festive forms that allow them to 'be merry and yet honest too' (4.2.100). To what extent is the shaming of Falstaff also a symbolic expulsion of the court? The play associates his licentious attempts at seduction with courtly behaviour, and the court itself is nearby during the action of the play – either in residence at Windsor Castle or on its way to Windsor or from it. *The Merry Wives of Windsor* exists in two distinct early texts, one of which is clearly more hostile to the court than the other; the two may well record different possibilities for the play in performance.[25]

As Michael Bristol has recently argued, 'rough music' or Skimmington also provides an important context for early modern response to *Othello*.[26] The play begins with an incipient communal shaming in which Iago and Roderigo hurl epithets from the street to deride the 'irregular' union of Othello and Desdemona: 'an old black ram / Is tupping your white ewe' (1.1.87–8). Fool figures in blackface were a staple of contemporary rituals of misrule, particularly Maying and morris dancing, and of some versions of the Skimmington. To what extent would the noble figure of Othello in the play have aroused contemporary associations of blackface with the 'disorder' of popular festivity? It seems likely that Othello on the early modern stage was played not as a 'tawny' Moor, but as a blackamoor or black man. The part of Othello would have been played by a white man in blackface, and Desdemona by a boy dressed as a woman – both familiar figures from the Skimmington. Depending on the manner in which an audience engaged with them, the tragic protagonists could register as noble and courageous, or as comic butts – the symbolic representatives of miscegenation displayed for public mockery. Given this profoundly disturbing reading, the rest of *Othello* can become an extension of the ritual shaming inaugurated by Iago at the beginning of the play. At present, an *Othello* that capitalized on the traditional associations between blackface, 'rough music' and misrule would be almost impossible to stage because of its racist overtones: the play could generate powerful connections between the stigmatization of blackness through the persecution of Othello and more recent incidents of ritual shaming, such as those practised against racially mixed couples in the American South. To imagine an Othello in performance who was always poised on a fine line between tragic hero and black-faced buffoon is to realize how remote our more customary readings of the play may be from Elizabethan and Jacobean cultural forms. To consider Shakespeare's plays in terms of popular festivity is not necessarily to recreate an idealized 'Merry England' of fellowship and 'good neighbourhood'; in cases like *Othello*, echoes of popular festivity can instead cause us to recognize our distance, even estrangement, from elements of early modern culture. Part of Shakespeare's power as a dramatist lies in the range and complexity of his explorations of popular festivity – its benevolence, charm, volatility and menace.

Chapter Three

SHAKESPEARE'S CLOWNS

Alex Davis

L et those that play your clowns speak no more than is set down
for them – for there be of them that will themselves laugh, to
set on some quantity of barren spectators to laugh too, though in
the meantime some necessary question of the play be then to be
considered. That's villainous, and shows a most pitiful ambition in
the fool that uses it.

(Ham 3.2.38–45)

Hamlet's instructions to the players in Elsinore bespeak a desire for a
decorous and socially elevated theatre: for a stage of restrained gesture
and performances bounded by the 'modesty of nature' (3.2.19). He
wants (as he has just explained) a style of speech clearly differentiated
from the common bawlings of town criers, plays unfettered by the banal
capacities of their plebeian audiences – 'the groundlings, who for the
most part are capable of nothing but inexplicable dumb-shows and
noise' (3.2.11–12). This analysis culminates in a particularly harsh set
of strictures directed at one class of performer in particular, the clown.
He must not improvise, or play up to the audience, and the jokes that are
his stock-in-trade seem to be regarded with suspicion. At issue here is the
way sixteenth- and seventeenth-century theatrical companies employed
specialist players to perform comedic parts such as Bottom, Touchstone
or Dogberry – professional humorists such as Richard Tarlton, Will
Kemp and Robert Armin, who often (to judge from the frequency of contemporary references) attained a celebrity exceeding that of the authors
of the works they performed. Positioned at the end of a long list of

theatrical crimes, the antics of the clown evidently represent for the Prince of Denmark the very nadir of the early modern stage's tendency towards lowest-common-denominator crudity.

Hamlet's comments therefore constitute a catalogue of the diverse ways in which a sixteenth- and seventeenth-century theatrical company might fall into the trap of producing popular drama – 'popular' in a quite specific sense. There is little suggestion here of the possibility of a work being 'popular' in the sense of having general appeal. On the contrary: you can perform a play as Prince Hamlet would like it performed, or you can perform it for the 'groundlings', those too poor to afford seats in the theatre; and if you do the latter, you will produce poor, vulgar, 'popular' art. The theatre offers no prospect of rich and poor meeting on the ground provided by shared literary experience. Hamlet's is therefore an aesthetic critique, but also a social one. His speeches additionally represent an obvious starting point for a discussion of the Shakespearean clown, not least because it has always been tempting to see in Hamlet's words a manifesto for Shakespeare's own dramatic theory and practice. The problem with viewing Hamlet as his creator's mouthpiece is that Shakespeare's works singularly fail to conform to these standards. His plays are full of clowning and laughter, of shocking juxtapositions of high and low, mixing comedy and tragedy in a way that later dramatic criticism came to regard as distressingly indiscriminate. Indeed in *Hamlet* it is to a large extent the Prince himself who ends up playing the clown's part, not only defacing his princely discourse with deliberate nonsense and vulgar sexual innuendos, but also, as David Wiles points out, casting himself as the clown in the performance of 'The Mousetrap': first prefacing the play with 'jesting and singing', then offering non-scripted interjections (variously ribald and enigmatic), and finally producing at the close a display of song and even perhaps dance, to the tune of 'Why let the strucken deer go weep' (3.2.265) – an echo of the clown's jig that would have followed the performance of a play.[1] And when the prince plays the clown, he is not just behaving in a manner at variance with his stated literary preferences and previous character. For an early modern audience, the aristocratic clown was, potentially at least, a contradiction in terms. To understand why this might have been the case, we need to look more closely at the figure of the clown himself.

It is clear that the clown was a hugely popular feature of the early modern theatrical experience. But many of the contemporaries who bear witness to this fact also bemoan it. Sir Philip Sidney's *Defence of Poesie* complained that modern plays were 'neither right Tragedies, nor right Comedies, mingling Kinges and Clownes, not because the matter so carrieth it, but thrust in the Clowne by head and shoulders to play a part in maiesticall matters, with neither decencie nor discretion'.[2] The clown was so popular with audiences that he had to be 'thrust' into the action, whether it warranted it or not (the same accusation is literalized in a university play, *The Pilgrimage to Parnassus*, when the clown is physically dragged on stage with a rope).[3] Having absorbed Horatian principles about the rules of decorum – the notion that there was a language and a generic format appropriate for each social class – authors and critics such as Sidney were clear that such an intrusion was not in fact justified. Clowns belonged in comedies, kings in tragedies, and nothing good could come of their meeting. 'Manye tymes', George Whetstone complained of playwrights, '(to make mirthe) they make a Clowne companion with a Kinge: in theyr graue Counsels, they allow the aduise of fooles: yea they vse one order of speach for all persons: a grose *Indecorum*, for a Crowe, wyll yll counterfet the Nightingales sweete voice: euen so, affected speeche doth misbecome a Clowne'.[4]

A 'clown' was a peasant or rustic – ignorant and uncouth. A spurious Elizabethan etymology derived the word from the Latin *colonus*, 'farmer'.[5] To behave clownishly was to make oneself ridiculous through ill breeding. More broadly, the word 'clown' might denote a position in society, the very lowest of the low, emblematically opposed (in the 'clowns and kings' formula) to the very highest – the monarch. Shakespeare's clowns are therefore not, in fact, exclusively rustics: the Dromios of *The Comedy of Errors*, for instance, descendants of the slaves of Roman New Comedy, occupy a distinctly urban milieu. What ties all these clownish figures together is their low social status relative to the central characters of the plays. Clowns then are a problem, firstly because they exemplify what Sidney calls the 'scurrillitie' and 'doltishnesse' of modern comedy, but also because of their status as embodiments of the popular in the sense we have been examining, the vulgar. Mixed in with aristocratic characters, they conjure up an unsettling image of social promiscuity.

So the clown was not just an aspect of popular culture, although he certainly was that, if we are to believe Hamlet's characterization of his antics as appealing to the groundlings in particular. He was also a symbol of it in general. But he therefore also exemplifies the problems that modern scholars face when they attempt to pin down this slippery and elusive concept. To take just two points from a very substantial discussion by Tim Harris of the simplifications imposed by the binary model it implies:

> The use of the term 'popular culture' in the singular encourages us to think of the culture below the elite as if it were a coherent whole, and directs our attention away from a consideration of the diversities within popular culture . . . Likewise, formulating the question in terms of a conflict between elite and popular culture which the elite eventually (and inevitably) won distracts us from considering the degree of interaction between the cultural world of the educated and the humbler ranks of society.[6]

If we shift our focus from the clown in the sense of the low-status character in the play, to the clown in the sense of the specialist actor who played him, these complexities quickly become apparent. Consider for instance possibly the most famous clown of them all, Richard Tarlton. According to Thomas Fuller, Tarlton (born in Shropshire) was

> in the field keeping his Fathers Swine, when a Servant of *Robert* Earl of *Leicester* . . . was so highly pleased with his *happy unhappy* answers, that he brought him to Court, where he became the most famous *Jester* to Queen *Elizabeth*.[7]

Tarlton then was a clown in the sense of being an uneducated countryman, but his verbal talents – his ability to 'clown' – allowed him to attain a social position far removed from his origins. But this position was not a fixed one. Tarlton occupied a variety of different social milieux. So we

FIGURE 6   Richard Tarlton, from *Tarltons Jests* (1938).

have, for instance, courtly Tarlton: starting life as a swineherd, he ended up on terms of limited intimacy with the queen herself (many of the stories about him relate to risqué exchanges with the monarch). He was appointed – along with his fellows in the Queen's Players – an Ordinary Groom of the Queen's Chamber (admittedly an honorary position). Sir Philip Sidney acted as godparent to his child. If Fuller is to believed, Tarlton's position at court even afforded him a limited degree of political influence: 'Her highest *Favorites*, would in some Cases, go to *Tarleton*, before they would go to the *Queen*, and he was their *Vsher* to prepare their advantagious access unto Her.'[8] Tarlton was a court clown, but he also belonged in the theatre, as a specialized theatrical performer. He was named as one of the Queen's Men when the company was formed in 1583; many surviving anecdotes relate to his onstage witticisms. Nor is this all: in 1587 he was admitted as a Master of Fence – an accredited teacher of fencing. He owned taverns in London. And he was an author; in 1570, Tarlton composed a ballad on floods in Bedfordshire.

The careers of other sixteenth- and seventeenth-century clowns were similarly diverse, although authorship appears in the record with surprising frequency. Will Kemp published an account of his famous morris dance between London and Norwich (Figure 7). Robert Armin, who began life as an apprentice of the Goldsmiths' company, first broke into print as the author of the preface to a work of religious controversy, *A Brief Resolution of The Right Religion* (1590), and was to go on to produce a verse translation of an Italian ballad, plays of his own devising, and histories of fooling such as his *Fool Upon Fool* (1600). Like Shakespeare, for whom he performed so many roles, Armin ended up being awarded a grant of arms, the mark of a gentleman.[9] William Rowley, who acted in his own *All's Lost by Lust* as Jacques, 'a simple clownish Gentleman', co-authored with Thomas Middleton one of the finest tragedies of the period, *The Changeling*. These performers may have made a living out of playing idiots and country bumpkins (pictures of Tarlton seem to indicate that his stage persona was that of a rough peasant), but it is perfectly clear that they themselves were considerably more sophisticated individuals than that.

Kemps nine daies wonder.

Performed in a daunce from
London to Norwich.

Containing the pleasure, paines and kinde entertainment
of *William Kemp* betweene *London* and that Citty
in his late Morrice.

Wherein is somewhat set downe worth note; to reprooue
the slaunders spred of him: many things merry,
nothing hurtfull.

Written by himselfe to satisfie his friends.

LONDON
Printed by *E. A.* for *Nicholas Ling*, and are to be
solde at his shop at the west doore of Saint
Paules Church. 1 6 0 0.

FIGURE 7   Will Kemp as morris dancer, from *Kemps nine daies wonder* (1600).

Clowns as performers were more than anything social anomalies. Consider the medieval court jester, one of the ancestors of the early modern theatrical clown. As John Southworth notes:

> in some of the earliest European records [the fool] is designated *nebulo* . . . a paltry, worthless fellow, a nobody. It was not merely that his position in the feudal hierarchy was low . . . he was altogether excluded from it. Being neither lord nor cleric, freeman nor serf, he existed in a social limbo . . . it was only in relation to his master that he was able to gain identity.[10]

The opportunities afforded to the adroit operator such as Tarlton by such an ill-defined social position should be equally clear. Another oft-cited antecedent of the early modern clown, the figure of the Lord of Misrule or summer lord, is again a socially ambiguous figure, a paradoxical blend of high and low, temporarily elevated to high office precisely because of his position as the most negligible member of the community.[11] Beneath the simplistic formula that would divide society into gentry and commoners, clowns and kings, we can begin to discern the potential for a sophisticated toying with social expectations.

If clowns themselves occupied a surprisingly diverse range of social positions in real life, the same can be said when it comes to the consumption of 'clownish' jests, anecdotes and antics. The aristocratic Beatrice in *Much Ado About Nothing* is insulted to think anyone might imagine 'that I had my good wit out of the "Hundred Merry Tales"' (2.1.119–20) – this being a jest book first published in 1526, and regularly identified as the very quintessence of vulgar reading[12] – but Queen Elizabeth had the very same volume read to her on her death bed.[13] We can see a similar situation, of presumed vulgarity obscuring genuine diversity, in the first Quarto of *Hamlet*. This edition, like subsequent ones, contains the prince's attack on clowns and 'barren spectators', but also mentions the gentleman auditors, who admire the clown and copy his jests 'in their tables, before they come to the play'.[14] And we do in fact have examples of jest-book material turning up in gentlemen's commonplace books (their 'tables'): for example, an anecdote about Tarlton, who was hissed by the audience in a town, and 'brake forth at last into this sarcasticall taunt':

> I livde not in ye Golden Age, when Jason won ye fleece
> But now I am on Gothams stage, where ffooles doe hisse like Geese.[15]

The jest appears in a miscellany compiled by an unknown but unquestionably gentlemanly figure, educated in Latin and linked to the Cambridge area, who seems to have been particularly interested in such highbrow topics as matters of religious controversy and court politics. And yet this man was also an avid collector of 'vulgar', clownish jests and anecdotes. In such a context, we might ask, does Tarlton figure as a representative of popular or elite culture? His persona is rustic and his humour coarse, yet he reveals a possibly surprising acquaintance with classical myth. And why might this story be recorded by a university-educated intellectual? Is it its very vulgarity that makes it appealing? And if so, why is it then framed within such an apparently incongruous context?

Beneath the binary distinction between high and low implied by the term 'early modern popular culture', closer examination reveals a much more complex and fluid set of relationships between individuals, their rank, and their association with or consumption of 'popular' culture. The figure of the clown could have been practically invented to muddle matters further, pointing as it does in two directions – on the one hand, towards a clarity of social distinctions, and on the other, towards a messy reality in which the relationship between individuals and the labels applied to them is often imprecise, potentially unstable, and even downright deceptive. The interest of Shakespeare's clowns lies precisely in the ways in which these two senses are played off against each other, in a series of increasingly complex variations upon a theme, thus creating the distinctively 'mixed' nature of his drama. The remainder of this essay contrasts the roles played by specialized comic performers in Shakespeare's early comedies with those in his later ones, a contrast that might be crudely summarized as one between clowns on the one hand and witty fools on the other. This is not a terminological distinction in the plays themselves. Lavatch in *All's Well that Ends Well* and Feste in *Twelfth Night* are designated 'clown' throughout the original stage directions, although they belong in the second category. Clowns are defined as much as anything by their rank, whereas with fools we are presented with a profession of sorts. In the first case, the interest in exploring social distinctions predominates; in the second, the figure of the fool produces a more uncertain sense of the force of such categories.

In the early plays in particular, then, the clown is an inadvertent and therefore amateur comedian. He is a weaver, a constable, a servant. Dogberry in *Much Ado* litters his speech with humorous errors, and the laughter he elicits is only amplified by the contrast with the very different sort of comedy generated by the aristocratic wit of his betters, who are in full command of their verbal resources. (He would moreover have been played by Will Kemp, generally felt to have been a relatively physical, bawdy type of comedian.) It is Dogberry who declares that 'comparisons are odorous', and when the governor of Messina, Leonato, complains that he finds the constable's discourse 'tedious', Dogberry takes the word to mean 'rich':

DOGBERRY   It pleases your worship to say so, but we are the poor Duke's officers; but truly, for mine own part, if I were as tedious as a king, I could find in my heart to bestow it all of your worship.

LEONATO   All thy tediousness on me, ah?

DOGBERRY   Yea, and 'twere a thousand pound more than 'tis, for I hear as good exclamation on your worship as of any man in the city, and though I be but a poor man, I am glad to hear it.

LEONATO   And so am I.

(3.5.18–27)

Dogberry's verbal confusions comically misrepresent the world of *Much Ado*, in which wit goes hand in hand with social status: kings may be rich, but in these plays they are rarely tedious. That quality is reserved for the lower orders, although their linguistic deficiencies are also a source of amusement: there is a sense in which even the bored Leonato might be 'glad' to be subjected to Dogberry's malapropisms. We end up edging towards a use of the clown that is expressive of a certain viewpoint: that the lower classes are funny.

Elsewhere in these plays, however, Shakespeare's use of the clown and the way he provides a means of talking about matters of rank and status takes on a more analytical character, via the notion of performance. It is notable how often in the early comedies his clowns appear framed within metatheatrical, play-within-a-play situations presented before an aristocratic audience. In *The Taming of the Shrew*, the clownishness of

Christopher Sly is best manifested through a 'jest' in which he is persuaded that he is an aristocrat watching a play (Induction, scenes 1–2). In *Love's Labour's Lost*, we have the pageant of the Nine Worthies, proposed by the King of Navarre as a means of courting the Princess of France and her ladies. Responsibility for arranging the entertainment devolves onto the actors: the affected Spaniard Armado; his page, Moth; Holofernes, the schoolmaster; Nathaniel, the curate; constable Dull; and the clown, Costard. At Holofernes's suggestion, they decide to collaborate on a pageant of the Nine Worthies – renowned heroes of classical, Jewish and Christian history. (Holofernes has no hesitation in bagging the role of Judas Maccabeaus for himself, unaware of any possible incongruity between a rural pedant and the great Jewish war hero.) Particularly interesting here is the curiously 'flattening' effect the play has on the social status of these players. Only the rustic Costard is a clown strictly speaking, the others being what are sometimes called 'fantastics': 'Don' Armado is in theory some sort of Spanish nobleman, whilst the curate Nathaniel and the schoolmaster Holofernes clearly occupy a different rung on the social ladder from Costard, the clown proper – but the effect of the pageant is to 'clownify' its actors – to push them down the social ladder – through contrast with legendary heroes and historical figures and in opposition to the French and Navarrese aristocracy. Certainly, the pageant of the Nine Worthies does not go quite to plan for the king and his lords: comprehensively humiliated by the French ladies beforehand, the frustrated noblemen immediately move to recover their lost face by disrupting the pageant with carping comments that ultimately move Holofernes to the surprisingly dignified protest that 'This is not generous, not gentle, not humble' (5.2.623). First the performers look absurd; then the Navarrese nobles look cruel. It is a complex effect that leaves us unsure where our sympathies really lie, and we get a good sense of the potential ambivalence of the clown, poised as he is between laughing at those above him and being laughed at by them.[16] But the effect is perhaps only permitted by a prior simplification: as we watch the pageant, we may get a sense of teams lining up against each other, as if at a sporting fixture. The tendency of the play-within-a-play format is to reach out towards the binary social opposition: clowns and kings.

In *A Midsummer Night's Dream* we have the play of Pyramus and Thisbe presented by the 'rude mechanicals' of Athens as a part of the concluding nuptial celebrations. As Theseus' Master of Revels suggests, in recommending some other entertainment, the pleasure afforded by this performance cannot lie in the play itself, but only in the incompetence of the performers: 'it is nothing . . . Unless you can find sport in their intents' (5.1.78–9). Pyramus and Thisbe is indeed just as deliciously awful as this introduction has led us to expect, beset as it is by inadvertent obscenity, malapropism and a persistent infringement of literary and linguistic conventions. The tradesmen of Athens are evidently all at sea when it comes to the sort of Ovidian drama that might have been the special preserve of the humanistically educated young gentleman in Shakespeare's day. Peter Quince's Prologue sets the tone for what is to follow:

> *If we offend, it is with our good will.*
> *That you should think, we come not to offend,*
> *But with good will. To show our simple skill,*
> *That is the true beginning of our end.*
> *Consider then, we come but in despite.*
> *We do not come, as minding to content you,*
> *Our true intent is. All for your delight,*
> *We are not here. That you should here repent you,*
> *The actors are at hand; and by their show,*
> *You shall know all, that you are like to know.*

(5.1.108–17)

The carpenter's mispunctuated introduction formalizes the divide between the significance of the play for its players, and its significance for the Athenian grandees, in effect producing two different speeches. Intended as a graceful *apologia* for any defects in the ensuing performance, once mangled by Quince the Induction becomes a genuine if inadvertent admission of the actors' incompetence and inability to satisfy an aristocratic audience on the actors' own terms.[17] Rather than taking pleasure in a nicely versified compliment, the spectators' enjoyment is focused on the way Quince inadvertently rewrites himself – not as the sort of charmingly awe-struck subject that Theseus had fondly recalled just before the performance began (5.1.89–105), but as a rebellious subject who refuses to participate in an aristocratic economy of pleasure in which it is the purpose of commoners to provide 'delight' for their betters, setting out instead to offend with a good will and threatening (in one feasible reading) to extort repentance from the Athenian gentry. Indeed, Quince's speech is shot through with subliminal hints as to the possible conclusion of such an act of rebellion, be that the judicial 'end' of the actors' lives, or, more obliquely, of the audience themselves – as the speech concludes with the menacing prediction that by the end of the performance, 'you shall know all, that you are like to know'. Just to make the joke all the funnier, we, the real-life audience of the play, know that the notion of inserting a Prologue was originally conceived by Bottom so as to reassure the audience that 'we will do no harm with our swords' (3.1.17) – that the death of Pyramus need not be a cause of 'fear'. Bottom's innocence about fiction is entirely typical of the mechanical, marking their actual performance when Snug the joiner reassures the ladies in the audience that he is no real lion; but it is a particularly sweet irony that a speech explicitly designed to allay the fears of an aristocratic audience should instead end up threatening them with 'despite', forced repentance, even with death.

In reality, of course, the Prologue's confession of seditious intent merely renders Quince all the more delightfully ineffectual, prompting a flurry of puns about his linguistic incompetence:

THESEUS   This fellow doth not stand upon points.

LYSANDER   He hath rid his prologue like a rough colt; he knows not the stop. A good moral, my lord: it is not enough to speak, but to speak true.

HIPPOLYTA   Indeed he hath played on this prologue like a child on a recorder; a sound, but not in government.

(5.1.118–23)

The rest of the performance amply confirms these impressions of the mechanicals' talents.

Once again, the clown in the play-within-the-play serves to underline the cultural and social gulf that separates high and low. Robert Weimann has written on the contrast on the early modern stage between the locus, the space of the world created by the author, and the platea, the in-between space so often inhabited by the clown, with his traditional licence to step away from the world of the play and engage with the audience directly.[18] Here, the clown's ability to distance himself from the boundaries of the theatrical part he is playing is reframed within a new performative context, wherein the inability of these commoners to inhabit their dramatic roles results in self-incrimination; they end up playing themselves, putting themselves on display – making an exhibition of themselves. But although 'Pyramus and Thisbe' ends with a Bergomask, a dance 'after the manner of the people of Bergamo, commonly ridiculed for their rusticity',[19] and therefore the antithesis of the refined aristocratic masque, the mechanicals are not much associated with specifically lower-class cultural practices here. Rather, their clownishness is manifested as an inability to handle non-clownish material: humanistic, classical drama.

Placed in context, this seems particularly significant. Much of the action of *A Midsummer Night's Dream* is set within a framework of popular culture: specifically, the fairy world of the forest, derived from old wives' tales, childhood stories and ballads. When scrutinized closely, however, this fairy lore underlines the point about the elusive nature of popular culture, proving again less clearly vulgar ('popular') than it might seem at first glance, to the point of undermining any clear binary distinction between high and low based on cultural practice. As Mary Ellen Lamb points out, many early modern gentlemen would have been 'culturally "amphibious" – reared in a community of "Country-people" and "old woemen" [sic] before . . . education in the texts and values of a literate society'.[20] This social reality, in which 'popular' tales and customs might in fact be the shared property of many social groups, finds its analogue in the confusing world of the Athenian forest. Quite apart from the romantic chaos the world of the forest engenders, it also destabilizes the norms that underpin the hierarchical world-view re-established in the mechanicals' performance. There, Snug the joiner's speech prompts Demetrius' quip that 'one lion may [speak] when many asses do' (5.1.152), but in the forest we have seen an ass, a weaver, consorting with a queen. The world of traditional fairy lore, far from operating to separate out high and low on the basis of their response to popular culture, instead ends up promiscuously mingling the two.

After such disorder, the play of 'Pyramus and Thisbe' has a stabilizing effect. Just two scenes previously, Theseus was being asked to bring the full force of Athenian law to bear against the young lovers (4.1.153–8). Now, the play of wit that the performance elicits from the aristocrats serves to remind them of what they have in common. To do so successfully, the mechanicals must appear as clowns, emblems of the popular, but *not* in such a way as evokes actual popular practice. As David Wallace suggests, 'these Athenian artisans are guildsmen without a guild', each named for their profession (so that 'Bottom the weaver is named after the skein on which yarn is wound', Peter Quince after the 'quoins' or wooden wedges used by carpenters, and so forth). But guilds do not exist in Athens, and, as Wallace notes, the play of Pyramus and Thisbe sits oddly when placed against the guild pageantry of the Middle Ages.[21] Rather than creating their own meanings by celebrating their own civic or religious culture, as for instance in the Coventry cycle of mystery drama,[22] the mechanicals perform in a play in which meaning is foisted upon them unawares.[23]

If the clowns of *A Midsummer Night's Dream* are at their most clownish – that is, their most clearly popular, most capable of effecting that distinction between high and low – precisely when they feature in a neoclassical drama performed before an aristocratic audience – that is, when severed from popular ritual and practice – then the two halves of the verbal equation 'popular culture' here exist in an inversely proportional relationship to one another. The more clearly popular a figure, the less linked to actual cultural practice, and *vice versa*, since, in the faerie world of the forest, the world of traditional folklore, popular and aristocratic become confused, forming bizarre and disorienting hybrids, of which Bottom – that union of beast and man, a mere weaver yet also a queen's lover – might well stand as an emblem. Such confusion demands a response. Preceding or concluding the action of the play proper, what we see in the use of this play-within-a-play motif is an understanding of how the broad, muddied categories of high and low, elite and popular, can be brought into view and clarified within the context of performance. This clarification takes place not at the level of custom and practice, but on that of inherent character, nature, or disposition, the disposition revealed precisely when we see commoners wrestling with unfamiliar cultural formats: rude mechanicals unwittingly mangling classical tragedy, or a tinker struggling to get to grips with the linguistic protocols and behavioural customs of the nobility. Shakespeare deploys the image of the theatre here not just to reflect metadramatically upon his own practice, but also to thematize the structural relationships he sees at work between high and low in Elizabethan England. Theatre becomes a symbol of the difference in outlook between his nobles and his commoners, the perceptual gap between how his clowns view themselves and how they are viewed. The clowns' inferior rank in these early plays is manifested as a chronic, amateurish artlessness, an inability to perceive that the entertainment they provide exceeds that of the play they are playing. They are the unwitting participants in a larger piece of social theatre, the verbal content of which exactly corresponds with that of their own production, even while its meaning outstrips it. Modern literary criticism is fascinated by the interactions between dramatic representation and high politics in early modern England – the theatricality of power, as it has been termed. Shakespeare is equally interested in what one might term the theatricality of impotence, a theatricalization of the popular, in which commoners exist only to provide an opportunity for 'practice' and 'jest',[24] for spectacles of inadvertent humour that confirm their betters in their sense of innate superiority. Here, it is clowns as much as kings who are 'set on stages, in the sight and viewe of all the world duly observed'.[25]

'It was', Peter Burke writes in his pioneering study, 'in the late eighteenth and early nineteenth centuries, when popular culture was just beginning to disappear, that the "people" or "folk" became a subject of interest to European intellectuals.'[26] One might quibble as to dates, but it can be agreed that the precondition for such an interest is, as Burke suggests, the ability to perceive the popular as somehow different, the repository within one's own national life of an alien culture that suddenly becomes visible as such. To exist as a conceptual category, a distinct and separate object of study, popular culture has to be brought to visibility, must always first appear framed or as it were 'onstage'. Much modern

literary criticism has concerned itself with the way in which the interactions between high and low in Shakespeare's plays themselves relate
to the structural inequalities of early modern England. Theatre and performance provide images and situations that permit Shakespeare some
perspective on the processes in which his drama participates: they allow
us to see Shakespeare reflecting on the ways in which 'high' and 'low'
might themselves emerge as viable conceptual categories, as objects of
analysis. At his most complex, the Shakespearean clown represents a
tool for thinking about 'the popular', long before it ever emerged as a
term of academic analysis.

* * *

As his career progresses, Shakespeare's use of the play-within-a-play
motif and his understanding of what performance might signify become
ever more sophisticated. Shakespeare's later clowns tend to be professionals, not amateurs; consciously rather than unconsciously funny.[27] This
shift is often linked to a change in the personnel of Shakespeare's playing
company. In 1599, Will Kemp, the company's clown and one of its principal shareholders, left the Chamberlain's Men for unknown reasons. His
replacement was Robert Armin, whose introduction to the company may
be signalled in *As You Like It*, when Jaques's comments after first encoun-
tering Touchstone seem designed to pinpoint Armin's distinctive style, as
much a novelty to the audience as it is to the melancholy courtier: 'A motley fool', he exclaims – and yet, one capable of expressing himself 'in good
set terms' (2.7.16). As indicated here, the essence of Armin's comedy was
its disorienting juxtaposition of sense and folly. Whereas it seems that
Kemp was distinguished by a relatively broad and even physical comedic
approach – he was particularly famous for his jigs – Armin is often painted
as offering a much more refined form of entertainment.

For modern literary critics concerned with the relationship between
the Shakespearean stage and the society he lived in, this shift is sometimes seen as an act of betrayal. Assembling a variety of apparently
diverse circumstances – the replacement of Kemp, the move to the Globe,
later performances at the indoor Blackfriars theatre, Shakespeare's

acquisition of a grant of arms – it is possible to discern in the careers of the Chamberlain's Men and their principal playwright an upwardly mobile social trajectory that (it is argued) also necessitated an attempt to dissociate themselves from popular culture – a loss, as Richard Helgerson puts it, of the common touch. Acknowledging the enormous range of popular forms that are incorporated within Shakespearean drama, Helgerson's account nevertheless stresses the efforts Shakespeare and his company made 'to exclude and alienate the popular, the socially marginal, the subversive, and the folk'. Within such a narrative, the departure of Kemp – the rustic clown, famed for his skill in the jig – and the introduction of Armin – the fool as a purveyor of classy Erasmian paradoxes about the folly of wisdom and so forth – symbolizes the desire of the Chamberlain's Men to purge themselves of any taint of vulgarity. It is emblematic of 'the alienation of the clown from the playwright, of the players' theatre from the authors' theatre, of the people from the nation and its canonical self-representations'.[28]

Shakespeare's style certainly adapts to fit Armin's, but it is less clear that this must necessarily imply a wholesale rejection of popular culture. Rather, his plays seem to turn towards a different kind of exploration of the ambiguities inherent in the notion of 'the popular' itself. Although I have argued that Shakespeare's early comedies intermittently offer an anatomy of sixteenth- and seventeenth-century social relations, there can be no doubt that, with their malapropisms and their talent for unwitting self-humiliation, his early clowns correspond far more closely than his later ones to the aristocratic notion of a man who is funny simply by virtue of his status. Boisterous, physical and earthy though they may be, they therefore also embody some of the most notorious clichés regarding popular culture. In the plays of Shakespeare's mature period we see something subtly different. First, Shakespeare's clowns become both more ambiguous and more diverse in the social positions they occupy; and second (extending and modifying the play-within-a-play theme of the earlier works), they are consistently written not just as entertaining characters, but as characters placed in the position of entertainer, often professionally. And while the dialogue of Shakespeare's later clowns is undoubtedly tailored to the distinctive features of Armin's comedic style, these shifts actually somewhat predate Kemp's departure from the Chamberlain's Men, since the changes I am concerned with here are also visible in the figure of Falstaff – a part it is thought Kemp played[29] (the wisdom-and-folly theme is, moreover, thoroughly canvassed in the early *Love's Labour's Lost*). The result is ultimately something less narrowly sociological than the early plays – something closer to a general vision of human interaction.

The likes of Lavatch, Feste and the Fool in *King Lear* are professionals: but what exactly is the rank of such characters? Where do they fit into the social hierarchy of the worlds they inhabit? The origins of the theatrical clown, as we have seen, lie in figures whose rank is indeterminate or confused – the medieval jester as *nebulo*, for instance, or the kings-for-a-day of seasonal festivities. Whereas the likes of the Athenian mechanicals have their clownishness refined and clarified within the context of theatrical performance, the capacity of these later fools to provide entertainment lets them escape easy classification. What for instance are we to make of Lear's Fool – a 'knave' (1.4.42), at his master's beck and call, continually threatened with whipping (1.4.108) – and yet one on a mock-familial footing with his 'nuncle', the king himself – and this in an era when power could be measured in terms of a person's intimacy with and ready access to the person of the monarch, as in the case of Richard Tarlton? What of Touchstone, who is introduced to us in the context of his being a 'natural' fool (1.2.47), who is again threatened with whipping (1.2.78), but who evidently possesses more sense than such an introduction might suggest, as Jaques's comments on first meeting him indicate? Touchstone is characterized throughout by his appetite for the attributes of a courtly identity. Right from the start, we find him asserting his right to swear by his honour (1.2.57), and once in the forest of Arden, he rapidly adopts the traits of the stereotypical courtier, culminating in the following self-appraisal:

> I have trod a measure, I have flattered a lady, I have been politic with my friend, smooth with mine enemy, I have undone three tailors, I have had four quarrels, and like to have fought one.

> (5.4.44–7)

When Jaques satirizes Touchstone as the epitome of the witless courtier, it appears that he has actually accepted him in his new identity (2.7.36–43). The world of the forest is full of transformations and disguises, but Touchstone's self-fashioning is one of the most curious in the whole play, balanced as it is between imposture and genuine mutability. Far from reaching towards some ultimate clarification, it serves only to cast doubt upon his initial status at court.

Feste in *Twelfth Night* similarly floats free from any sort of simple social categorization. In a play wholeheartedly committed to an exploration to the ties of association (be they of marriage or kinship or service) that might bind individuals and communities together, and of their relative strengths and vulnerabilities, Feste is one of the most socially unmoored characters in Shakespeare's works. Even the two orphaned aliens, Viola and Sebastian, move with extraordinary rapidity to integrate themselves into the households and hierarchy of Illyria, ultimately transforming them through marriage. Feste, by way of contrast, remains something of an outsider throughout. He describes himself as Olivia's 'corrupter of words' (3.1.37), but as the play progresses it becomes increasingly unclear in what sense he is 'hers' at all. He is introduced to us being playfully threatened with hanging for his long absence from his mistress, but throughout *Twelfth Night* this domestic retainer is actually to be found continually moving back and forth between the two worlds of Orsino's court and Olivia's household, begging and receiving money. When Viola comments on the fact that he is to be found in both places, Feste's response is to note that 'Foolery, sir, does walk about the orb like the sun, it shines everywhere' (3.1.39–40).

Even in his late plays – with their romance-derived plots, their foundling princes and princesses, and their attendant interest in innate social characteristics – Shakespeare includes figures such as Autolycus, from *The Winter's Tale*. The Clown in this play ends up a 'gentleman born' (5.2.137 – 'these four hours') – but this is a joke that really underlines his distance from true gentility. The ballad-seller Autolycus, on the other hand, is genuinely disturbing in his ability to impersonate his betters, with no more than a change of clothes. Simon Forman, an early viewer of the play, noted 'howe he changed apparrell wt the kinge of Bomia his sonn, and then howe he turned Courtiar'. 'Beware', he added, 'of trustinge feined beggars or fawning fellouss.'[30] But to 'turn courtier' implies a more radical transformation than mere disguise, or imposture.

This social ambiguity finds its counterpoint in a third class of comic character, the aristocratic clown: noblemen whose association with popular culture somehow renders their status indeterminate. For instance, Sir Toby Belch: unquestionably a knight, and yet, so unremittingly 'below-stairs' is the company he keeps, so persistent his association with the 'cakes and ale' of traditional festivities, it is sometimes hard to see that his marriage to Maria really constitutes a social transgression equivalent to that represented by Malvolio's desire to marry his mistress. Like his drinking companion, Sir Andrew Aguecheek, Sir Toby has 'slipped', socially. He lives in Olivia's household on sufferance, and this position is crucially intertwined with the notion of entertainment. As long as he is there, he can enjoy an 'ale-house' (2.3.90) life of late nights, song and revelry; but if he steps over the line, he will be dismissed – as both Malvolio and Maria warn him. As with Feste, another character living on sufferance, far from confirming his status, Sir Toby's propensity for clowning performance renders it ambiguous.

In this Sir Toby appears similar to, but is actually the opposite of, another decayed knight, and Shakespeare's first attempt at this new style of aristocratic clown. For Falstaff, performance represents the opportunity to redeem his tarnished social position. Again, it is sometimes difficult to remember that Falstaff is in principle a member of the aristocracy. He is mainly associated with a seedy tavern underworld and popular festive culture, complemented by references to the Vice of the mystery plays (2.4.441) – another ancestor of the early modern clown. And yet this lowlife character is on intimate terms with the Prince of Wales, the heir apparent to the throne of England. Although the play is separated by scene divisions into clearly separate locales – court and city, centre and regions – the England of *Henry IV* is not in fact a strictly regimented social world, but rather one in which high and low mingle indiscriminately, the lines between the two becoming blurred, so that 'while the Prince masters the argot of Eastcheap, the clown is cast as a knight'.[31] For Falstaff, Hal represents the opportunity to cross one of these permeable barriers and leave Eastcheap behind him for an altogether more elevated life. Modern criticism, alerted by the prince's first soliloquy, tends to be justifiably hard on Hal for his ultimate intention of casting off his friend. But of course the two are mutually exploiting one another. From the very beginning, their interactions are threaded through with implicit and explicit references to Falstaff's great expectations of the reign of Henry V.

Certainly, these exchanges tend to have rather ominous overtones. 'I prithee sweet wag', Falstaff is introduced as saying, 'when thou art king, as God save thy Grace – Majesty I should say, for grace thou wilt have none' – as indeed he will not, so far as Falstaff is concerned (1.2.16–18). Later, Falstaff seizes on a comment that suggests he will be a judge. But no, says Hal, bursting his bubble: he meant him for a hangman (1.2.59–65). Falstaff's hopes for the future are entirely dependent upon his continued association with Hal, which is in turn contingent upon his ability to entertain – 'to keep Prince Harry in continual laughter' (2H4 5.1.76) – and Hal knows it, and plays upon the fact. This is most notably the case in the 'mock king' game, a 'play extempore' (2.4.276) in which Falstaff first plays the father and Hal himself, following which Falstaff is deposed (2.4.429) and the roles reversed. When Hal plays his father, he takes the opportunity to abuse his friend, and Falstaff's pleas for himself – 'banish not him thy Harry's company, banish not him thy Harry's company, banish plump Jack and banish all the world' – elicit only the chilling declaration: 'I do, I will' (2.4.472–5).

This seems somewhat like the plays-within-plays of Kemp's early roles. Yet beneath this intimation of the coming separation of the popular and the regal lies a deeper equivalence. After all, a consistent thread running through these tavern scenes is the way in which Hal is edged towards the paradoxical realization that his regal persona may ultimately be reinforced if he surrounds himself with common things and 'can drink with any tinker in his own language' (2.4.18–19). In the post-sacral monarchy of *Henry IV*, the king is a role, a part one can play – as is suggested by the episode at the battle of Shrewsbury, in which decoys swarm across the battlefield dressed as the king, and in which the real king is unrecognizable (5.4.24–37).[32] Henry IV's concern was that his son was bringing the royal image into contempt like Richard II, who 'Grew a companion to the common streets, / [and] Enfeoff'd himself to popularity' (3.2.68–9); but the plays show Hal to be a more astute politician than either. Consorting with thieves and whores, Hal is merely preparing the ground for a radical extension of the range displayed in the role of king, in the direction of popular monarchy. He resembles nothing so much as some medieval method actor, diligently researching his part in the stews of Eastcheap. The almost anthropological gaze with which the high regards the low persists from the early plays, then.[33] Hal is fascinated by his education in the language of tapsters and tinkers, although equally adroit in side-stepping when life with his lowlife friends threatens to become a fraternity of pleasure, inventing games and plays that maintain a certain distance from the objects of his study. But that merely underlines the deeper equivalence. Both Hal and Falstaff are fully aware of the possibilities for social transformation implicit in an engagement with popular culture and entertainment. The sophistication of the Hal–Falstaff relationship is that it is mutually parasitic: a zero-sum game over who will get to convert his acquaintance with the other player into public standing. Unlike the plays-within-plays of the early comedies, both are acting in the same performance; it is the outcome that is in doubt. Hal will indeed ultimately banish Falstaff, but in so doing he is revealed as just another popular entertainer, cementing his position as monarch through the ultimate *coup de théâtre*. In the early comedies, to be a sophisticated consumer of drama was to be a noble; to be the unwitting participant in a play was to be a commoner. Here performance as a route to advancement is ubiquitous, theatricality the exclusive property of neither the powerful nor the weak, but simply the medium within which social interaction takes place.

Falstaff is a transitional figure: Kemp's last role and Shakespeare's first attempt at a wholly new exploration of the thematic potential of the figure of the clown. 'Popular culture', as we have seen, is a problematic concept, and many of the plays we have looked at hint that early modern writers might have been well aware of that fact. Shakespeare's later clowns, his fools and aristocratic clowns, develop this sense of the unstable relationship between cultural preferences and social status – the very sense that the plays-within-plays of his earlier work serve to suppress by removing culture from the equation altogether. In the later plays, clowning performance has a very different function. Far from sorting the world of the play in an orderly fashion into gentlemen and commoners, clowns and kings, it opens up a perspective on a very different social landscape, one in which, while the brute reality of social hierarchy is never forgotten, identities appear fluid and even confused. Playing the clown signifies social opportunity. It is also risky. Those who play the clown might be found at the bottom of the social heap, or at its very top. More than that: the blurring of social signals involved in playing the clown render the player's exact social position intriguingly indeterminate.

The situation of the clown – in its broadest sense of a clownish figure in the play – ultimately comes to seem uncannily like that of the early modern actor – the clown doing the playing. On the one hand, a common player was in principle a vagrant, classed with the very lowest of the low; on the other, he might enjoy the patronage of some of the most powerful noblemen in the land – the Lord Chamberlain or even the king. Social critics were lavish in their insistence that actors were in fact nothing more than mere nobodies, their impersonation of the great and the good on stage a gross impropriety, their claims to status an open affront; but this only indicates the worrying extent to which performance might (as for Shakespeare) open an avenue to respectability.[34] As text after text written in the sixteenth and seventeenth centuries testifies, Renaissance England was a society hungry for a clarity of social distinctions; but the reality of early modern life was inevitably messier, more fluid and dynamic, than that outlined in the social taxonomies generated by Shakespeare's contemporaries.

While most accounts of the relationship between elite and popular culture agree in painting a picture of increased differentiation between high and low throughout the early modern period, Shakespeare's plays seem to become increasingly interested in the ways in which clowns and performance offer a means of evading such distinctions. Even Hamlet, the prince who despises popular culture, might find himself playing the clown.

Chapter Four

SHAKESPEARE AND POPULAR ROMANCE

Helen Moore

The literary category of 'romance', let alone 'popular romance', is notoriously difficult to define, in that it overlaps with the classical genres of epic and comedy, harks back to the ancient Greek fictions (often called, anachronistically, 'romances'), and both colonizes and repudiates ancient, medieval and modern forms of historical writing. All of these elements are brought to the fore in 'elite' romances such as Chaucer's *Knight's Tale*, Spenser's *Faerie Queene* and Sidney's *Arcadia*, and have been the subject of academic interest for many years. Recently, however, increasing attention has been paid to the subcategory of medieval texts whose composition and audience have earned them the designation 'popular' romances. These romances are usually written in rhyming verse, and may show evidence of a debt to oral culture through the use of tags and formulae. Their subject matter is usually a straight-forward tale of love, adventure or religion, presented in a simply structured narrative.[1] Prose romances such as the tales of Arthur or continental chivalric fictions may also be described as 'popular' texts in the sixteenth century because they were read by popular as well as elite audiences. In one sense, romance is the popular genre *per se*, carrying in its very name a powerful signal of its ties to the language and culture of the people. The term derives from Old French *romans*, which was first used in the twelfth century to refer to the vernacular language, in an explicit contrast with Latin, the literary language of the elite. As Paul Strohm has demonstrated, the meaning of *romans* extended to indicate not only the language in which a narrative was written, but also the whole work and, ultimately, the genre.[2] Latinity is the most important factor dividing the intellectual elite from the rest of the population in the Middle Ages, and from the outset the readership of romance was envisaged as being non-Latinate: Benoît de Sainte-Maure, for example, explained that he wrote his *Roman de Troie* 'en romanz' for those 'qui n'entendent la letre' ('who do not understand letters', i.e. Latin).[3] However, it should be emphasized that this category of the non-Latinate encompasses members of both the social elite and the populace, or to use the medieval terminology, the second and third estates (the clergy, who often fulminated against reading romances, being the first estate).

Discussions of modern popular culture often treat intellectual and social elites as though they are one and the same. However, this supposition must be abandoned if we are to understand the powerful appeal of romance to readers and audiences of all social strata in the medieval and early modern periods. Romances formed part of the common literary culture spanning all social groups in Shakespeare's day, and the evidence they present, like that offered by ballads, urges us to be cautious about assuming the existence of homogeneous groups of 'elite' and 'popular' readers in this period.[4] Medieval romances that either originated in elite contexts (for example those about King Arthur) or that were enjoyed by both elite and popular medieval audiences (for example *Bevis of Hampton* and *Guy of Warwick*) retained their currency in both elite and popular contexts in the early modern period because they were issued in Tudor printed editions, and therefore made accessible to readers such as Shakespeare.[5] *Bevis of Hampton* was printed at least eight times, *Guy of Warwick* three times, and there were doubtless other editions that have not survived. The romances of *Bevis* and *Guy* were staple elements of the 'cheap print' studied by Tessa Watt and Margaret Spufford, retailing wholesale at between 4d and 7d per copy in Edinburgh and York.[6] *Sir Eglamour* and *Robert the Devil*, which may also have been known to Shakespeare, were among the books sold by the Oxford bookseller John Dorne in 1520 for a few pence each.[7] The tales of Arthur, Guy and Bevis were favourite subjects for ballads. George Puttenham, in *The Arte of English Poesie* (*c*.1570, printed 1589), recalls the 'small and popular Musickes' including *Bevis of Hampton, Guy of*

Warwick and 'other such old Romances or historicall rimes, made purposely for recreation of the common people at Christmasse diners & brideales, and in taverns & alehouses and other such places of base resort'.[8] There were at least four ballads of King Arthur in the period 1565–1620, and three Guy ballads between 1592 and *c.*1640.[9]

Richard Langham's description of the library of Captain Cox, a Coventry mason, attests to the popular taste for printed versions of medieval romances. Captain Cox is known as a participant in the entertainment staged for Queen Elizabeth at Kenilworth in 1575, and among the books he owned were listed the following:

> king Arthurz book, Huon of Burdeaus, The foour suns of Aymon, Beavys of hampton, The squyre of lo degree, The knight of curteyzy, and the Lady Faguell, Frederik of Gene, Syr Eglamoour, Syr Tryamoour, Syr Lamwell, Syr Isenbras, Syr Gawyn, Olyver of the Castl.[10]

According to Henry Parrot, the same tastes in reading are shared by a 'Countrey-Farmer':

> Shewe me King *Arthur*, *Bevis*, or *Syr Guye*,
> Those are the Bookes he onely loves to buye.[11]

The three great heroes of English popular romance are King Arthur, Guy of Warwick and Bevis of Hampton, and their stories were familiar to both learned and popular audiences. Thomas Nashe mocks the rhymes employed in *Bevis* as 'worne out absurdities', but the fact that he can cite four examples from the poem shows that he had read it with some degree of attention.[12] Not all educated readers were quite so dismissive: George Puttenham, for example, claims to have written a 'litle brief Romance or historicall ditty in the English tong', featuring the deeds of Arthur and his knights, of Bevis and of Guy.[13]

References to Arthur, Guy and Bevis recur in Shakespeare's plays, indicating that the playwright's own conception of popular romance accords with that of the populace at large.[14] Shakespeare was also familiar with other medieval metrical romances such as *The Squire of Low Degree*, romances translated in the early Tudor period (such as *Huon of*

Bordeaux), and the high Elizabethan vogue for translations of Spanish chivalric romance. Shakespeare doubtless knew the names of the main romance protagonists by repute or from the ballad tradition, and he would have encountered plentiful references to Arthur, Guy and Bevis in the work of historians such as Holinshed. The uses to which Shakespeare put this knowledge are diverse. In the history plays and *King Lear*, Arthurian material is deployed for both historical and mythic purposes, in order to construct a heroic genealogy for the nation's kings, but also to meditate upon the ultimate unknowability of both past and future. Popular romance plays an important role across the canon in the depiction of demotic, low, or carnival figures and contexts, such as the Eastcheap tavern in the Henriad or the London hordes that mass to greet the Princess Elizabeth at the end of *Henry VIII*. And in *Love's Labour's Lost*, romance is one of the elements of worldly popular culture that threatens to unseat Navarre's rarefied 'little academe' (1.1.13).

Whether or not Shakespeare had actually read the romances – perhaps in his youth, like later readers such as Francis Kirkman and John Bunyan in the seventeenth century, or Samuel Johnson in the eighteenth – he would have been familiar with them from popular report and communal memory. This is particularly true of the legend of Guy, with its powerful local associations. Guy's killing of the Dun Cow, a sixteenth-century addition to the legend, originated from oral rather than written culture, and Guyscliffe, where Guy was reputed to have lived as a hermit, was a local landmark, described by William Dugdale in *The Antiquities of Warwickshire* (1656) as 'the very seat it selfe of pleasantnesse', with its wood, springs, caves and meadows (p.564). A sword and armour reputed to belong to Guy were kept at Warwick Castle, and in the chapel at Guy's cliffe there was a bone supposedly taken from the Dun Cow killed by Guy.[15] Shakespeare's familiarity with popular forms of drama, such as the mumming play, may also have contributed to his knowledge of popular romance, especially if he performed in a 'calf-killing' stunt reminiscent of Guy's killing of the Dun Cow.[16] A final possibility, but one for which there is sadly little surviving evidence, is that Shakespeare witnessed, or even participated in, some of the lost romance plays of the 1590s such as *Huon of Bordeaux*, *Uther Pendragon* and *King Arthur*.[17]

FIGURE 8 Guy, Earl of Warwick, shown fighting the dragon rather than the Dun Cow, from Samuel Rowlands, *The Famous Historie of Guy Earl of Warwick* (1625).

'SKIMBLE-SKAMBLE STUFF'

Shakespeare's use of Arthurian material is complex, in that his references allude not so much to literary texts as to para-literary texts and cultural traditions: his main source for Arthurian material is Geoffrey of Monmouth's *Historia regum Britanniae* (*History of the Kings of Britain*), a quasi-historical narrative written between 1130 and 1136, and the origin of much of the material that later found its way into Arthurian romance. It is unlikely that Shakespeare used a manuscript version of Geoffrey; instead, his knowledge probably derived from chroniclers such as Holinshed, who relied heavily on Geoffrey's account of the early history of Britain, or from poems on historical themes, such as *A Myrroure for Magistrates* (1559), which makes extensive use of Geoffrey's *History*. Arthurian material is deployed by Shakespeare in the history plays and *King Lear*, where its historical and mythic facets are fully exploited. In *1 Henry VI*, for example, the figure of Arthur's father, Uther Pendragon,

is deployed in order to forge an analogy between the heroic achievements of past, present and future British kings. Gloucester's reminis-
cence of Henry V, the king whose 'arms spread wider than a dragon's
wings' (1.1.11), hints at a heroic genealogy stretching from Uther
Pendragon to Henry V and beyond to Henry VII, who exploited the
iconography of the British red dragon in the early days of his reign.[18]
Pendragon returns later in the play as an example of undaunted
courage, when Bedford proclaims his intention to participate in the siege
of Rouen:

> for once I read
> That stout Pendragon, in his litter sick,
> Came to the field, and vanquished his foes.
>
> (3.2.92–4)

This incident refers to Uther's siege of Verulam, recounted in Book 8 of
Geoffrey's *History*.[19] Uther's appearance in a litter leads the Saxons to
make an arrogant miscalculation and leave the gates of the city open.
The Saxons realize 'how grievously they had erred in their pride' but are
defeated, causing Uther to rise from his litter and rejoice that he had con-
quered them while 'half-dead'. These allusions to Uther form part of the
play's conscious deployment of heroic prototypes from history, which is
intended to bolster the reputation of the English. As Edward Burns
writes, 'Male heroic figures . . . represent the continuity of heroic history;
they are both its progenitors and its memorials.'[20] Heroic history of the
kind represented in *1 Henry VI* blurs the boundaries between the 'facts'
of historical record and the 'fiction' of the legendary prototypes invoked
by the play. It also participates in the creation of a proto-mythical present,
and thus underlines the innovative nature of Shakespeare's historical
drama in which past, present and future coexist. As Geoffrey Bullough
observes, '*1 Henry VI* is not so much a Chronicle play as a fantasia on
historical themes' (vol. 3, p.25).

  The complexity of the relationship between history and fiction, and the
contingent nature of historical narrative, are particularly evident in
1 Henry IV. Such an observation is usually made during discussions of
Shakespeare's treatment of Prince Hal and his interpolation of the comic
plot focused on Falstaff, but it is also true of the play's treatment of the

pseudo-historical Arthurian material derived from Geoffrey.[21] Shakespeare's use of Geoffrey means that the influence of Arthurian traditions is seen, perhaps surprisingly, not in the depiction of the chivalric Hotspur, but rather in the Welsh leader Owen Glendower. Indeed, Hotspur the man of action has little time for what he believes to be Glendower's rhetorical and spiritual delusions, and in particular his internalization of the prophecies of Merlin contained in Book 7 of Geoffrey's *History*:

> Sometime he angers me
> With telling me of the moldwarp and the ant,
> Of the dreamer Merlin and his prophecies,
> And of a dragon and a finless fish,
> A clip-winged griffin and a moulten raven,
> A couching lion and a ramping cat,
> And such a deal of skimble-skamble stuff
> As puts me from my faith.

> (*1H4* 3.1.144–51)

Merlin's prophecies, which Geoffrey claims to have translated from a Welsh original, speak of cosmic and earthly disruption and figure future persons, especially a leader who will liberate the Welsh, under the guise of animals. These oblique and riddling predictions comprise the most influential early example of the genre called 'political prophecy' which attained a new forcefulness and relevance following the religious and political turmoil of the Reformation.[22] In his summary Hotspur mixes fabulous animals with animals from Merlin's prophecies; Shakespeare's sources for the latter are Holinshed and *The Mirror for Magistrates*, in which the 'moldwarp', or mole, is Henry, and the conspirators Glendower, Hotspur and Mortimer are signified by the dragon, lion and wolf.[23]

Hotspur's frustration with Glendower seems to be that of a man of action who also despises poetry (3.1.130), brought into uneasy alliance with an inveterate dreamer. It would be easy to take his dismissal of Merlin's prophecies at face value, perhaps even implying a Shakespearean view of Glendower as a 'braggart',[24] and a certain scepticism about political prophecy (a view that has been advanced in relation to the Fool's Merlinesque prophecy in *King Lear* 3.1).[25] However, Hotspur's dismissal of

Merlin's prophecies as 'skimble-skamble' stuff[26] may have played differently to an early modern audience familiar with such prophecies, who would have felt the political *frisson* inherent in opacity. As Howard Dobin explains, 'the earliest vaticination in Welsh probably began as ardent regional patriotism; its obscurantist style served to shield both the prophet and the prophesied hero from easy identification'.[27] So it is possible that, far from being a dismissal of Welsh Arthurian whimsy designed to raise a knowing smile from an English audience, this speech of Hotspur's actually reveals the naivety manifested in his failure to identify the political purposes that mythic obscurantism may serve. Hotspur's speech makes an implied contrast between his own clarity and Glendower's confusion, while in fact demonstrating that it is Hotspur himself whose impatience prevents him from identifying the alternative language of political action embodied in Glendower's tales.[28] This interpretation is supported by Hotspur's earlier impatience with romance allusion manifested in conversation with Northumberland and Westmorland, the latter of whom offers to 'unclasp a secret book' to Hotspur:

> I'll read you matter deep and dangerous,
> As full of peril and adventurous spirit
> As to o'erwalk a current roaring loud
> On the unsteadfast footing of a spear.
>
> (1.3.189–92)

The reference is to the sword-bridge of Arthurian romance, such as that crossed by Lancelot in Chrétien de Troyes' twelfth-century romance *Erec et Enide*,[29] but Hotspur's response, beginning 'If he fall in, good night' (1.3.193), shows that he has no more time for such allusions than he has for Glendower's accounts of the portents that attended his birth. Both incidents show that the 'skimble-skamble stuff' of Arthurian narrative is not mere confusion and nonsense, but may actually operate as a 'secret book' of meaning.

King Lear also exploits the dual function of Geoffrey's *History* as both historical authority and repository of 'skimble-skamble stuff'.[30] The *History* contains the earliest version of the story of the ancient British King Leir and his daughters Gonorilla, Regan and Cordeilla, but

Shakespeare probably derived his knowledge of the story from Caxton's version of the fourteenth-century prose romance *Brut*, from Polydore Vergil's *Anglicae Historiae* (1534), from Robert Fabyan's *New Chronicles* (1516), or, most likely, from Holinshed's *Chronicles*.[31] During the storm on the heath, Lear, Kent and the Fool take refuge in a hovel, and the Fool utters a 'prophecy' foretelling abuses in the state and 'great confusion' in Albion, concluding with the words 'This prophecy Merlin shall make, for I live before his time' (3.2.95–6).[32] Chronologically, the Fool does come before Merlin, of course: on one level, then, his prophecy is part of the play's tendency towards dehistoricization, seen in its sporadic flights from the historically specific moment and its embracing of mythic time. It would be in keeping with this aspect of the play for the Fool to live in a time before Merlin, yet to be granted an anachronistic knowledge of Merlin's prophecies.

On another level, this prophecy addresses itself to the subject of wisdom that is examined from so many different angles in *Lear*. From this perspective, the Fool is suggesting, tongue in cheek, that he possesses a wisdom greater than that of the most famous British seer, indeed that he is the genesis of that prophet's sagacity.

In *1 Henry VI* and *1 Henry IV*, a knowledge of Arthurian material is shared by Welsh and English aristocrats and military men. The situation is very different in *2 Henry IV*, in which the Arthurian legend forms part of the mentality of the Eastcheap tavern world, arguably Shakespeare's most sustained depiction of a 'popular' setting. Scene 2.4 is the last occasion on which the regulars of the Boar's Head tavern are brought together, and it is an exuberant celebration of the culture they embody. It is a whirling, almost chaotic assemblage of slang and cant terms, quotations, and snippets drawn from Elizabethan popular and stage culture, all combining to provide a fine example of the 'demotic energy'[33] that drives the Henry plays. There are references to the 'roaring boy' phenomenon that found its way onto the stage (2.4.69), parodies of popular drama (the fashion for stage ranting, 2.4.153–7; Marlowe's *Tamburlaine*, 2.4.160–2; Peele's *Battle of Alcazar*, 2.4.175), and quotations from ballads (2.4.47). The Arthurian reference belongs with the last of these categories: Falstaff enters the tavern singing the ballad of *Sir Lancelot du Lake*, 'When Arthur first in court' (2.4.33).

The earliest surviving version of this ballad is found in Thomas Deloney's
Garland of Good Will (*c.*1586),[34] and it is an appropriate choice for Falstaff,
exemplifying the vainglorious excesses into which Arthurian texts can
descend when rendered in ballad or chapbook format. Fittingly, *2 Henry
IV* is also the play in which Shakespeare reveals his knowledge of some
Londoners' enthusiasm for Arthurian imitation. Justice Shallow offers as
his qualification for commenting on matters of arms the fact that he participated in 'Arthur's Show', the exhibition of archery held at Mile End
Green by a society called 'The Auncient Order, Society, & Unitie Laudable,
of Prince Arthure, and his knightly Armory of the Round Table':[35]

> I remember at Mile-End Green, when I lay at Clement's
> Inn – I was then Sir Dagonet in Arthur's show.
>
> (3.2.274–6)

The fact that Shallow played the part of Sir Dagonet, King Arthur's fool,
is surely no accident.

The popular world of Arthurian ballads and citizen play-acting may
seem a long way removed from the courtly intellectualism of Navarre's
'little academe' in *Love's Labour's Lost*. Yet this play incorporates a powerful undercurrent of popular culture similar to that of Eastcheap, manifested in its obscene wordplay, allusions to popular culture, and use of
proverbs.[36] The encroachment of the festive, sexual and popular upon
Navarre's academy is often attributable to the ready and wide-ranging
wit of Boyet, who is mocked in the terms of popular culture by Berowne
('He is wit's pedlar and retails his wares / At wakes and wassails, meetings, markets and fairs', 5.2.317–18). During a merry exchange in
which hitting a target with an arrow becomes a sexual metaphor,
Rosaline fires a witty dart at Boyet:

> Shall I come upon thee with an old saying that was a man when
> King Pepin of France was a little boy, as touching the hit-it?

to which Boyet replies:

> So I may answer thee with one as old, that was a woman when
> Queen Guinevere of Britain was a little wench, as touching the
> hit-it.
>
> (4.1.118–23)

(Henry Woudhuysen, the Arden 3 editor, explains 'hit-it' as 'a popular song and dance, with the innuendo of "hitting" as having sex'.) The play's undercurrent of 'low' culture is much in evidence in this scene, and the allusions here work in accord with this aspect of the play's comic sport. Pepin (father of the eighth-century Frankish hero Charlemagne, one of the Nine Worthies) and Guinevere are deployed here to exaggerate the idea of an 'old saying': both are located in a past so distant that any saying that existed in their time must be old indeed (and therefore of great oral authority, it is implied). A further dimension to the Boyet/Rosaline exchange is also worth noting. Boyet's Guinevere reference matches Rosaline's Pepin reference (one ancient historical example for another), but, as so often in the play, also overgoes it. Scene 4.1 is a hunting scene, and Boyet and Rosaline's witty 'hitting' of one another began with the well-worn subject of cuckold's horns. In answering Rosaline's Pepin reference with Guinevere, Boyet therefore provides a doubly meaningful 'hit': Guinevere is not merely associated with the ancient past; her husband was one of history's most famous cuckolds. The way in which Pepin and Guinevere are used here as examples of the past suggests not so much the learned world of the chroniclers and antiquarians, but rather the world of 'wakes and wassails' that constantly encroaches upon the play yet is excluded from its action. The King of Navarre's academy, which he describes as 'still and contemplative in living art' (1.1.14), is founded upon a rejection of the worldly desires celebrated by popular culture, but the arrival of the Princess of France's entourage offers a direct challenge to his intent. The action of the play dramatizes this struggle between intellect and nature through the realities of sex and death that form the staple matter of popular puns, jokes, tales and worldly wisdom.

The play's interest in the conflicts and negotiations of elite and popular culture is also seen in its treatment of the Spanish romances such as *Amadis de Gaule* and *Palmerin* that became extremely popular in the 1580s and 1590s, thanks to the translations undertaken by Shakespeare's fellow playwright, Anthony Munday.[37] In Spain and France these romances found favour with aristocratic and popular audiences successively, but in late Elizabethan and Jacobean England the

English translations were primarily associated with popular tastes. Their style, and their influence upon popular audiences, is lampooned in Francis Beaumont's play, *The Knight of the Burning Pestle* (1607), in which the apprentice Rafe models his heroic deeds upon those of the Spanish heroes such as Palmerin and Amadis. Shakespeare had already remarked the popularity and the idiosyncracy of the genre in *1 Henry IV*, in which Falstaff mocks Bardolph's nose, calling him 'the Knight of the Burning Lamp' (3.3.26–7); this, like the title of Beaumont's play, is a parody of the elaborate pseudonyms bestowed upon or adopted by the heroes of Spanish romance. The particular inspiration for this insult is Amadis of Greece, hero of the ninth book of the *Amadis* cycle, who is known as the Knight of the Burning Sword.[38] In *Love's Labour's Lost* these romances, inhabitants of both elite and popular worlds, are evoked during the King's assessment of 'the refined traveller of Spain' (1.1.161), Don Armado:

> A man in all the world's new fashion planted,
> That hath a mint of phrases in his brain,
> One who the music of his own vain tongue
> Doth ravish like enchanting harmony,
> A man of compliments, whom right and wrong
> Have chose as umpire of their mutiny.
> This child of fancy, that Armado hight,
> For interim to our studies shall relate
> In high-born words the worth of many a knight
> From tawny Spain, lost in the world's debate.
>
> (1.1.162–71)

This description of Armado's reading gives a very accurate impression of the reputation of the romances of chivalry. They certainly established a 'new fashion' of fiction in France and Spain, the dominance of which lasted for much of the sixteenth century. One of the reasons for their success was their refined and elegant style of rhetoric, particularly in erotic contexts: *Amadis* and *Palmerin* are replete with love letters, amorous orations and complaints, uttered by both men and women. The

King's characterization of Armado's rhetorical innovation and exaggeration ('mint of phrases', 'compliments', 'high-born words') accurately captures the tenor of these works, and alludes to the widespread imitation of Amadisian rhetoric among courtiers, and, as the fame of these books spread, popular audiences as well. It is clear that Shakespeare was aware of the linguistic characteristics of these romances, and the rhetorical fashion they launched. The King's words also reveal the playwright's knowledge of the criticism these romances received as a result of their extreme fabulation. Like Don Quixote, the most famous victim of romance reading, Armado is a 'child of fancy' (i.e. imagination) and has entered the solipsistic world of Amadisian self-creation, 'ravish[ed]' by 'the music of his own vain tongue'. This passage does not reveal whether or not Shakespeare had read any of the Spanish romances, but the precision with which it describes their linguistic and social influence reveals a detailed knowledge of the literary-critical debate sparked by their popularity. It is striking just how closely the terms Shakespeare employs here mirror those used across Europe when debating the virtues and vices of these books, and how acutely he describes the characteristics that ensured their appeal in both elite and popular contexts.

'FIE, FOH AND FUM'

It is well recognized that Shakespeare's evocation of the past, whether Roman or ancient British, is syncretic, mingling 'authentic' detail culled from historians such as Plutarch or Holinshed with medieval and early modern anachronisms; the clock in *Julius Caesar* is perhaps the best-known example of this syncretism of past and present. In *King Lear* a fascinating anachronism occurs in the context of popular romance, when Edgar as Poor Tom adapts a couplet from the medieval romance *Bevis of Hampton* during the storm. In answer to Gloucester's enquiry 'What are you there?' (3.4.124) Edgar releases his own storm of allusion relating to his assumed identity:

> Poor Tom, that eats the swimming frog, the toad, the tadpole, the wall-newt and the water –; that in the fury of his heart, when the

foul fiend rages, eats cow-dung for salads; swallows the old rat and the ditch-dog; drinks the green mantle of the standing pool; who is whipped from tithing to tithing and stocked, punished and imprisoned – who hath had three suits to his back, six shirts to his body,

> Horse to ride and weapon to wear.
> But mice and rats and such small deer
> Have been Tom's food for seven long year.
>
> (3.4.125–35)

The allusions here depict the vagrant's struggle to find food as a defining characteristic of his plight. His social and mental alienation is broadcast, first, in his consumption of the culturally inedible (amphibians, dung, rats, dead dogs and the scum on stagnant water), and second, in the reference to the vagabond's forced exclusion from the rudimentary structures of social care in the parish. The adaptation from *Bevis* occurs in lines 134–5 and the lines adapted are as follows:

> Rattes and myce and suche smal dere
> Was his mete that seven yere.[39]

The inclusion here of the quotation from *Bevis* is on one level symptomatic of Poor Tom's disordered raving, which at this juncture is very similar to the mish-mash of allusion employed earlier in the play by the Fool. Yet, like the Fool (and indeed like Glendower), Poor Tom speaks sense through his confusion. The quotation in its original context refers to the sufferings undergone by Bevis during his seven-year imprisonment in Damascus at the hands of King Brademond. During this time, Bevis is deprived of human society and incarcerated underground 'in penaunce and in moche stryffe' (l. 1342).[40] The detail with which his diet is recorded recalls the significance attributed to food in Poor Tom's speech: Bevis receives no 'mete ne drynke', which is restated as no 'bred ne corne', and he eats only a 'sympull messe' (meal) of bran with water once a day (ll. 1337–44). It is possible, therefore, that Poor Tom's reference to Bevis answers Gloucester's question about identity in the 'secret book' style of romance allusion seen in *1 Henry VI*, revealing to his father that Tom's state of alienation is a temporary phenomenon, a forced hiatus in an otherwise active and righteous, even heroic, life. This interpretation may be supported by the closing lines of the scene, in which Edgar binds a literary allusion to Roland, hero of the Old French epic *Le Chanson de Roland*, with a snippet from the folktale of Jack the Giant-Killer:

> Childe Rowland to the dark tower came,
> His word was still 'Fie, foh and fum,
> I smell the blood of a British man'.

$$(3.4.178-80)[41]$$

R.A. Foakes, editor of the Arden 3 *King Lear*, designates these 'nonsense verses' but speculates that the lines 'may also point to Edgar, who will turn into a hero and kill the "giant" Edmund'. Given the likely coding in Edgar's reference to Bevis discussed above, this would seem a distinct possibility. Indeed, Bevis is himself a folklore giant-killer, in that one of his most renowned exploits is his defeat of the giant Ascopart, following which Bevis spares the giant's life and Ascopart becomes his page (Kölbing 119-20).[42] It would seem, therefore, that these two references work to create a suffering, yet giant-killing alter ego for Poor Tom, in coded references that could, if interpreted correctly, provide a revealing and accurate answer to Gloucester's question 'What are you there?' The interpolation of these allusions to romance and folklore may seem incongruous, even indecorous in generic terms, but they are aptly chosen to reveal the truth-speaking, giant-killing Edgar cloaked in the persona of Poor Tom. This is not giant-killing nonsense, but proof of the complex blend of learned and popular wisdom that is typical of Poor Tom.

The exaggerated, giant-killing, folklore element of *Bevis* seems particularly to have impressed itself upon Shakespeare's imagination. In *The First Part of the Contention* (1594), formerly described as a source for *Henry IV* but now viewed as a 'bad' quarto,[43] there is a combat between the armourer and Peter, in anticipation of which the armourer makes the drunken threat 'have at you Peter with downright blowes, as Bevys of South-hampton fell upon Askapart'.[44] In *Henry VIII*, a reference to

Bevis occurs at the climax of Norfolk's description of the 'earthly glory' that was the Field of the Cloth of Gold. Norfolk's account emphasizes the otherworldly splendour of the occasion, with descriptions of pages like cherubim, 'all gilt', and allusions to the riches of the East. His speech closes with an extravagant flourish:

> When these suns –
> For so they phrase 'em – by their heralds challenged
> The noble spirits to arms, they did perform
> Beyond thought's compass – that former fabulous story
> Being now seen possible enough, got credit
> That Bevis was believed.
>
> BUCKINGHAM   O, you go far.
>
>   (1.1.34–8)

Buckingham's remonstration, with its implication of 'surely not!', suggests a common understanding of *Bevis* as an example of extreme fabulation: how, he seems to be saying, could anything make *Bevis* seem believable? The critical question is whether the allusion works to amplify the greatness of the occasion or to undermine it; the *Bevis* reference therefore plays a part in establishing the tone of the play's opening scene and indicating the way in which regal splendour and Henrician display are to be handled in the drama to come. Throughout the scene Buckingham operates as the means by which the apparent admiration of Norfolk's description is peeled away to reveal the aristocratic scepticism that characterizes the noblemen's view of royal performance. For example, when Norfolk attributes the organization of the occasion to the 'good discretion / Of the right reverend Cardinal of York' (i.e. Wolsey, 1.1.50–1), Buckingham replies 'The devil speed him! No man's pie is freed / From his ambitious finger' (1.1.52–3). He then goes on to describe the splendid events of the royal meeting as 'fierce vanities' (1.1.54). Thus the reference to *Bevis* operates not merely to capture the sense of general awe at the proceedings in France, but also to raise the question of whether the Field of the Cloth of Gold really was the great occasion it was proclaimed to be, or instead a fabulous and insubstantial fiction of the kind typical in folklore.

The third great English hero, Guy of Warwick, is also a giant-killer, and he appears in *Henry VIII*, in the controversial porter's scene (5.3) attributed to John Fletcher, who collaborated with Shakespeare on this play. The scene is often cut from performances, partly because of its supposed authorship, and partly because it introduces a demotic, carnivalesque atmosphere before the play's dignified climax in the christening of Elizabeth and Cranmer's prophecy of England's greatness under her reign.[45] Yet the scene plays an important part in the closing stages of the play through its vivid evocation of the life and mentality of the nation that is to be governed by Elizabeth. To this end it evokes many aspects of popular culture during the porter's castigation of the multitude that flocks to the entrance of the court in order to witness the christening procession. In the course of his chastisement of the people, the porter alludes to popular customs such as the 'ale and cakes' eaten at holidays, entertainments such as bear-baiting and playgoing, and items of gossip such as the tendency of apprentices to prefer brawling to work. Appropriately, it is the giant-killing, folklore Guy who is invoked by the porter's man as he defends himself against the charge of ineffective action against the invading commons:

> I am not Samson, nor Sir Guy, nor Colbrand,
> To mow 'em down before me; but if I spared any
> That had a head to hit, either young or old,
> He or she, cuckold or cuckold-maker,
> Let me ne'er hope to see a chine again
>
> (5.3.20–4)

Guy's fight against Colbrand, like Bevis's defeat of Ascopart, is one of two incidents to achieve particular emphasis in the popular renditions of his story; the other is his killing of the Dun Cow, discussed above. Colbrand was the Danish champion, another 'giant'. At the request of King Athelstan, Guy fought with Colbrand and beheaded him, thereby causing the Danes to leave England and hence liberating his country.[46] This political dimension to the story meant that the legend of Guy was often incorporated into histories such as Fabyan's *Chronicle* (first printed 1516).[47] It also appears in two accounts contemporary with

Shakespeare: Holinshed's *Chronicles* (1577; sig. P2ʳ) and John Stow's *Summarie of the Chronicles of Englande* (1587). Stow emphasizes the national and political importance of Guy's giant-killing with his observation that it 'brought this lande into one Monarchie, for he expelled the Danes, and quieted the Welshmen' (sig. C2ᵛ). Although opposed as enemies in the historical and folklore account, the proverbial reputation of Guy and Colbrand united them in their character as strong men, and this is the primary signification here.[48] However, it is entirely fitting that the folklore hero who defeated a foreign 'giant' and advanced the cause of English national identity should be embedded into this scene celebrating Elizabeth's birth, just as it is appropriate that her christening should be depicted against the vivid background of London's popular culture.

The porter's scene may be wholly or partly by Fletcher, but its juxtapositioning of popular culture and high solemnity is a fully Shakespearean trait. In a fine moment of comic seriousness in *Henry V*, the myth of Arthur becomes conflated with Christian tradition during a discussion on Falstaff's resting place:

BARDOLPH Would I were with him, wheresome'er he is, either in
    heaven or in hell!
HOSTESS Nay, sure, he's not in hell; he's in Arthur's bosom, if ever man
    went to Arthur's bosom.

(2.3.7–10)

The mistaking of 'Arthur' for 'Abraham' in this idiom, which refers to the resting place of the happy departed, is in keeping with the comic impieties ('carnation' for 'incarnate', and so on) of the Hostess throughout this scene. Remembering how Falstaff cried out 'God, God, God!' on his deathbed, she explains 'Now I, to comfort him, bid him 'a should not think of God; I hoped there was no need to trouble himself with any such thoughts yet' (2.3.19–21). This recollection of Falstaff on his deathbed parodies the preceding scene depicting Henry's judgement on the traitors Cambridge, Scroop and Grey, his injunction that they should repent and endure death, and his dedication of the French expedition into the hands of God. Together with the supplanting of

Abraham by Arthur, the confusion over 'incarnate', and the Hostess's literalization of the Whore of Babylon, her advice removes Falstaff from the realm of Christian judgement and locates his passing in a world of spiritual ignorance and mangled mythico-Christian traditions. The overall effect is simultaneously comic and tragic, highlighting as it does both the cheerful, crowded worldliness of Eastcheap and its fragile grasp on questions of eternity.

Popular culture is again juxtaposed with serious matter in 5.1, which depicts the bickering and brawling between Pistol and Fluellen, and is sandwiched between the solemnity of the Chorus's description of Henry's return to England and the concluding scene paving the way for Henry's marriage and future rule. In contrast with the great events unfolding around it, 5.1 contains Fluellen's defence of the custom of wearing the Welsh leek. Seeking to revenge Pistol's insults, Fluellen cudgels Pistol into eating leek, and incorporates a popular romance, *The Squire of Low Degree*, into his mock heroics:

> You called me yesterday mountain-squire, but I will make
> you today a squire of low degree.

(5.1.36–7)

The reference is intended primarily to effect a contrast with 'mountain', and does not in itself suggest any particular familiarity with the romance. It is worthy of comment, however, because it fleshes out the mental world of the populace represented by Fluellen and Pistol, and because the romance itself possesses some affinities with the circumstances of the speakers, dealing as it does with the adventures of a lowly squire during an enforced absence from his beloved. This scene serves a comparable purpose in *Henry V* to the porter's scene in *Henry VIII* by invoking comedy and depicting popular culture at the moment of a sea-change in monarchy, being here the final transformation of Prince Hal into King Henry. The scene also helps to bind the Henry plays together by perpetuating the 'demotic energy' noted by David Scott Kastan as a characteristic of the Henriad, and it keeps something of the Eastcheap world alive to the end of the play, despite the passing of Falstaff.

Shakespeare's knowledge of popular romance, like that of his learned and popular contemporaries, was derived from a mixture of sources. From the chronicle tradition he gained a sense of Arthurian legend as politically charged and fundamental to an understanding of national origins. He was familiar with the phenomenon of Elizabethan Arthurianism that was manifested with equal enthusiasm in elite and popular contexts, and he possessed a surprisingly detailed knowledge of the continental debate concerning the virtues and vices of Spanish chivalric fiction. Oral tradition and local legend provided him with further information about popular heroes, especially Guy of Warwick, and he may have read one romance, *Bevis of Hampton*, with some degree of attention. In Shakespeare's plays, Arthurian romance enjoys a dual signification as both history and myth. As history, it may point up connections and comparisons with the present (witness the references to Uther Pendragon in *1 Henry VI*), while as myth it offers many opportunities for truth-telling in the guise of riddles. Both Arthurian and native popular romances, with their local associations and proximity to folklore, are integral to Shakespeare's writing of the nation. They form a common core of reference from court to tavern, and bind not only elite and popular, but also past and present.

Chapter Five

SHAKESPEARE AND ELIZABETHAN POPULAR FICTION

David Margolies

INTRODUCTION

R obert Greene, Shakespeare's most prolific contemporary, is less well known today for his own work than as the writer who accused Shakespeare of climbing to success on the backs of his fellows:

> there is an upstart Crow, beautified with our feathers, that with his Tyger's heart wrapt in a Players hide, supposes he is as well able to bumbast out a blanke verse as the best of you: and being an absolute *Iohannnes fac totum*, is in his owne conceit the onely Shake-scene in a Countrie.[1]

Greene was referring to Shakespeare's use of other writers' plays, but his attack would have been more justified in relation to fiction because Shakespeare based *The Winter's Tale* on Greene's hugely popular *Pandosto* (though nearly two decades after Greene's death), and there was a large body of fiction being produced in Elizabethan England that Shakespeare knew well. The fiction that entered the Elizabethan world in abundance was undoubtedly important to Shakespeare as a playwright, but its importance was not, as is often assumed, only as a store of plots. Today, when so much theatre consists of plays that are adaptations of novels (or journals, court records, or even films) rather than original drama, there is a natural tendency to superimpose current practices on Shakespeare's method of working; his use of 'sources' is thus often regarded simply as a change in the mode of presentation of the 'raw material' of plot. This notion tends to conceal the complex role that sources play in his work. In fact, plot is often the most superficial element of Shakespeare's 'borrowing', and concentration on it has obscured the variety of ways in which his experience of fiction affected his dramatic production – as well as undervaluing the richness of the fiction itself.

Traditional hierarchies of literary production also contribute to the difficulty of seeing the importance of popular fiction for Shakespeare's plays. Although not regarded as a 'mechanical' activity like that of the actor, the writing of fiction, as distinct from poetry, was not considered part of the liberal arts by the Elizabethans. The mode of distribution for the vast bulk of fiction was commercial, and the writing of most fiction suffered from a taint of mercenary motives which deprived it of gentlemanly flavour. As a consequence it has often been denied serious status, and this, in turn, has led to an assumption that it cannot be of much significance as a source for Shakespeare. There are, of course, major exceptions, and not all fiction was considered common. Sidney's *Arcadia* was not just a literary *tour de force*; it was also 'validated' by his aristocratic pedigree and its amateur (i.e. non-professional) status. Thus it is not viewed as at all surprising that Shakespeare should have used it in the Gloucester plot of *King Lear*. Lyly's *Euphues*, a masterpiece of rhetorical wit which set the style for at least a decade, is grudgingly accepted because its primary audience was the court.[2] Nashe has also gained acceptance, despite a reputation for confrontational individualism, perhaps because his verbal virtuosity overflowed with learning and his wild imagination ultimately supported the status quo. But these exceptions do not diminish the distrust of the popular. Greene, though a master of arts in both the universities, and therefore technically a gentleman, never escaped his 'common' reputation and never achieved a positive literary image.

While there were some excellent pieces of Elizabethan fiction that have gained a place on the margins of the canon, it is also true that there were many publications in which it is difficult to find virtues. But it has to be recognized that there was a flourishing and expanding publishing trade that entertained a cross-section of society.[3] Books, or pamphlets, were affordable in price, and there were many of them, sold by the stationers around St Paul's (later also by chapmen) and advertised by title pages that often included a plot summary and elaborated claims to instructional value. Greene's *Never too Late* (1590), for example, includes on the title page the description 'sent to all youthfull gentlemen; to roote out the infectious follies, that ouer-reaching conceits foster in the spring time of their youth . . . As pleasant as profitable, being a right pumice stone, apt to race out idlenesse with delight, and follie with admonition'. Most importantly, there was a public that could read.[4] It did not matter if they moved their lips while they read; fiction was mostly in the oral mode, in effect written speech, and the manner of consumption was characteristically group reading.

For Shakespeare and his contemporaries it is also significant that the very production of fiction was experimental. When Shakespeare was born no one knew how to write a novel because the genre did not yet exist. Problems of how to represent experience – what to tell, how to order the presentation of events and organize release of information (is it better if the reader gets the letter when it is written or when it is received?), how to present character – all were live issues. Experimentation with form was relevant to anyone concerned with verbal modes of representation, dramatists as well as fiction writers. It was also the case that much fiction had progressed but a short distance from oral narrative, and the writing retained a ceremonial and a performative quality which overlapped with dramatic construction. 'Character' as the psychologically developed individual of the modern novel is no part of Elizabethan fiction; its authors usually dealt with personages who were given typical qualities. Similarly, their speech was not the lifelike interchanges we are accustomed to seeing naturalized in the novel; rather, speaking was represented as formal speeches from which the character type could be understood, in the same way as in the drama.

The experimental character of Elizabethan fiction had as much to do with testing social attitudes as with literary-technical exploration. It provided a perspective on the experience of readers that was embodied in elements of concrete living. 'Concrete' may seem an inappropriate term to apply to the stylized narration of Elizabethan fiction; but it is concrete both in drawing its material from concerns of everyday life and in the down-to-earth, proverb-like character of the narration. In contrast, the hierarchical view of social order, the single coherent world-view available to the Elizabethans, had an abstract character that failed to engage with many important aspects of day-to-day life. Fiction went some way to closing this gap because it was often rooted in the kind of situations and interactions people knew from their own lives. For example, in Austen Saker's *Narbonus* the eponymous hero becomes a soldier and his miserable diet and living conditions are given extended description. Similarly, Emanuel Forde in *Ornatus and Artesia*, although he draws on Sidney's *Arcadia*, remarks the rude behaviour of one aristocrat towards his social inferiors and comments that another worries about being too costly a charge on his humble host.[5] Even when the fictional hero is a king, as in Greene's *Arbasto, The Anatomie of Fortune* (1584), the narration is likely to be less concerned with matters of state than with romantic attachments. This change in the sense of what is important is part of fiction's strength and appeal. The attraction is not just the alternative perspective but also the familiar detail or situation of its embodiment. Thus in *Tamburlaine* or *Doctor Faustus* Marlowe's heroes rebel against a severely restrictive hierarchical definition of the world, but that rebellion is on a heroic scale; and however attractive it may be to an audience, being 'larger than life' it does not suggest how it can be fitted into life on a human scale. In a practical sense – i.e. in relation to what people do – there is no model of behaviour offered. In fiction, on the other hand, Robert Greene's protagonists, for example, make rebellious choices, but they are also immediately understandable in terms of the reader's world. Thus one of his heroines in *The Defence of Conny-Catching* rescues her family from a treacherous, lascivious usurer by nailing his ear to the window frame. Even if this cannot serve as an exact template for behaviour, it is grasped in terms of a personal resistance such as readers could themselves make. The fiction relates to their lives in a way that is not possible for the writ-large, representative approach of Marlowe.

What I am trying to suggest is that Shakespeare's use of Elizabethan fiction was far from just the simple gathering of plots. Fiction had a function in terms of ideas and values that was at least as important to him, but is less immediately evident because it is more diffused. I want to look first at the nature of some of the standard borrowing discussed in

Bullough, Muir and Gillespie.[6] Then I shall examine one instance of the influence of popular fiction that has been obscured by the long-standing high-culture bias of English studies: Shakespeare's use of Richard Johnson's crude but popular *Tom a Lincoln, The Red-Rose Knight* in *Cymbeline*, and, more importantly and at greater length, its use in *Hamlet*. I shall then turn to the matter of fiction's importance in preparing the audience to accept particular attitudes, and finally to the possibilities of organizing meaning that Shakespeare may have gained from fiction.

SHAKESPEARE'S WHOLESALE USE OF FICTION

The two best-known examples of Shakespeare's wholesale use of English prose fiction are Thomas Lodge's *Rosalynde* in *As You Like It* and Greene's *Pandosto* in *The Winter's Tale*. The use of *Rosalynde* is fairly straightforward. Shakespeare was working with a popular text which, published in 1590 and reissued in 1592, 1596 and 1598, had a sustained appeal that continued after *As You Like It* appeared (editions in 1604 and 1609). *Rosalynde* already had performative qualities, which may have suggested transfer to the stage. Its verse sections, for example, are sometimes eclogues, live poetry or singing competitions which, although still formal, have a dynamic quality not achieved when a poem is simply inserted into a prose text to add variety. Shakespeare maintained the eclogue element with intervals of singing, and preserved the charming pastoral quality of *Rosalynde*, but he also added elements to the simple, self-contained world that go beyond it. Although Lodge's story is clearly not uni-dimensional, his narrative, verse and internal monologues are compartmentalized. This separation of the conventions from other perspectives means that Lodge provides nothing that challenges or questions the conventions. Shakespeare, however, opens the closed world of the pastoral to other perspectives that do challenge its assumptions. Lodge's shepherds exist only at a pastoral level – a world of country air and pleasant sheep – whereas Shakespeare's introduction of conflicting elements (e.g. the need for food and shelter juxtaposed against the sung praise of the greenwood) highlights the conventions and makes them a subject to play with. Lodge has neither a fool nor a melancholic in his work. Shakespeare's addition of Touchstone, and to a lesser degree of Jacques, brings a court consciousness, an urban/urbane perspective to bear on country conditions.

When Corin and Silvius first enter with their dialogue on the pains of love, Touchstone makes a caricature of it (which is necessarily from a different point of view), and when Rosalind empathizes with Corin's plaint as 'much upon my fashion', Touchstone shows the court perspective, saying the fashion 'grows something stale with me' (2.4.58–9). The contrast of different ways of looking at the world occurs most sharply where Corin politely enquires of Touchstone how he likes the shepherd's life. Touchstone replies at some length:

> Truly shepherd, in respect of itself, it is a good life; but in respect that it is a shepherd's life, it is naught. In respect that it is solitary, I like it very well; but in respect that it is private, it is a very vile life. Now in respect it is in the fields, it pleaseth me well; but in respect it is not in the court, it is tedious. As it is a spare life, look you, it fits my humour well; but as there is no more plenty in it, it goes much against my stomach.
>
> (3.2.13–21)

Again, with punning consciousness, Touchstone is in effect opposing the pastoral image to the reality he is experiencing. 'Solitary' and 'spare', for example, are fashionable notions, the opposite of urban excess; but for Touchstone they are unpleasant in the actuality – without ceremony and deprived of the abundance to which he is accustomed. He views the actual life of the shepherds not through a literary representation but in terms of the life lived at court – attractive as image but not as reality. Similarly, when Corin gives a conventionalized picture of the satisfactions of the humble occupation of animal husbandry, Touchstone's reply wittily interprets it from the contrary perspective of court sexual corruption:

> That is another simple sin in you, to bring the ewes and the rams together, and to offer to get your living by the copulation of cattle; to be bawd to a bell-wether, and to betray a she-lamb of a twelve-month to a crooked-pated old cuckoldy ram, out of all reasonable match.
>
> (3.2.76–81)

The element of disguise is also used in a more complex, reflective way by Shakespeare. For Lodge, the effectiveness of Rosalind's disguise is a given: Rosader (the Orlando figure) 'took him flat for a shepherd's swain'. In the interchange leading up to their mock marriage Rosalind asks, 'Did not Rosalind content her Rosader?' and Rosader makes a witty, rather literary reply which shows that the reality he thinks he sees is Ganymede, not Rosalind:

> Truth, gentle swain, Rosader hath his Rosalind but as Ixion had Juno, who thinking to possess a goddess only embraced a cloud. In these imaginary fruitions of fancy I resemble the birds that fed themselves with Zeuxis' painted grapes, but they grew so lean with pecking at shadows that they were glad with Aesop's cock to scrape for a barley cornel. So fareth it with me, who, to feed myself with the hope of my mistress' favors, soothe myself in thy suits and only in conceit reap a wished-for content. But if my food be no better than such amorous dreams, Venus at the year's end shall find me but a lean lover. Yet do I take these follies for high fortunes and hope these feigned affections do divine some unfeigned end of ensuing fancies.[7]

In a text assimilated through reading, disguise can pass unchallenged; on the stage it is obviously a more complicated matter. Ganymede for Shakespeare moves more completely into the Rosalind role; that is, as Ganymede she plays Rosalind in an elaborated way. In Lodge, Ganymede's enactment of Rosalind serves merely as a marker, not like the real thing, as Rosader makes clear; whereas in *As You Like It* the doubleness is constantly brought to the audience's attention. For example, when the mock Rosalind and Orlando have just been 'married' and she recites a litany of the contrary qualities of wives, he asks 'But will my Rosalind do so?' Her reply plays on the doubleness: 'By my life, she will do as I do' (4.1.149–50). The play necessarily adds complication because the layers of reality are not kept separate. That is, even if we discount the further complication that would arise from considering also the boy actor's relation to the part, what we see is Rosalind impersonating Ganymede playing Rosalind. We are given all three levels of being at once, and they leak into each other. The different behaviours and levels of relation occurring in the same dramatic interaction make the conventions very obvious, and this is part of the pleasure of the play. Lodge wrote a delightful, relaxed, gently witty pastoral; Shakespeare transformed it into a piece that retains the charm but also has a local edge in displaying the sharp wit of Elizabethan London and playing on heightened urban awareness of changing fashion, of rhetorical and conventional postures, and of the gap that always exists between image and actuality.

The other popular work of prose fiction Shakespeare used as a whole is Robert Greene's *Pandosto*. It appeared in 1588, although it was not used by Shakespeare until 1610 in *The Winter's Tale*, when, like *Rosalynde*, it was in its fifth edition. But *Pandosto* is quite a different matter from *Rosalynde*. Superficially a fairly simple narrative with a pastoral setting for the greater part, it has what amounts to a dual focus. The narrative, after the opening scenes of jealousy, is concerned with the development of an amorous relationship between a shepherdess (who, unbeknown to herself or any other character, is a princess) and a prince. However, the matter given greatest narrative density is the shepherdess's resolution to follow her own romantic inclinations rather than the social rules that forbid cross-class unions. Unlike his use of *Rosalynde*, where he kept the pastoral character but added another dimension, with *Pandosto* Shakespeare follows the plot closely but dispenses with the social comment, which produces a play of an entirely different character.

Pandosto, at once fantastic yet with a sense of real issues that characters have to resolve, and combining literary and popular style, provided an excellent basis for the mixed modes of the last plays. It happily violates the unities of time and place (there is a sixteen-year gap between the two parts of the story, and the action moves from Bohemia to Sicily and back to Bohemia again); it had elements of concealed identity, mortal danger, sexual attraction (including incestuous attraction), noble fortitude, comic caricature and an oracle; and it also had a plot set in motion by one of the period's most saleable motives, jealousy.

Greene combined his romantic elements with a witty social commentary that Shakespeare chooses to ignore, using only the socially neutral narrative. He opens *The Winter's Tale* with jealousy in action, endowing Greene's conventional situation with a psychological depth that surpasses that of almost all his other plays. He then moves into action based on the second part of Greene's plot, with the discovery of the infant princess who has survived abandonment. Shakespeare has the abandonment preceded by a long (more than forty lines), humorously formulaic, moralizing speech by Antigonus, and it is immediately followed by Shakespeare's most famous stage direction, 'Exit, pursued by a bear', which is an ironic use of a romance convention. There is no bear in Greene. The device Greene uses for bringing the shepherd to the rescue is that he is searching for a sheep he cannot afford to lose, and his reflection on seeing the infant is that he must save it from freezing and starvation but cannot afford to foster it. This gives the scene a strong sense of social location. The commentary of Shakespeare's shepherd has less social focus – he identifies 'waiting-gentlewoman in the scape' and says, 'they were warmer that got this than the poor thing is here' (3.3.72–6). Shakespeare then moves immediately into the music-hall comic exchange between the stage rustics.

Greene also had a conventional comic scene. When the shepherd returns home with the baby, his wife thinks it is his bastard,

> marveling that her husband should be so wanton abroad, sith hee
> was so quiet at home . . . and taking up a cudgell (for the most
> master went breechlesse) sware solemnly that she would make
> clubs trumps, if he brought any bastard brat within her dores.[8]

But the comic interchange soon yields to practical discussion and then, with no sense of comedy, to jumping the narrative forward sixteen years.

Shakespeare frames the plot element – Perdita's rescue – with elements that send up the whole scene: Antigonus' conventional, moralistic speech, the stage direction and finally the chorus, Time, which emphasizes the absurdity of the sixteen-year gap – all of which would suggest that, contrary to the view generally held, Shakespeare is using *Pandosto* to parody the conventions of romance. He signals this directly in a gentleman's comment on the play's denouement: 'Like an old tale still, which will have matter to rehearse, though credit be asleep and not an ear open' (5.2.62–4). Yet Shakespeare proceeds from send-up, through the elaborated guilt of Leontes, to the very moving 'resurrection' of Hermione and the complex of emotions associated with this scene. In Greene, when the queen dies she stays dead, and the function

of guilt is that after the happy reunion of father and daughter, Pandosto
(the Leontes figure) reflects on his behaviour and commits suicide:

> Pandosto (calling to minde how first he betrayed his friend Egistus,
> how his jealousie was the cause of Bellariaes death, that contrarie
> to the lawe of Nature hee had lusted after his owne Daughter)
> mooved with these desperate thoughts, he fell in a melancholy fit,
> and to close up the Comedie with a Tragicall stratageme, he slewe
> himselfe.

(p.121)

Shakespeare, then, relies very heavily on Greene but changes the balance of the plot, emphasizing the potentially tragic jealousy, adding pastoral in a formal way (the sheep-shearing festival) and eliminating the
social questions almost entirely. Greene's work may be careless and
inconsistent in many respects, but in others, such as his shifting of the
social perspective, it is sophisticated and significant. Rather than trying
to make a good play out of a flawed romance, Shakespeare (as I would
see it) is sending up romance, and at the same time setting for himself an
extremely difficult comic obstacle to achieving a moving conclusion. To
turn a witty parody and a 'show' with song and dance into a serious-
seeming play that evokes genuine emotion is an extraordinary demon-
stration, not of profundity, but of Shakespeare's dramatic skill and his
power as a theatre artist.

The role of Greene for Shakespeare is too often treated reductively
because, unlike Sidney or even Lodge, Greene has traditionally been
regarded as having appealed to a lower-class audience, and is dismissed as
entirely commercial in his orientation. This judgement does him an injustice, but, more important, it makes it difficult to recognize that his work is
not just a crude story which Shakespeare turned into a sophisticated play.

SHAKESPEARE'S USE OF
LOWER-CLASS ROMANCE

Shakespeare's reputation gives prominence to his artistic refinement,
which means that the possibility of his using crude fiction as a source is
often discounted. Even if Shakespeare's use of Greene is incontestable, the

role played by others such as Richard Johnson, declassé and lacking in artistic skills, tends to go unremarked. Johnson characterized himself as 'a poore apprentice' in one of his first publications, *The Nine Worthies of London* (1592), a verse celebration of London heroes. His address to 'Gentlemen readers, as well Prentices as others' signals his resistance to hierarchy, and he says he will not be discouraged by being called 'mechanicall'. Art is no prerequisite for publication, and he claims none: 'Every weede hath his vertue, & studious trauaile (though without skill) may manifest good will' (sig. A3^r). Shakespeare drew significantly on Johnson's *Tom a Lincoln* (1599) on at least two occasions. Indeed, the anonymous editor of the 1872 edition of Johnson's most enduring work, *The Seven Champions of Christendom* (it went through some sixty editions before 1800 and became a children's book), observed in his introduction, written at a time when the book's jingoism might have struck a more resonant chord: 'it is generally believed that Shakespeare was as familiar with this work of Richard Johnson as with those of Plutarch or Chaucer'.[9] Arthur Burrell introduced the 1912 edition of *The Seven Champions* to 'the Young Reader' as 'one of the important books of the world': it has led young people to a love of reading even though 'your histories of English Literature either do not notice it or contemptuously give it a word or two'. Southey, Hallam, Scott and 'a number of great writers devoured it'.[10] Although Shakespeare's use of *The Seven Champions* was much more limited than that of *Tom a Lincoln*, it still seems to have had a minor role in *Hamlet*, providing a model for the letter that was to ensure the prince's speedy death on landing in England with Rosencrantz and Guildenstern. King Ptolemy of Egypt plots to dispose of St George in the same way, sending him to the Soldan of Persia with a letter calling for his execution:

> This is the request upon the League of Friendship betwixt us, to show the bearer hereof, thy Servant Death: for he is an utter enemy to all Asia and Africa, and a proud contemner of our Religion. Therefore fail not in my request, as thou wilt answer on the Oath, and so in hast farewell.[11]

Tom a Lincoln, the Red-Rose Knight, is the bastard son of King Arthur. Left at a shepherd's gate with a purse of gold, like Fawnia/Perdita he is

The moſt Pleaſant

HISTORY
OF
TOMALINCOLN
That Ever Renowned Souldier,
THE
Red-Roſe Knight.

Printed by *H. B.* for *W. Thackery* at the Angel in *Duck Lane,* 1682.

FIGURE 9   Tom a Lincoln, from Richard Johnson, *The Most Pleasant History of Tom a Lincoln* (1682).

raised by the shepherd as his own child. After a brief period of banditry, he is installed as a Knight of the Roundtable and thereafter follows a heroic career. Red-Rose and his choice crew of English gentlemen soldiers, returning from several months' stay on an island inhabited only by women – whom they graciously agree to assist in re-populating the island – find themselves becalmed, and Red-Rose asks Sir Launcelot du Lake to entertain the company with a story. This story, just over 4000 words long, provides the framing plot of *Cymbeline*.[12] Valentine, a prince, and Dulcippa, the daughter of a country gentleman, intend marriage and thereby incur the hatred of the Empress, Valentine's mother, who 'thinks it a scandal to her son's birth to match in marriage with one of so base a parentage' and considers 'how she might end their loves and finish Dulcippa's life'. To that end she summons her doctor to procure poison, and gains his assistance, though against his will. He gives Dulcippa, not poison, but a draught that sends her into a death-like trance. Valentine, when he hears of Dulcippa's 'death', leaves the Court,

> and conuerted his rich Attire to ruthfull Roabes: his costly coloured Garments, to a homely russet Coat; and so trauailing to the solitary woods, he vowed to spend the rest of his dayes in a Shepheards life: His royall Scepter was turned into a simple Sheepehooke, and all his pleasure was to keepe his Sheepe from the teeth of the rauenous Wolues.[13]

Dulcippa, woken by the goddess Diana, joins the party of forest nymphs, and, some time later, shepherd and nymph joyfully rediscover each other. An old hermit (a casual entrant to the forest scene, without other narrative function) informs them that the wicked Empress will be killed if no champion comes forward for her, and the good son Valentine and Dulcippa agree to return to the court.

> But being no sooner arriued in the Court, and seeing his Father to take the combat vpon himselfe, presently he kneeled downe, and like an obedient Sonne, discouered himselfe, and withall Dulcippas strange fortunes: whereupon the Empresse and the Doctor were presently deliuered, and did both most willingly

consent to ioyne these two Louers in the bands of Mariage: where after they spent their dayes in peace and happinesse.

(sig. F2ᵛ)

As romance, the plot is simple. Shakespeare uses it as only one thread in the complex weaving together of a number of plots. In the basic story he reverses the social positions of the lovers, changes the evil mother into a wicked stepmother, and increases the number of relationships.

Shakespeare's use of Launcelot's tale does indeed suggest the 'raw material' role of fiction – a simple tale is used as the framework for a complex play. But the main tale of *Tom a Lincoln* has greater significance for Shakespeare, and would appear to be one of the shaping elements of *Hamlet*. We know from Thomas Lodge that there was a popular *Hamlet* playing in London; in 1596 he wrote of a character who 'looks as pale as the Visard of the ghost which cried so miserably at the Theator like an oisterwife, Hamlet, revenge'.[14] Lodge's reference, in a popularly oriented work, suggests general awareness of the play. In the manner of tragedies in ancient Greece and Hollywood remakes of today, a well-known story can be used with a new significance, although the basic outlines of the plot must remain the same. As a revenge play the missing *Hamlet* is unlikely to have concentrated on psychological depth. For Shakespeare, revenge frames the plot, but the conditions that determine its significance, such as Hamlet's alienation and the complacently corrupt court at Elsinore, assume a greater prominence. Despite being shallow and disconnected, *Tom a Lincoln* would seem to make a major contribution to that change.[15]

When King Arthur reveals on his deathbed that he is the father of Red-Rose, Anglitora, wife of Red-Rose, is outraged to discover she has been married to a bastard. She leaves England with their son, the Black Knight, to return to the land of her father. Red-Rose's behaviour at this point would seem also echoed in *Pericles*: he

made a solemne vow to Heauen, neuer to cut his Haire, neuer to come in Bedde, neuer to weare Sho, neuer to taste Food, but onely Bread and Water, nor neuer to take pleasure in humanitie, till he

had eased his griefe in the presence of his deerest Anglitora, and
that her loue were reconciled to him.

(sig. I2^v)

Anglitora and her son, lost in a strange land, take hospitality from the
Knight of the Castle. The Knight and Anglitora become lovers, and
the Black Knight, while hunting, becomes lost in the forest. Seven years
later, when Red-Rose finally finds Anglitora, she and her lover murder
him. His ghost then comes to the Black Knight, still lost in the forest,
guides him back to the castle and encourages him to take revenge.

There are other elements that find clear echoes in *Hamlet* but are not
themselves significant. The ghost condemns the sensuality of the adul-
terous mother, whose frailty he bewails – her 'weake nature, that so
easily was woon to lewdnesse' (sig. I4^v). The Black Knight, like Hamlet,
bemoans the profitless use of his time; he swears to revenge his father
with Hamlet-like elaboration; he makes a graveside speech that suggests Hamlet's in Ophelia's grave. But it is the closet scene, one of the
most vexed scenes for critics in the play, that seems to derive most from
Tom a Lincoln. The action in the play can be described as Hamlet con-
fronting Gertrude over her relationship with Claudius; Johnson has
effectively the same action, but without nuance. The Black Knight,
urged on by the ghost, approaches his mother and her lover asleep in
bed. He kneels, whispers a prayer to the furies, and 'Hauing spoken
these words, hee sheathed his Sword vp to the hiltes in the boosome of
the Knight of the Castle'. Anglitora wakes and cries out, 'Oh what hast
thou done my cruell Sonne? Thou hast slaine the miracle of humanitie; and one whom I haue chosen to be my hearts Parramour, and thy
second Father' (sig. L4^v) (which suggests Gertrude's crying out over
Polonius, 'O me, what has thou done?', 3.4.24, and Hamlet's asking
whether it is the king). Then the Black Knight is wracked by guilt over
conflicting duties:

Oh Heauens; how am I grieued in minde. Father forgiue mee, I
cannot kill my Mother And now againe, mee thinks I see the pale
shaddow of my fathers Ghost glyding before mine eyes; mee thinkes
hee shewes me the manner of his murther; mee thinkes his angry

lookes threatens mee and tels how that my heart is possest with cowardice, & childish feare; Thou doest preuaile, O Father euen now receiue this sacrifice of blood and death; this pleasing sacrifice, which to appease thy troubled soule, I heare doe offer. And thus in speaking these words, with his Sword hee split the deare heart of his mother; from whence the blood as from a gushing Spring issued.

(sig. M1^{r-v})

The problem of guilt which Johnson raised was obviously of interest to Shakespeare, but its influence was suggestive, not a direct transfer. Hamlet insists that Gertrude listen to his view of the significance of her behaviour: 'You go not till I set you up a glass / Where you may see the inmost part of you' (3.4.18–19). Gertrude's response, however, shows a fear in excess of any threat that Hamlet's anger seems to pose: 'What wilt thou do? Thou wilt not murder me? / Help, ho!' (3.4.20–1). Like Gertrude, Anglitora confesses, but to no avail; the Black Knight kills her, and it is probably this that Shakespeare echoes in Gertrude's panic.

Johnson deals with moral absolutes. As soon as Anglitora and the Knight of the Castle begin their affair, he gives immediate condemnation: 'she that in former times was accounted the worlds admiration for constancie, was now the very wonder of shame' (sig. K3). He has no concern for consistency, and details of plot frequently contradict each other. He shares the characteristic tabloid contradiction of offering attractive models of immorality while moralizing against them. Even so, the moral problem, with some aspects that go back as far as Greek tragedy, remains interesting. It helps Shakespeare make what was probably a popular bloodthirsty play of revenge into a profound tragedy of social corruption and individual responsibility.

NATURALIZING ATTITUDES
THROUGH FICTION

The fiction of the day played an important role in establishing attitudes that Shakespeare could expect his audience to recognize, whether or not they accepted them. While this may seem unimportant for literature – for books – it is a fundamental requirement of drama. Taking *Rosalynde* and *As You Like It* again as examples, Lodge opens his work with a background explanation of considerable length before he comes to the point where Shakespeare's play opens (roughly 2500 words out of some 42 000). Giving the family history, Lodge makes clear the positions of the various characters and provides the reader with the attitudes that make Rosader's rebellion understandable and justified. Shakespeare's audience has neither the interest nor the patience to endure so much discussion before the action starts, so he opens the play with Orlando's rebellion:

> the spirit of my father, which I think is within me, begins to mutiny against this servitude. I will no longer endure it, though yet I know no wise remedy how to avoid it.

> (1.1.21–5)

In the few lines that lead up to this statement, Shakespeare sketches a character type: Orlando is a youth of noble nature, a gentleman born, who bitterly resents the injustice and indignity he suffers at the hands of his brother. While Lodge has the leisure to paint the full picture, the theatre audience must already have a familiarity with this kind of issue in order to be able to recognize it from the minimal brush strokes Shakespeare uses. In this respect drama must be much more efficient than fiction; to get on with exploring what the elements mean, it must be able to ensure that they are established very quickly.

Sometimes the 'recognition factor' is dependent on familiarity with conventions coming from the theatre. Thus when Richard III enters he is almost immediately recognizable as the traditional Vice. The audience know in general what to expect from such a character and, in that sense, they can feel at home with him. But there are of course other factors that contribute to this familiarity which originate outside the theatre, and the popular fiction of the period is certainly important among these. At the simplest level, *The Two Gentlemen of Verona* opens with Valentine's parting from his friend Proteus, whom he would persuade, were he not tied to Verona by romantic attachment, rather

> To see the wonders of the world abroad
> Than (living dully sluggardis'd at home)
> Wear out thy youth with shapeless idleness.
>
> (1.1.6–8)

Travel to broaden the mind and expand one's fortunes did not have to be explained to the audience because they could recognize it immediately as a stock theme from fiction, from John Lyly's *Euphues* (1578), several of Greene's works, and much minor fiction of the period. The topic of friendship versus romantic love, out of which the plot develops, is another standard theme, naturalized from the wide currency it gained through *Euphues*. Its literary roots are in fact kept before the audience when Valentine responds to Proteus' saying he will pray for him – 'And on a love-book pray for my success?' (1.1.19). Even the role of Gower as Presenter in *Pericles* has been made familiar for the audience by the somewhat mocking use made of him in *Greene's Vision* (1592).

For audiences today, and perhaps those of Shakespeare's own day, preconceptions about the place of women are one of the most fraught areas when it comes to establishing exactly what may be properly thought of as conventional expectations. Not only students but many directors seem very uncertain about Shakespeare's attitude to women and to marriage. Are we supposed to feel happy that Helena wins back Bertram in *All's Well that Ends Well*? Is Shakespeare making a point about marriage when the main characters of the plot of *Much Ado about Nothing* are far less memorable than Beatrice and Benedick? Is it significant that, unlike *As You Like It*, the marriages that would conclude the action of *Measure for Measure* do not take place in the play? Does 'taming' break or make Kate in *The Taming of the Shrew*? A great deal of the uncertainty, I would say, comes from not knowing what would be the standard attitudes held by Shakespeare's audience. The problem is not the difficulty of articulating an abstract definition but of recognizing the attitudes themselves in the limited social embodiment of the play. Fiction, in giving a much more extended embodiment, did much to overcome the difficulty, and can still offer help with it.

The most straightforward instance of the problem today is probably *The Taming of the Shrew*, because the main action does not deviate from the matter of the marriage relationship. The Induction sets a tone that is broad and somewhat bawdy, and the slapstick when Petruchio enters would seem to confirm we are to witness a comedy of the interplay of depersonalized types. Petruchio, like other young men (as in *The Two Gentlemen of Verona*), has gone to seek experience and fortune, 'farther than at home, / Where small experience grows' (1.2.50–1). He intends to 'wive and thrive' (1.2.55) as best he may, an intention which is reduced to any kind of marriage where there is sufficient cash, even if she is old or ugly or shrewish: 'If wealthily, then happily' (1.2.75). The action continues mostly at that slapstick level until Katherine has responses that are not simply combative (4.1) and the individual emerges out of the folkloric shrew type. From then on Katherine's individuality is prominent, as when she engages creatively in role-play with old Vincentio in 4.5. The problem arises in the last scene, where the obedience of Kate is tested, and her final speech about the roles of husband and wife indicates either that her spirit has been crushed or that it has been liberated.

Katherine's speech is forty-four lines in length, which is a very long time on the stage. It is different in style from her previous conversational utterances, stilted and with mostly end-stopped lines. Its ideas are also quite different from those offered earlier; they are old fashioned, very like something from outmoded marriage instructions, outside Petruchio's type:

> I am asham'd that women are so simple
> To offer war where they should kneel for peace,
> Or seek for rule, supremacy, and sway
> When they are bound to serve, love and obey.
> Why are our bodies soft, and weak, and smooth,
> Unapt to toil and trouble in the world,
> But that our soft conditions and our hearts
> Should well agree with our external parts?

> (5.2.162–9)

The responses of Vincentio, Lucentio and Hortensio are short and simple; they agree with the attitudes of the speech and therefore accept it at face value, and think Kate has become docile. The possibility of a contrary response – that Kate is sending up old-fashioned hierarchical views on marriage – depends upon audience awareness of a different perspective on marriage. The play does not itself confirm that the conclusion moves towards gender equality; such a judgement must be based on attitudes brought to the play from outside.

Thus, for the audience to be able to understand Kate's speech as a mark of her liberation, it is necessary that they have already been exposed to flaws in the patriarchal system and are familiar with positive images of women. Greene's fiction would have been an important factor here; it would have allowed Shakespeare to use types that had what could be called a 'prepared significance'. Greene's contemporary Thomas Nashe called him 'the Homer of Women' for his positive images of women, and probably because most of his heroes – i.e. the characters who face crises and have to make decisions – are women.[16] As the most popular author of his day, Greene's images should have had some influence in shaping the ideas of gender roles held by Shakespeare's audience. His first piece of fiction, *Mamillia* (1580), parodies Lyly's *Euphues* and its traditional humanist misogyny. In Lyly's work male friendship is more important than romantic love, and women are inconstant. Greene reverses this; his heroine is principled and she even has to rescue her irresponsible, two-timing suitor.[17] His framework tales, such as *Perimedes the Blacke smith* (1588), also present women who lead their lives with integrity and occasional heroic resistance to oppression. In his final works about con-men, the 'conny-catching' series, the characters that most stand out are women who defend themselves against various injustices (especially in *The Defence of Conny-Catching*). But his most important construction of a positive image of women, one consistent with seeing Katherine in the *Shrew* as liberated, was in *Pandosto*, an aspect Shakespeare did not reflect in *The Winter's Tale*.

TECHNIQUES OF MAKING MEANING

More than simply taking a positive attitude, Greene developed ways of validating women in his narrative which deserve more attention. They were actually techniques of making meaning that did not rely on an appended moral or on the outcome of the plot. The way he establishes Fawnia as the heroic centre of *Pandosto* is a function not just of her particular qualities but also of how he embodies them in the narrative. As is probably the case with most fiction and drama, he is producing a structure that interprets and makes sense of experience. However, as well as the Elizabethan world itself undergoing rapid change, the tools of interpretation were also changing. Traditional images of order were no longer adequate – actuality and interpretation did not fit together. In literature this can be seen at the simplest level in the frequent irrelevance of concluding morals to the experience in the narrative. Thus the first moral Lodge draws in *Rosalynde* – 'that such as neglect their fathers' precepts incur much prejudice' (p.227) – has little application to the concerns of the story. Greene avoids this problem, not by moralizing more accurately, but by privileging one of the conflicting perspectives and giving the experience of certain of his characters more intense narration. This density of narration, more than the logic of the argument, serves to validate a character's perspective. The 'narrative density' principle can be seen clearly early on in *Pandosto*, when Pandosto asks his servant Franion (Camillo in *The Winter's Tale*) to poison King Egistus. Franion's internal debate about royal threats, conscience, rewards and reputation is equal in length to all the narration in the story up to that point. Thus this problem is given more narrative space per moment of fictive event, and the concerns are more fully realized – that is, there is greater density.

Greene's most important use of such density is to give importance to the perspective of Fawnia, the heroine of *Pandosto*. She is 'heroine' not just as protagonist but also in her integrity in the face of crisis. Her dilemma is that she is a shepherdess in love with a prince. To pursue her desire she must violate hierarchical codes; to follow the codes she must abandon her desire. Greene allows her lengthy internal monologues where she weighs the issues. Deciding eventually that the principle of love takes precedence over adherence to codes, she elopes with her prince. Dorastus, the prince, in contrast, loves Fawnia, but finds crossing the social gulf shameful. In his internal monologues he says that if he must love, then he should 'choose flowers, not weedes; Diamonds, not peables: Ladies, which may honor thee: not shepheards which may disgrace thee' (p.102). His decision to elope with Fawnia the shepherdess is not the assertion of a positive disregard of hierarchy but an admission of his weakness in not living up to the code. Similarly, when it looks as if their elopement will end in disaster, Dorastus berates himself for failing to follow the codes, whereas Fawnia, who must choose between yielding to Pandosto's lust or leaving Dorastus in prison, holds fast to the principle of love while bemoaning the injustice of fortune.

What is technically interesting is that it is not so much the arguments of Fawnia's internal monologues that validate her decision – the audience is sufficiently accustomed to the form to regard the details of the content as conventional – but that Greene presents the world of the fiction from her perspective. When Dorastus first meets resistance from Fawnia he threatens with his power – 'for thou knowest I can commaund and constraine' – to which Fawnia replies, 'but not to love: for constrained love is force, not love' (p.100). She can love Dorastus, she says, when he becomes a shepherd. He acquires a shepherd's outfit, returns to Fawnia, and demands that she fulfil her part of the bargain. Fawnia's response switches the perspective from conventional pastoral of playing shepherds to actual sheep-keeping: 'shepheards are not called shepheards, because they weare hookes and bags: but they are borne poore, and live to keepe sheepe: so this attire hath not made Dorastus a shepheard: but to seeme like a shepheard' (p.103). This is different from *As You Like It*, where the distinction is between pastoral convention and the court. Here the work of the shepherd is made the base reality, the standpoint from which all events can be viewed, and judged. It is the perspective of someone who must work for a living. The importance of this must not be exaggerated – we are not given a proletarianized pastoral – but it is significant that Greene makes a narration reorganized to give voice to a different point of view.

The focus on the everyday became fairly general in the fiction of the age. *Narbonus, Ornatus and Artesia* and *The Adventures of Lady Egeria*[18] – across the whole spectrum of prose fiction, writers were increasingly concerned with the details of a changing reality. Judgements were made, sometimes in inappropriately antiquated formulations, but the moral effect of the fiction derived from its elaboration of experience, from the much-derided but powerful principle of proof by anecdote. Eschewing the super-heroic images of individualism shown on the stage by Marlowe, Greene, as well as many of the other authors of popular fiction, created down-to-earth situations, even if they were set within fantastic plots, many elements of which were on the same level as readers' lives, and which could therefore serve as models.

Shakespeare's own use of a variable density shows his development of the technique Greene displayed. This is different from an argument made by slanting the selection of material; it is the way the material is realized that is the important thing. In *The Merchant of Venice* Shylock's domination of so much of the play is not simply a matter of his centrality in the plot; it results also from the way that he articulates his experience in comparison to other characters. The bond of a pound of flesh is not seen as entirely serious by the Venetians; the audience, in any case, knows the comic side of a bodily pledge from the Faustbook (1592).[19] In 3.1 Salerio says to Shylock, 'Why I am sure if he forfeit, thou wilt not take his flesh, – what's that good for?' (3.1.45–6). Shylock moves the vaguely abstract sense of bond immediately into the concrete – Antonio's flesh will feed fish, and, in a metaphor only slightly removed from the material, feed his revenge. His 'hath not a Jew' speech follows directly, and this is usually understood as an appeal to shared qualities that assert the humanity of the Jew. The argumentation has a quasi-rational form – 'if you prick us do we not bleed? if you tickle us do we not laugh? if you poison us do we not die? and if you wrong us shall we not revenge?' (3.1.58–60) – but its power lies in Shylock's greater specificity. What he is saying can be visualized immediately; it is concrete. Salerio's speech is abstract in comparison – 'Antonio hath a ship of rich lading wrack'd on the narrow seas' (3.1.2–3). What Shakespeare is doing is comparable to Greene's establishing Fawnia's shepherd perspective in *Pandosto*; like Fawnia, Shylock has a more material vision, more immediate to reality, and his perspective dominates. Similarly, in the courtroom scene, when Antonio acknowledges the bond, Portia says, 'Then must the Jew be merciful'. Shylock, undercutting the vagueness of Portia's 'must', reduces it to a specific legal matter – 'On what compulsion must I?' (4.1.178–9). This is not merely the adoption of a contrary position; Shylock's view is embedded in a more specific reality and thereby controls the dramatic argument. When he sharpens his blade on the sole of his shoe it is not just a symbolic reminder of the threat to Antonio; it is the material reality of the scene. The quality of Portia's introduction of mercy – 'And earthly power doth then show likest God's / When mercy seasons justice' (4.1.192–3) – is too abstract to outweigh Shylock's materiality. Even though Shakespeare has Shylock defeated in the plot, Shylock's perspective is not overcome – creating a conflicted closure which is usually uncomfortable for an audience. This technique of 'tactfully' establishing a perspective in opposition to the socially dominant values may well owe much to Greene.

Greene was the most popular author of popular fiction in the Elizabethan period, but there were many others who wrote narratives that reflected everyday life and offered alternative ways of understanding the world. Although their books were mostly designed to entertain readers, that inevitably meant reflecting the changing conditions of the age, and, in various ways, finding significance in standard narrative materials. This in turn meant not only reflecting but also shaping the understanding and attitudes of readers. Thus, as well as plots, Shakespeare gained from popular fiction an audience that was already primed to respond to the complexities of social change that enlivened so many of his plays.

Chapter Six

SHAKESPEARE, GHOSTS
AND POPULAR FOLKLORE

Diane Purkiss

Unlike Marlowe and Milton, Shakespeare is often seen as an author who bridges social divisions to embody a universality that makes him a repository of all his possible contexts. However, in the past twenty years, those who have chosen to write on Shakespeare and the supernatural, unlike their predecessors earlier this century, have seemed oddly inclined to consider only elite cultures, or at any rate – since that term is itself a very troubled one – only educated and literate culture as antecedents for the plays. Writing on ghosts, for example, Stephen Greenblatt considers the apparition of Hamlet's father's ghost almost entirely from the perspective of Reformation developments in conceptions of the afterlife. Of course, these issues were not exclusively the concern of the well-educated and the literate; many middling and even labouring people also pondered them. But Greenblatt's interest in the reflection of the Reformation in theatre leaves little room for other strands of popular culture, and he gives little consideration to ghosts in ballads, pamphlets and oral recollections except where these illuminate what he takes to be the central concern of ghost-lore: the nature of the afterlife.[1] There is a danger of implicitly overwriting popular cultural representations with elite and educated concerns, reducing the former to a redaction of the latter. And there is little evidence that Shakespeare saw ghost stories in this way – as a medium for the representation of theological debating points.

Since the elite and educated view of ghosts has already received a good deal of attention, it can be summarily described here. The pioneers in this field, who judiciously examined the plays ghost by ghost, were first Moorman in 1906, who argues that the pre-Shakespearean ghost was always Catholic in its origins, coming exclusively from Purgatory, and thus set the agenda for all future discussion.[2] In *What Happens in Hamlet*, and in his edition of Lewes Lavater's treatise *Of Ghosts and Spirits Walking by Night* (which may have suggested some details for *Hamlet* and *Macbeth*), J. Dover Wilson argued that the play invites the audience to speculate upon whether the ghost is actually the spirit of the late king, or a demon sent to tempt Hamlet to murder and suicide. This influential idea is based on part of Lavater's book, which expounds the notion that ghosts are a Popish lie. A Protestant audience would have seen the spirit's description of the afterlife as duplicitous: since no spirit can be released from hell (at least in Protestant eschatology, though in the legends of medieval Catholicism the Virgin Mary obtains a temporary remission for the damned from Good Friday to Easter Sunday), and since no other penal form of afterlife exists, then the ghost must be a liar, and hence a demon.

This entire argument is both over-ingenious and over-literal. Discovering something hidden in the text that cannot be brought into the open is rarely a scrupulous form of criticism. Dover Wilson is certainly right to argue that the play – like other ghost stories – invites the audience to consider what the ghost is. But we shall see that the arena of theological definition is precisely the one the play's characters eschew, in favour of a lengthy discussion of folklore and folktales. By contrast, other critics – Robert West in *The Invisible World*, and Katharine Briggs in *The Anatomy of Puck* – are more interested in tracing connections between ghosts across theatrical traditions.[3] Briggs correctly calls the idea that fairies and ghosts were both merely demons in disguise an 'extreme Puritan' belief, and she stresses instead the literary antecedents of the theatrical ghost in the tragedies of Seneca. For Briggs, the Senecan ghost is like the deities of Greece and Rome, an ornament which does not give rise to questions of belief. But Briggs also correctly points to the remarkable fact that even the most overtly vengeance-hungry spectre of Seneca has counterparts not only in the plays of the classically educated, but also in ballads such as 'The Unquiet Grave'.

In Marston's 1599 play *Antonio's Revenge*, an entirely Senecan ghost named Andrugio shares with a ghost in that ballad the oddity that each is called forth by grief, the grief of a son for a father. We shall see that the same motif recurs not only in *Hamlet*, as Briggs herself notes, but also with the ghosts that haunt Posthumus in *Cymbeline*, and perhaps even to Caesar's ghost in *Julius Caesar*.

For Greenblatt, however, the complexities and contradictions of Hamlet's ghost all relate to the abolition of Purgatory as an idea, and to a set of stories which made it possible to negotiate with the dead. Though scrupulous in recording the seductions of this set of stories and their lingering power, Greenblatt's neglect of folklore means that he probably underestimates the survival of essentially Catholic ideas in the post-Reformation era: angels and even saints had not altogether vanished from imagination by the 1600s, even if they had gone from theology. The stubbornness of folklore makes it a cosy nesting-place for ideas discarded by elites. The notion that the theatre had to substitute for a lack or loss in religion is less attractive if one considers that it was not the only way of telling stories about the dead. There were also pamphlets, ballads and plain oral storytelling as ways of speaking to and about the dead. A ballad such as 'The Cruel Mother' was not subject to the same scrutiny and censorship as the stage: could it afford to be less careful about the views of an educated and Protestant elite?[4]

Another difficulty with Dover Wilson and Greenblatt's approaches is that neither takes into account the fitfulness of folklore's appearance in Shakespeare's plays. We shall see that while the ghost in Hamlet is saturated in diverse folkloric motifs and draws after him additional strands of folklore, Shakespeare's other ghosts have a much more distant relationship to folkloric texts, and to popular culture in general. They are dominated not by cultural but by literary models, which derive principally from classical drama. Ironically, Seneca and other classical dramatists draw on the folklore of their own day, but by Shakespeare's time the turbulence of this folkloric material has been subdued until it has become literary convention.[5] However, it does not cease to signify. In particular, the Senecan ghost stands for the breakdown of linear time, and hence becomes a metaphor for the (tragic) loss of order, stability and sometimes even reason, and their dissolution into chaos and confusion. At the same time, the Senecan ghost seeks to restore the order whose absence he represents, through reparation, revenge or (more subtly) through the assertion of the stability of patrilineal succession. The ghost of folklore too is tirelessly concerned with inheritance: with buried treasure, wills and legitimate descent of property. The categories of high and low overlap.

The New Historicist method does not address the problematic relations between popular cultures and high cultures highlighted by Tim Harris, Miri Rubin and Roger Chartier, all of whom have argued that there is no single, unified popular culture.[6] And yet their approach, too, risks drawing attention *away* from that elusive, multifaceted object and towards an elite power or powers that act upon it, a tendency very visible in Chartier's own work. Equally, Greenblatt's method neglects Shakespeare's own agency in constructing both early modern *and* our own notions of what is 'popular'. As Mary Ellen Lamb has recently argued, Shakespeare and his contemporaries have often seemed to be drawing on deep wellsprings of popular culture when they were in reality inventing a culture of folklore and calling it 'popular' in order to mark out its difference from their learned selves.[7]

So when trying to understand the origins of Shakespeare's ghosts, a task the plays positively invite us to complete, we cannot locate a single wholesale alternative to elite ideology in the sphere of the popular. But equally, we cannot neglect the processual popular cultures of the supernatural simply because it is difficult to pin down what they are. It is especially important to try to map the fugitive and sometimes elusive traces of the popular in the case of *Hamlet*, because it is there that they are most marked, and yet it is also in that play that the influence of folklore has been most consistently overlooked.

* * *

We might begin by asking whether this area of representational antecedent has been neglected because it is impossible to write about. If we were tackling a question in the history of ideas – evolving notions of monarchy, for example – we would be hoping for a large cache of written material to which an author might have had access, ideally produced within about twenty years either side of the literary text in which we interested ourselves. But in the present case there are no large quantities of surviving 'contemporary pamphlets' (taking 'contemporary' to mean within two decades either side of the first performance of the plays under discussion). Rather, what we have (at popular level) is much more scattered chronologically, some of it dating from the early eighteenth century or even from nineteenth-century folklore collections. It goes without saying that this chronological scattering generates interpretive problems. If we find a parallel between, say, an early eighteenth-century pamphlet and a Shakespeare play, should we conclude that both have an anterior source in folklore which both re-interpret, or should we entertain other possibilities – including, of course, the possibility that the play has exerted a shaping influence over the later pamphlet? How can we tell?

Problematic as it seems, this kind of difficulty need not be an insuperable obstacle to the discussion of popular culture, for three reasons. First, it is apparent that Shakespeare's ghosts do in fact have characteristics which cannot be explained solely with reference to learned sources (theological treatments of various kinds, classical drama, Elizabethan drama). Second, these characteristics can best be explained through a discussion of the transmission of folklore as an aspect of popular culture, an important issue for the present volume since popular culture was not, of course, confined to print. But the fact is that folklore is notoriously difficult to date. Folklorists commonly use the historic present for everything they write about, because although it is possible to date the moment when a piece of folklore *surfaces*, in print or in a piece of oral storytelling that happens to have been recorded, this is obviously not the same as the date when it was first composed or created. Some such surfacings come accompanied by their own dates; that is, some ghost pamphlets date the phenomena they describe. But these dates are often unreliable. That a story about the Cock Lane ghost surfaces in the mid-eighteenth century can be known; what is far more difficult to ascertain is whether that story was told elsewhere about some other ghost 200 or even 500 years earlier. What is significant is that the story is *re*told. Folklore that seems static – an old story – is thus constantly processed to keep it current. For that reason, too, it is hard to say whether a story retold in 1715 is a story *of* 1715; definitiveness about chronology risks missing the point of the process.

The situation is further complicated by the difficult interactions between oral culture and print in the early modern period. What survives of folklore is often (though not invariably) print, and as soon as oral folklore is print, it becomes not the oral folklore in which the illiterate early modern public was immersed, but something that exists alongside it, in indirect and tangential relation to it. This is not to say that there is an originary oral folklore of which print is merely a trace; the opposite can as easily be true, and it can sometimes be demonstrated that an oral tradition has its origins in printed texts. We need to try to see both oral tales and motifs, and printed narratives, as circulating together – albeit unpredictably, unevenly, and in ways difficult to map. They circulate through the various layers of early modern writings upon ghosts, surfacing in learned texts (as part, for example, of the educated theological 'anti-sadduccee' controversy of the later seventeenth century), in popular play-texts, in pamphlets, in ballads, being revised and altered each time they appear, but also retaining common elements which may take on different significances in different contexts. These common elements, and these differences too, are alike the legitimate subjects of historical enquiry, but we need to be willing to look at the movements of ghost stories across wider than usual periods in order to trace them.

Folkloric issues require that we attend to traces of story and story type across a much broader time frame than would be appropriate for issues such as the transmission of political ideas. Folklore and folk practices do change and mutate over time, and they do so in response to the pressure of large-scale historical events like the Reformation. But it is an unwarranted assumption that elite changes are automatically reflected in popular beliefs. Most writers on ghosts, for example, take it for granted that the Reformation has an enormous impact on all representations of ghosts, but this ignores the way ghost stories are told and retold as entertainment, or as negotiations of fears and desires that have little to do with theological controversies. Driven by forces extrinsic to theological debate, the ghost story may survive any amount of laborious disproof by reason. This is one reason that folktales can be oddly stubborn, continuing to circulate long after their apparent social usefulness has evaporated.

What this suggests is that it is worth searching for parallels between folkloric traces and the plays themselves as sufficient warrant for further investigation and comparison, even comparison that stretches the boundaries of period in ways not normally considered acceptable. In this sense, the study of folklore calls into question the narrowness of historicism by bringing to bear the subtle movements of popular as opposed to high cultures. 'Popular cultures', remarks Barry Reay, 'do not follow the tight chronologies of political history': they have their own unfolding timetable.[8] We might also note Reay's careful use of the plural. There is not one popular culture of the supernatural but many, and a term such as 'ghost' is not only contested at the level of high cultural investments in theology, but also at that of the telling of tales. Characteristically, ghost stories engage the listener in careful forensic interpretation of events. A figure appears, and listeners must actively decide who or what it is, what its purposes are. Often – most often – the narrative fails to disclose a definitive answer, perhaps leaving room for argument. We will see that this is precisely the structure of onstage ghost sightings, a structure which invites the plurality of popular cultures to make themselves visible in the characters' dialogue. What this illustrates is that alignments between dramatic and popular cultures on the terrain of the supernatural can allow the latter to illuminate the former.

Given all this, we might expect the stage ghost to be a figure who embodies the cultural contradictions and dilemmas thus generated. That is, the kind of conversations characters might have about it could be arranged not around polarities derived solely from learned culture – polarities involving questions about the afterlife – but around the polarity between the learned and the popular or around polarities and differences within the popular. To understand how this might work, we need to understand both popular and high cultural interpretations of ghosts.

* * *

Richard III is a play about the conflict between two ways of interpreting the world. For four acts it looks as though everyone is crazy except Richard, since everyone but he believes history to be the unfolding of the will of providence, and since evidence for providential intervention in historical processes is at best fleeting in the early action. Richard usurps the throne and God does not punish him. But suddenly, in Act V, God acts. Richard's enemies turn out to have been correct. God *is* in charge, and he has sent Richmond to end the tyrant's rule. Richard himself believes the world is run on Machiavellian lines; that man can fashion himself, that authority derives not from God but from putting on a good show, that an authentic self does not exist, that man is nothing but a series of roles. Now he becomes an existentialist transported to a cosmos where providence is real, crimes are punished, and God exists. This providential universe is ushered in by the parade of ghosts who entertain him before Bosworth. They represent the historical hiatus between a providential world and the modern world Richard tries unsuccessfully to incarnate. This points forward not only to *Macbeth* with its single and more telling ghost, but also to Hamlet, afraid that death may prove the gateway to a world in which his humanist values have no place. Seductiveness and rhetorical efficacy are alike useless in a providential world, and Richard's talents and achievements are reduced to nothings.

Richard's ghosts simply recount their deaths: 'I, that was washed to death' (5.3.133); 'my anointed body / By thee was punched full of deadly holes' (5.3.125–6). They are embodied narratives, so that though they are apparitions they are also and primarily stories, animated stories of death. Such ghosts are common in pamphlet literature; they appear stuck, able to repeat only a single phrase or action, or unable to speak at all, a motif that also recurs in *Hamlet*.[9] Banquo's ghost is similar. In that play there is an interesting movement away from the word and into the realm of spectacle. Compared with the ghosts of Richard's victims, all of whom exist to tell their hidden stories, Banquo's ghost is inarticulate. His ghost acts as a riddle that has to be interpreted by Macbeth. This tricky ghost first appears not as a ghost but as a host, as a double of Macbeth, usurping the usurper's seat as if part of the feast, a gory Christopher Sly. This symbolic usurpation foreshadows their rivalry for the royal 'seat', and also foreshadows the unquenchability of Banquo's body (and hence his survival through his heirs) and his identity in occupying it. Yet elements of folklore surface too: his appearance is also a common and particularly Scottish folklore motif. The untimely dead often return in search of food or hospitality denied them in life, and must be satisfied; in general, ghosts often keep appointments made when living, as if still subject to the laws of time.[10] Yet when Banquo is revealed as dead, he turns into the antithesis of comely seemliness expected of a guest, with gory locks, the monstrous spectacle of violated hospitality that Macbeth tries to conceal. Unlike the pre-Reformation dead, whose passing could be celebrated by an outpouring of bodily excess, including feasting on the top of the coffin itself, Banquo cannot be both dead and a guest.[11] Instead, his presence signifies the absence of festive order.

Banquo in particular is murdered because of patrilinearity. His ghost therefore stands for the disruption of patrilinearity by a tyrant, but paradoxically, as a ghost, Banquo also stands for the dead, and thus for the kind of connection, lineage and descent that his murder attempts to suppress. If Banquo's murder offers to disconnect Banquo and his heirs from their proper ancestry, and hence threatens patrilinearity, his reappearance as a silent spectacle says that such discontinuities are themselves subject to time or are reversible.

Similarly Brutus and Cassius in *Julius Caesar*, seeing Caesar's ghost at Philippi, are confronted by the spectacle of what they had hoped to conceal. While the Ricardian ghosts represent nothing except a universe in which crimes have a kind of power of recoil installed in them by providence, Caesar's ghost also represents necromantic prophecy. Of course, it is only that Caesar makes articulate what the other ghosts do not say in so many words. While the ghosts of *Richard III* primarily look back to tell the stories of their own deaths, the ghost of Caesar primarily looks forward to the defeat of his foes. Like Banquo's ghost and many folkloric ghosts, he initially presents himself as a riddle, one who demands that those who see him find the right story about him: 'Art thou some god, some angel or some devil / That makst my blood cold and my hair to stare? / Speak to me what thou art' (4.3.277–9). Also like Banquo's ghost, Caesar first manifests himself as if he were an abstracted aspect of

Brutus: his reply to this question is 'Thy evil spirit, Brutus' (4.3.280). This conclusion is supported when ghost and Brutus keep repeating, as if mesmerized by each other, that they will meet again at Philippi. The ghost has succeeded in transforming Brutus into a kind of echo of itself; this is almost a form of possession by witchcraft. When Philippi is attained, Brutus is all but obsessed with Caesar, 'O Julius Caesar thou art mighty yet! / Thy spirit walks abroad, and turns our swords / To our own proper entrails' (5.3.93–6). Possession makes its victims suicidal, and it is a paradox that being possessed with Caesar's 'proper' spirit should have this very Roman effect on Brutus, who kills himself precisely to lay this ghost. 'Caesar now be still / I killed not thee with half so good a will' (5.5.50–1): Caesar can only be laid by *self*-slaughter. Ironically, summoning up the dead brings with it the risk of joining the dead; trafficking with ghosts inaugurates tragedy.

By contrast, the masque of ghosts of Posthumus' family in *Cymbeline* is much more productive, bringing not death but a commitment to life. Here, as often in the romances, Shakespeare seems to rewrite the most evocative parts of the tragedies, turning them inside out to bring out new significances. Folklore is invoked in Fidele's dirge, in which ghosts are specifically banished from Innogen's specious bier: 'Ghost unlaid forbear thee!' (4.2.278). The presence as well as the absence of ghosts, however, is required to resolve the tension between past and present. The ghosts of Posthumus' family, like Banquo's, look towards a future, but a future of life and marriage, a comic future and not a tragic one. They remind us of the pre-Reformation traditions of feasting and playing sexual games around the dead body. If the ghosts in the tragedies are testimony to the disruption or breakdown of patrilinearity and order, the ghosts of Cymbeline represent its restoration.

And restoration is required. Posthumus makes the most misogynistic speech in all of Shakespeare, beginning 'Is there no way for men to be, but women / Must be half-workers? We are all bastards' (2.4.153–4). When the ghosts come, they confer the legitimacy Posthumus denies, as Posthumus himself immediately says: 'Sleep, thou hast . . . begot / A father to me: and thou hast created / A mother, and two brothers: but, O scorn! / Gone! they went hence so soon as they were born' (5.4.123–6).

Like Macduff, Posthumus is ripped from his mother; she is not the cause of his death, but he is the cause of hers, and she begins by recounting this, as if like the ghosts in *Richard III* she is concerned to set the record straight. Like them, too, she has been cut off before her time, but the play is not infected by disruption because she survives in Posthumus, once he can accept enough of her part in him to take a wife and have sons himself. Through the ghosts, Posthumus becomes known to himself, and thus known to the audience as part of their ancestry too. The ghosts in *Cymbeline* represent the power of the theatre, and the dramatist, to restore the audience and the nation to a real identity through the summoning of such authentic ancestral spirits. It is vital to restore truth to Posthumus, so that Innogen can resume her place as a noble British/Roman wife and mother, and in this restorative role the ghost becomes a way of pretending that the past has no fissures, that it was solid in a way the present could only imagine.

* * *

Most fissured of all is the ghost of *Hamlet*, and it is this ghost that carries the thickest marks of folklore on his grim person. *Hamlet* is a play that catches up all its characters in discussion of folklore and the retelling of folktales. The ghost which is its most spectacular feature is not the sole focus of all this talk, and one of Hamlet's most fascinating speeches about a ghost pertains only indirectly to it. Here, Hamlet moves beyond tale-telling and intellectual speculation to embrace an identity drawn from folklore:

> 'Tis now the very witching time of night,
> When churchyards yawn and hell itself breathes out
> Contagion to this world. Now could I drink hot blood,
> And do such bitter business as the day
> Would quake to look on.

> (3.2.371–5)

In this remarkable and slightly neglected speech, Hamlet imagines himself as a kind of dead creature quite alien to the play's elegant, theologically well-informed and well-read Senecan apparition. Hamlet is speaking as if he were a revenant. This kind of folklore ghost was a bloodsucker who needed the warmth of the blood of the living, and who revelled in evil – a kind of vampire.[12] Hamlet is inhabiting the part of early modern nightmare; for the moment, he is the creature that kept his culture awake and sweating, clutching the sheets.

We might say that Hamlet's speech lays bare the repressed popular culture that is the underside of the play's better-known ghost. That popular unconscious is also exposed when Hamlet first addresses the apparently literate and Senecan entity in the words: 'Be thou a spirit of health or goblin damned' (1.4.40). The Arden and Oxford editions unite in glossing 'goblin' as 'devil', so that the line simply opens out into the next line, 'Bring with thee airs from heaven or blasts from hell' (1.4.41).[13] This ignores the fact that a goblin is a demon only if Hamlet (and Shakespeare?) are in agreement with a fully demonological interpretation of fairies, an understanding of them as a guise for devils that deceive the folk. This understanding of fairies was certainly commonplace in educated and elite demonological texts, and it was adhered to by many justices presiding over witchcraft trials, especially in Scotland. But it is just possible that Shakespeare is glancing at the idea that the apparition is indeed a *goblin*, and it is significant in any case that he should use this term, redolent of popular rather than learned readings of apparitions.[14] Broadly, a goblin is a fairy of a particular kind, a revenant who is damned because he has met with an untimely death. The Greeks called this kind of being an *aoros*.[15] For some strands of early modern folklore, particularly those on the Celtic fringes, that was precisely what fairies were – those who had gone to death before their proper time. And of course that is exactly what the ghost says has happened to him just a few lines later. If this is indeed one of the possibilities through which the ghost might be understood, then it may be that the ghost is itself exactly the kind of revenant that his son declares his intention of becoming. In other words, it is only by becoming a revenant himself that Hamlet can hope truly to resemble his father.

The ghost first presents itself as a riddle or rebus, in the classic manner of ghost narratives. When the play begins, Francisco inexplicably claims to be 'sick at heart' and Barnardo asks 'Have you had quiet guard?' (1.1.9–10). The audience is invited to begin guessing at the being that lies behind these half-spoken allusions. Then Marcellus speaks – less obliquely, but his meaning remains elusive: 'What, has this thing appeared again tonight?' (1.1.24). This line offers the ghost not yet *as* a ghost, but as a some-thing, a mystery. It seems that everyone except the audience has heard it, but we never get to hear the story of the ghost – the ghost story – because it is interrupted by the ghost itself, so that the ghost appears not as confirmation of a told narrative that has been unfolded, but as a break in narrative. Next, the play itself introduces the question of who has the credentials to interpret the riddle of the ghost: 'thou art a scholar; speak to it, Horatio' (1.1.45). This line is usually understood and glossed by editors, following Dover Wilson, as referring to the exorcism of a demon, for which purpose Dover Wilson himself wrongly supposes one needs to know Latin; in fact, there were numerous English-speaking and Protestant exorcists in Tudor London, though eventually the Church shut them all down.[16] This would suggest that nothing so specific as exorcism is intended here. Rather, what Marcellus implies at once is the common Renaissance notion that books and book-learning – words – contained the means to handle the supernatural, an idea basic to Protestantism, and basic, too, to the idea of the Renaissance magician. This idea, however, is supremely alien to our tendency to place the supernatural in the category 'popular', so that the play itself equivocates between cultural categories. At first Horatio's volubility is silenced by the ghost, by his appearance which 'harrows me with fear and wonder' (1.1.47), emotions that silence its beholders, defeating their attempts to master it with words. Only folklore can be making them afraid of it (it is possible that what Horatio especially fears is that the ghost is a 'corpse-candle', a relative sent to carry off another of his family).[17] The ghost is doubly figured as the enemy of a scholar's words, and it becomes still more so when it becomes clear that book learning cannot compel it to speak. Before our eyes, the Renaissance faith in the power of learning over the supernatural is overthrown in favour of what will turn out to be the ghost's own truth, a truth of the body and relations of the body, rather than a truth of words, words which like the ghost will turn out to be untraceable signifiers, unmanageable and unmanaging. 'Stay, speak, speak, I charge thee, speak' (1.1.54). The ghost will not speak, and in the play his son will do nothing else. This is a kind of victory for popular culture.

When the ghost reappears, still it refuses to be anything other than a riddle, and now Horatio begins in much fuller form the process of trying out interpretations of spectral purpose on it, seeking confirmation, so that his speech is a kind of conspectus of possible ghost-beliefs:

> If thou hast any sound or use of voice,
> Speak to me.
> If there be any good thing to be done
> That may to thee do ease, and grace to me,
> Speak to me;
> If thou art privy to thy country's fate,
> Which, happily, foreknowing may avoid,
> O speak;
> Or if thou hast uphoarded in thy life
> Extorted treasure in the womb of earth,
> For which, thou say, you spirits oft walk in death,
> Speak of it, stay and speak.

(1.1.131–42)

He covers all the bases here: general revelation, political prophecy, buried treasure. And now it is the ghost that has been interrupted, though not by speech but by the arrival of dawn, which leads to more stories about ghosts, and a greater proliferation of supernatural possibilities. We now hear of witches, fairies, the supernatural crowing of the cock as a representation of the time of Christ's birth:

> Some say that ever 'gainst that season comes
> Wherein our Saviour's birth is celebrated,
> This bird of dawning singeth all night long;
> And then, they say, no spirit dares stir abroad,
> The nights are wholesome, then no planets strike,
> No fairy takes, nor witch hath power to charm,
> So hallowed and so gracious is that time.

(1.1.163–9)

– to which Horatio says 'So I have heard and do in part believe it' (1.1.170).

So where does that leave us? What are we to believe? Bundled together – not sorted or hierarchically arrayed – is a repertoire of possibilities from different layers of culture, advanced conversationally, some of which have little or nothing to do with the ghost before us. The narrative has not moved forward one jot. We are no nearer a solution to the riddle of the ghost. The ghost is left hanging, so to speak, as a question, while we meet those who will later figure in his narrative – Claudius, Gertrude and Hamlet the prince, who we know to be learned. And Hamlet was not trained at any old seat of learning: he comes from Wittenberg, which in England in 1600 had two connotations, both relevant to his relation to the ghost: it is the home of Luther and Lutheranism, so signifies precisely the break with Rome through learning, through words; and it is the home of Dr Faustus, so also signifies learning as supernatural power, together with the temptations of Protestant magic.

But folklore – traceable only in dispersed fragments – is also a factor in shaping the identity of ghost and prince as revenants. It is true that classical learning may have legitimated the central idea, the idea of death as a process rather than a moment, since the classical world envisaged ghosts as integrally related to the bodies of the dead. For Plato, for example, a ghost is the presence of the body in the world of the spirit due to the spirit becoming imbued with bodiliness, an outcome of fleshly indulgence.[18] For a well-educated Protestant like John Milton, this Platonic notion explained ghosts as a product of sin, and he writes about this in *Comus* when he speaks of ghosts thronging around tombs, unable to separate from the bodies they so enjoyed in life. In this eschatology, the ghost was visible because corporeal, because of sins which had incarcerated him in bodiliness. For Milton, this imprisonment was a special result of bodily sin: 'Such are those thick and gloomy shadows damp / Oft seen in charnel-vaults and sepulchres, / Lingering, and sitting by a new-made grave, / As loth to leave the body that it loved' (469–72).[19] Yet in thus stigmatizing the ghost, Milton was also moralizing what for European folklore was a natural state of affairs: death was often understood not as a dramatic change, but as a paralysis of the body in which the soul is dislocated, in pain, lost. Such a state resembled bewitchment rather than a natural process, a state in which the body of the victim was entered and controlled from outside itself by the spirit of the witch. This went along with the notion that the soul continued to inhabit a body for days, months, or even years after death – or at least hovered in the vicinity of its body. These understandings of death as gradual and processual went deepest in Scandinavia – interestingly for the Prince of Denmark – where the dead were understood to live in the churchyard.[20] Most famous was the revenant Glam of *Grettir's Saga*, an ill-tempered shepherd who was himself killed by a revenant, and became an angry, noisy poltergeist. Though not identified as such, many post-Reformation poltergeists resemble revenants. Chief qualification for becoming a revenant in all cultures is bad temper or generally hot blood. A second qualification is death by violence. Summarizing, the folklorist Thistleton-Dyer writes that 'those who have suffered a violent or untimely death are usually understood as baneful and malicious beings, for . . . they were driven unwillingly from their bodies, and have carried into their new existence an angry longing for revenge'.[21]

It is therefore relevant that memories of the late king are apt to be aggressively martial: that he smote the sledded Polacks on the ice, for instance. For Horatio he is so martial that his appearance in armour can only be a sign of war. Horatio is thinking like the scholar he is called, and understanding the ghost in principally omenological terms, but his thinking still assumes his warlike significance. And of course it is of crucial significance that Hamlet's father has died by violent means, for the whole point about dying by violence was that the individual was felt to have died less, so to speak, than other people who died at their just time. In the Celtic fringes, fairies were those who had died by violence or in childbirth (as they are in the medieval romance *Sir Orfeo*). As such, this class of the dead, the *aoroi*, are neither dead nor alive, but both.[22]

Just how embodied is the ghost of Hamlet's father? His son certainly understands him as embodied:

> thy canoniz'd bones, hearsed in death,
> Have burst their cerements, why the sepulchre

>Wherein we saw thee quietly inurn'd,
>Hath op'd his ponderous and marble jaws
>To cast thee up again.

(1.4.47–51)

These lines make nonsense of Victorian representations of the ghost as a vapour. And he has clothes, too. He first appears dressed in clothes which he wore in life, another common motif in folklore.[23] John Bowman of Greenhill, a tailor, saw the apparition of the long-deceased George Earl of Shrewsbury, 'a man lyke unto a prince with a greene doublet and ruff, and holding a brachete in his hande'.[24] Similarly, the restless spirit of Bishop Burgersh, of Lincoln, 'appered onto one of his sweyeres, with a bow, arrows, and horne, in a schort green cote' (green is itself a sign of a restless ghost; it is often a fairy colour and a witch colour too). But other ghosts appear in white robes. Anna Atkinson, a midwife who was said to have murdered some of the illegitimate babies she birthed, appeared as 'the apparition of a Humane Shape, with a white Hood, and very strange rolling eyes'.[25] Other apparitions brought with them the smell of sulphur, indicating their infernal origin (for whatever theologians decreed, the folkloric ghost could certainly come from hell), and still others 'an unsufferable Stench, like that of a putrified Carcase, filling the Room with thick Smoak, smelling like Sulphur . . . Striking them so that the next Morning their Faces were black with the Smoak and their Bodies swollen with Bruises.'[26] These accounts are again accounts of apparitions locked at various stages of the dying process. While those dressed as they were in life are still active and alive, even though they are dead, those dressed in white are moving towards death because they are wearing their shrouds or burial sheets. Those who smell of sulphur or putrefaction have crossed over into death, but are still not separated from their decaying or tormented bodies. They often have bodily needs – blood, for example – since they are still in the body. Such needs could be and often were interpreted as signs of a 'bad death'.

Where is Hamlet's father on this scale? And where is young Hamlet in his own vision of himself? Hamlet's father in his armour is barely dead, still attached to his living self. But when he returns, he is described in the

First Quarto as 'in his night-gown'. Many scholars have regarded Q1 as a reported text. If so, then 'night-gown' is not a name but a description of the kind of thing the ghost wore. It could be, as Hibbard suggests, a dressing-gown.[27] Or it could be something much more like a nightshirt. If the latter, it is possible that the reporter of the Q1 text actually saw the ghost wearing a burial gown, which resembled a nightshirt. If so, the ghost is making some progress towards death. The notion of the slow death of the murder victim might have helped the audience to see that King Hamlet has made as much progress towards death, towards rest-in-death, as he can without the enactment of justice.

Similarly, as well as making supernatural appearances in or out of the flesh, the corpses of the murdered, in particular, are often strangely active. Webster records the superstition that the body of a murder victim bleeds when the murderer approaches it; normally, of course, dead bodies do not bleed because circulation has stopped, so it may be that the very common notion of the bleeding victim testifies to its continued half-living state.[28] In the bizarre and chilling folktale 'The Flying Childer', the dismembered bodily parts of murdered children dance, speak, and do household damage.[29] Obviously this kind of story is far more straightforward than Hamlet can manage to be. There are so many similar stories that an audience member acquainted with folktales would have been surprised and disappointed, because what should happen in Hamlet is very different from what does happen. What should happen is that King Hamlet should appear and directly haunt or directly denounce his murderer. And of course Hamlet the prince adds his own – classical, tragic – obliquity to what in folklore is straightforward. Hamlet substitutes the theatre – the Mousetrap – not for the rituals of burial or reburial, but for the reappearance of the murder victim in or out of the body to discover his or her crime. This is indeed a rite of summoning, followed by a rite of exorcism. Hamlet calls up an actor to tell the story that his father cannot tell directly. And the Player King, not the real king, can haunt and encounter his murderer. Hamlet – and Shakespeare too – holds popular culture, popular superstition, at bay, and substitutes for it a process that looks more humanistic, more rational, more forensic. Shakespeare was a great propagandist for the stage, for here the Player

King can do what the ghost of the real king cannot: that is, provoke real fears of vengeance.

For the ghost marks the limits of self-fashioning, the limits of how far the humanist processes of education are allowed to drive a man from his father. Hamlet's words and books, his tendency to talk endlessly rather than acting as and for his father, might both represent nothing more complicated than grammar-boy guilt, of exactly the kind that was to be experienced by a later generation in the second great expansion of grammar-school education, the post-war era. The ghost's angry and ultimately impotent wish for a son who is like him, the vehicle of his will, might be an angry and guilty portrait of a father and a paternal culture which had to be discarded as part of education. It also marks the limits of the power of self-replication. Precisely because the ghost is and is not King Hamlet, he calls into question the son's power to be and not to be King Hamlet. It was not until later – much later – when writing *Cymbeline*, that Shakespeare imagined a spirit from the familial past who was not coming to arraign or accuse. Perhaps what enabled him to do so was that he had finally tamed the folkloric and popular impulses that surge upwards in *Hamlet*, unseating reason and logic and learning.

Chapter Seven

SHAKESPEARE'S SAYINGS

Neil Rhodes

Before writing there was only speech. There is no aspect of the popular culture of Shakespeare's own day more fundamental than this, and the printed texts of his plays are marked everywhere by the oral character of a world in which most people could neither read nor write. For the illiterate all knowledge was transmitted through speech. Ancient wisdom of both a moral and a practical kind was preserved in the capsule form of the proverb where 'saying' becomes '*a* saying', something both old and true. We can never really divorce the proverb and related verbal forms from their oral origins, which is why I have preferred the term 'saying' for the title of this essay. But saying held power not merely for the illiterate. The authenticity and authority of speech was recognized more generally long after script had become the normal means of most administrative business. This is particularly evident in legal procedure, for example. In the early fourteenth century the *veredicta* – verdicts or 'true sayings' of jurors – had to be presented orally at the bar of the court, despite having already been written down. In a turn away from the oral, however, a 'sentence', the judge's pronouncement of doom in response to those verdicts, came also to mean an aphorism, from Latin *sententia*, a more literary or artful form of proverb.[1] Both examples remind us of an earlier, entirely speech-based world.

Most people in the sixteenth century continued to inhabit such a world, though the new medium of print was beginning to make its mark on the illiterate as well as the literate.[2] Oral tradition required knowledge to be shaped into fixed verbal formulae, with alliteration, rhyme, or even song acting as mnemonic devices for easy transmission from generation to generation. This is why, from very early on, the saying was regarded as perhaps the very epitome of popular culture: 'what are Proverbs but the peeples voice? / Coin'd first, and current made by common choice', wrote James Howell in 1659.[3] Howell then makes some rather implausible claims for the democratic power of sayings, but his defining characteristics of the proverb ('sense, shortnesse and salt') also point to the paradox that a saying has to be both common and distinctive – distinctive enough to be memorable, for one thing.[4] A saying expresses a commonly accepted truth, but it does so in a way that will make an impact, so as well as using alliteration or rhyme, many proverbs are figurative. One swallow doesn't make a summer, but one of these devices could give a saying the distinctive flavour that would ease it into general currency.

Shakespeare's lifetime coincided roughly with the high-water mark of the saying in England. The common people may have had the privilege of making proverbs, but everybody used them. About 12 000 have been recorded from the sixteenth and seventeenth centuries.[5] This oral residue left its traces on almost all kinds of writing, not just on popular culture. Proverbs were learned at school, serving to drive home moral lessons at the same time as they facilitated Latin language acquisition. Humanist textbooks showed more advanced pupils how they could be used for rhetorical amplification, so although sixteenth-century education had a distinctly oral basis, its promotion of the proverb played a major part in the literary restructuring of sayings in the period. That development was underpinned by the commonplace or notebook method, a key element in humanist pedagogy, which systematized the collection and deployment of sayings and other notable expressions from the writers of antiquity.[6] Deriving from the *loci communes*, which Cicero and Quintilian described as the places where you could find persuasive arguments, the commonplace method evolved into a technique for stylistic adornment. The commonness of commonplaces was perceived differently as they were upgraded and redefined as a tool of eloquence. The effect of proverbs in education, then, was to move 'saying' in the direction of writing and therefore to act as the principal point of intersection between popular and elite cultures in the sixteenth century.

If that is one reason for the enormous prevalence of sayings in the mid-sixteenth century, the other, only a little paradoxically, is the spread of print culture. One of the earliest books to be printed in England was Anthony Wydeville's *The Dictes or Sayengis of the Philosophres* (1497). Other, more encyclopedic works found print the ideal vehicle for preserving and disseminating the commonplace tradition.[7] But there were also printed proverb collections of a demotic kind, the best known being John Heywood's *Dialogue of Proverbs* (1546), and it is this kind of book that represents what has been called 'the orality of popular print'.[8] Like ballads or romances, Heywood's loosely fictionalized compendium of popular sayings attempted to recreate the oral world through the medium that would eventually change it for ever. And print had its own devices for highlighting the oral character of the saying: the First Quarto of *Hamlet* (1603), for example, which is a more oral and less literary version of the play, however one might wish to account for its state, uses quotation marks for many of the 'wise sentences' of Corambis (the Polonius character). To his son he offers 'these few precepts in thy memory / "Be thou familiar, but by no means vulgare . . ."' , and to his daughter this advice: 'Come in Ofelia, such men often proue / "Great in their wordes, but little in their loue." '[9] In a play which is so sensitive to the media of representation, as well as to the relations between high and low cultural forms, this distinction between text and saying seems to complement the much more prominent distinction between theatrical performance within the play and the play itself. The quotation marks also flag these 'sentences' up as commonplaces, though not necessarily in the modern, derogatory sense of the term. That was to come, as oral tradition was superseded by mechanical reproduction. Print, in fact, was literally responsible for turning saying into cliché, since French *clicher* meant 'to stereotype', from the plate used in printing. 'Easier said than done' was once proverbial (with one Shakespearean example at *3H6* 3.2.90) and is now a cliché, which in view of its subject seems appropriate.

Education and print culture both helped to transmit sayings while maintaining a rather ambiguous relationship with this primitive, oral form. These contexts are particularly important for understanding how a writer such as Shakespeare might deploy sayings, since they carry the traffic between high and low culture. There is another context, however, that does not depend upon literacy, and to that extent would seem to be located more clearly in the realm of the popular: this is the dimension of the visual arts. In the mid-sixteenth century, Pieter Bruegel produced a number of paintings that might be considered as the visual equivalents of Heywood's *Dialogue of Proverbs*. 'Twelve Flemish Proverbs', originally painted on twelve wooden platters and dated 1558, was followed in 1559 by the single painting 'Flemish Proverbs', depicting about 120 popular sayings; one of the latter, 'the blind leading the blind' became the subject of the great painting of 1568, now in the Capodimonte in Naples (see Figure 10).[10] Sixteenth-century England did not enjoy such a rich visual culture as the Netherlands, but like other kinds of folk material, sayings appear in very similar forms in different countries, and in Europe all shared a common source in the Bible. Bruegel's picture of the blind leading the blind derives from Matthew 15:14 and reappears in Heywood: 'Where the blind ledth the blinde, both fall in the dike.'[11] In England, the story of the prodigal son

FIGURE 10   Pieter Bruegel, *The Blind Leading the Blind.*

(Luke 15: 11–32) may not have found its Bruegel, but it certainly featured on wall hangings and on painted boards. According to the Hostess in *The Merry Wives of Windsor*, Falstaff had his bedchamber 'painted about with the story of the Prodigal, fresh and new', and proverbs themselves, biblical or not, adorned both alehouse walls and more respectable domestic interiors: 'Who fears a sentence or an old man's saw / Shall by a painted cloth be kept in awe', reflects Shakespeare's Lucrece, presumably no frequenter of alehouses.[12] This moralistic aspect of popular visual culture is reproduced in dramatic form through the proverb play, almost a subgenre of the morality play and common in sixteenth-century England.[13] William Wager was fond of this form, turning out *The Longer Thou Livest the More Fool Thou Art* (1559) and *Enough is as Good as a Feast* (1560); Ulpian Fulwell wrote *Like Will to Like* (1568) and Thomas Lupton *All for Money* (1577). These are all from roughly the period of Shakespeare's childhood. They are part of the culture in which he grew up.

Perhaps the best way to indicate the extraordinarily wide cultural spectrum across which sayings operated in the sixteenth century is to point to its two extremes in Heywood's *Dialogue of Proverbs* and Erasmus' *Adagia*, both from the first half of the century.[14] Heywood, entirely populist, has already been mentioned. Erasmus on the other hand was the fountainhead of humanist wisdom and doyen of sixteenth-century textbook production. Yet proverb lore and the concept of the 'saying' remained a central element in his enterprises. This aspect of learning shouldn't be regarded as trivial, he claimed, arguing that the usefulness of proverbs could be broken down into four categories: philosophy, persuasiveness, grace and charm in speaking, and the understanding of the best authors. In the adage on 'Viva vox: The living word' he affirmed the authenticity of saying over script, quoting Seneca's Epistle V: 'The living voice and the intimacy of a common life will help you more than the written word.' But as a scholar and teacher, Erasmus' feel for the popular character of the proverb – and 'the intimacy of a common life' – is limited by other priorities, as well as by the fact that he was writing in Latin. In defining a proverb, he warns the reader that 'we cannot immediately rank in this category everything which has passed into popular speech, or contains an unusual image; it must be recommended by its antiquity and erudition alike', and he uses some of the adages as cues for reflective moral essays of his own.[15] So this is the upmarket version of the saying, presented with a nod to its origins in popular speech, but firmly directed towards loftier ends. And Erasmian material certainly percolated down to Shakespeare: to drive out one nail by another; a sea of troubles; said and done; at your finger tips.[16] The last, though, is from that hopeless pedant Holofernes, who manages to confuse *unguem* (fingernail) with 'dunghill', so returning the saying back to 'the dregs of the common people [*a vulgo . . . sumptum*]', as Erasmus rather fastidiously puts it elsewhere.[17] It is exactly this kind of detail that shows how Shakespeare slides along the register between the erudite and the popular.

John Heywood's *Dialogue of Proverbs* is a very different sort of work. Constructed as a dialogue between the author and a young man who is wondering whether or not to get married, it jogs along in rhyming couplets of a pretty rough and ready kind, dispensing page after page of proverbial wisdom. Again, there are plenty of expressions that can be tracked down in Shakespeare: 'Whan the sonne shynth make hey'; 'soone ripe sone rotten'; 'beggers shulde be no choosers'; 'put my hande betweene the barke and the tre'.[18] But Heywood's preface is the precise opposite of Erasmus': 'This write I, not to teache, but to touche' (1.9). The suggestion of physical intimacy in 'touche' seems to contradict the admission that he is merely 'writing', just as much as Erasmus' remarks on voice and 'common life' seem at odds with his disdain for the popular elsewhere. Perhaps the most interesting thing about Heywood's *Dialogue*, though, is not the fact that it offers a series of *reasons* for and against marriage, in the commonplace tradition, but that it does so in *rhyme*. The author tells his companion that his proverbs *are* reasons, as he complains that the young man has presented proverbs of his own to contend with his:

> But, reason for reason, ye so styffely ley
> By prouerbe for prouerbe, that with you do wey,

> That reason onely shall herein nought moue you
> To here more than speake.

(1.311–14)

In his later collection of epigrams (1562), Heywood refers to 'rhyme without reason, and reason without rhyme'. So what Heywood's *Dialogue* actually gives us is a gloss on one of his own proverbs, and one much favoured by Shakespeare: 'neither rhyme nor reason'.[19] The form of the saying seems to present them as alternatives, but they are in fact complementary. Heywood's marriage proverbs are rhymed reasons – rhyme, as we saw, being an oral mnemonic device – which in their own way bring elite and popular culture into alignment. Arguing for and against marriage was a school exercise developed by Erasmus. Eventually it found its way into Shakespeare's sonnets to the young man, which might also be described as rhymed reasons.

All this helps to explain why Shakespeare, born in 1564, would have been exposed to a culture saturated in sayings, and it also hints at some of the ways in which this would have been transferred to drama. Shakespeare himself seems to have been extraordinarily responsive to that culture. No writer in the English-speaking world is more quotable, or more quoted, and this is a reflection of a distinctive habit of mind; it has been perceptively said that 'It is often as if, at some deep level of his mind, Shakespeare thought and felt in quotations.'[20] He tapped into popular verbal culture, but his imaginative response to it was highly individual. So it is surprising that very little has been written about Shakespeare's sayings – on how he absorbed and transformed the proverbial, turning common matter into rare expressions.[21] There is, I should add, also a reverse process through which expressions apparently of Shakespeare's own invention pass into common, quasi-proverbial usage before finally descending into cliché. Macduff's 'at one fell swoop' (4.3.219), which refers to the deadly swooping down of the falcon on its prey, comes into this category, as does Macbeth's 'the be-all and the end-all' (1.7.5). A variation of this is a transmission from elite to popular culture where Shakespeare acts as a catalyst – for example, 'there's method in his madness' (based on *Ham* 2.2.200), which started life as a classical allusion and has ended up as a stock phrase.[22] But I am not principally concerned with these kinds of expression. What I want to do in the remainder of this essay is to explain some of the different ways in which Shakespeare refashions popular sayings, and suggest some of the themes that proverbs cluster around; then to look in slightly more detail at how they work in two plays, an early comedy and a late tragedy – *The Taming of the Shrew* and *Macbeth*.

Sayings in Shakespeare do come raw, especially early on. Some of the characters in the *Shrew*, for example, sprinkle their discourse with proverbs in a quite unselfconscious manner. But Shakespeare moves quickly to a more sophisticated use of the proverbial. *As You Like It*, for instance – certainly a proverb-laden and sententious work – offers various descants on sayings which construct a debate about elite and popular culture, inspected through the lens of pastoral. We shall return briefly to this play in a moment. First I want to suggest that the raw form of the saying in Shakespeare's work usually comes supplied with an ironic context, one obvious example being the boring parent. The quotation marks around Corambis's paternal advice in the 1603 *Hamlet* may not *quite* have been ironic, but irony is laid on heavily in *1 Henry IV* when Falstaff postures as King Henry, delivering droplets of moral wisdom to his surrogate prodigal son:

> There is a thing, Harry, which thou hast often heard of, and it is known to many in our land by the name of pitch. This pitch, (as ancient writers do report), doth defile; so doth the company thou keepest.[23]

(2.4.406–8)

The pompous dilation of the biblical maxim turns sentence into satire. Over a century later, Samuel Palmer observed of proverbs that their 'Original Method of Instruction was by Oral Tradition from Father to Son' – a point supported by Solomon himself in the biblical Book of Proverbs, who spoke of the wisdom to be learned from these sayings with the words 'Hear, my son, your father's instruction'.[24] Shakespeare was not entirely respectful towards this tradition. Falstaff cocks a snook at the supposed *gravitas* of fatherly advice from Solomon onwards.

Ringing the changes, Shakespeare puts the father himself on the receiving end of moral wisdom in *Othello*. Sanctioning Desdemona's elopement, the Duke attempts to soothe her furious father with a selection of glib 'sentences':

> When remedies are past, the griefs are ended
> By seeing the worst which late on hopes depended.
>
> (1.3.203–4)

And there is more in the same vein, the rhymes producing an insensitively trite effect that is hardly likely to placate Brabantio, who responds with a bitter analysis of them. Though Brabantio is the actual father here, the Duke's role is paternalistic both in its appropriation of the father's right to withhold consent to his daughter's marriage and in his dispensing of sententious moral counsel. His speech illustrates one traditional use of proverbs, which is to offer consolation in adversity: as Leonato advises another distraught father in *Much Ado*, 'Patch grief with proverbs, make misfortune drunk / With candle-wasters' (5.1.17–18). In *Othello*, however, what Brabantio actually says in response to this conventional wisdom highlights a quite different aspect of proverbs, namely their habit of contradicting each other:

> He bears the sentence well that nothing bears
> But the free comfort which from thence he hears,
> But he bears both the sentence and the sorrow
> That, to pay grief, must of poor patience borrow.
> These sentences, to sugar or to gall,
> Being strong on both sides, are equivocal.
>
> (1.3.213–18)

The fact that you can answer one saying by another was a point made in Heywood's dialogue where the author's advice to be cautious about getting married ('the more haste the less speed') was matched by the young man's examples of opportunity and expedition ('when the sun shineth make hay', 'when th'iron is hot, strike!'). In this exchange in *Othello* Shakespeare neatly sets the emollient function of sayings (sugar) against their contentiousness (gall). The same opposition was illustrated in book form, though in reverse order, by Nicholas Breton's *Crossing of Proverbs* (1616), showing how they can be contradicted, and his *Soothing of Proverbs* (1626). In *Othello* the transition from soothing to crossing precipitates the move from comedy to tragedy just as it sets out the terms of the relationship between husband and wife.

Advice from stand-in fathers provides one context where Shakespeare wants us not to take proverbial wisdom at face value. In these cases the sayings themselves are entirely visible, or perhaps we should say audible. Elsewhere, though, we may detect a concealed or suppressed proverb. One instance is the scene in *Titus Andronicus* where Titus gets his friends and relatives to shoot arrows into the Emperor's court as a protest at the impossibility of finding justice. The futility of this exercise is emblematic and proverbial: it is indeed the very epitome of futility, as well as expressing defiance, frustration and hopeless ambition. First he tells his companions that they might as well cast their nets in the ocean to find justice, or (echoing *The Spanish Tragedy*) dig down to the underworld – both *impossibilia*. He then gives them arrows, saying 'You were as good to shoot against the wind', and when they let them go, his brother comments, 'My lord, I aimed a mile beyond the moon'. There is a saying 'To cast beyond the moon', but what is surely concealed in this bizarre episode is the proverbial 'To piss against the moon', illustrated in one of Bruegel's 'Twelve Flemish Proverbs' (see Figure 11).[25] Combining the two statements by Titus and Marcus we are also reminded of the dangers of pissing against the wind, a useful lesson for would-be revengers. (This is very much a boys' game, I should add.) Scene 4.3 is not one of the scenes that has been attributed to Peele, and one wonders, in fact, whether rustic Shakespeare suppressed a more direct allusion so as not to offend that Oxonian gentleman's sense of decorum.

The saying in the passage from *Titus* is only half hidden. In other places we might have to dig deeper to strike the proverbial. To return to *1 Henry IV* for a moment: in Hal's soliloquy in 1.2 where he tells the audience of his scheme to make himself appear better in the future by behaving badly now, he compares himself first to the sun, 'breaking

FIGURE 11   Pieter Bruegel, 'Pissing at the Moon', from *Twelve Flemish Proverbs*.

through the foul and ugly mists / Of vapours that did seem to strangle him', and then to a gold coin lying in the dirt:

> And, like bright metal on a sullen ground,
> My reformation, glitt'ring o'er my fault,
> Shall show more goodly, and attract more eyes
> Than that which hath no foil to set it off.
>
> (1.2.207–10)

The two images are actually contradictory: the first represents the real self as the sun, but the second turns this inside out. It's the dirt that's real, and the golden self merely superficial. Hal's glittering reformation reminds us, as the Prince of Morocco learns in *The Merchant*, that all that glitters is not gold.[26]

In between the direct and the concealed proverbs come all those sayings which Shakespeare refashions so that we just half hear the original. 'To make the best of a bad bargain' is certainly audible behind the Duke's 'Take up this mangled matter at the best' in the scene with Brabantio (*Oth* 1.3.172). So it is after Coriolanus' death when a lord says 'Let's make the best of it' (5.6.146), though given the situation at the end of that play the remark seems almost on a par with 'Always look on the bright side' in *Monty Python's Life of Brian*. Making the best of things, however, is not just a theme of tragedy. It is an undercurrent of *As You Like It*, for instance, where we may well hear echoes of other, related sayings. The most quoted passage in this play, near the top of the list of Shakespeare's best-known sayings, is Jaques's speech beginning 'All the world's a stage'. But this is bookish, jaded, detached – certainly not from the popular lexicon. The exiled Duke makes the best of it in his own way with the fanciful 'Sweet are the uses of adversity', which is poetic and philosophical, but hardly in the popular idiom. The character who does negotiate between the poetic and the popular, and between high and low culture in this play, is Touchstone. *As You Like It* is, of course, a play about courtliness and rusticity, but also about home and homeliness. The Duke claims, rather improbably, that he has created a home from home in the forest of Arden, but Touchstone has a different view: 'now am I in Arden, the more fool I', he grumbles; 'when I was at home I was in a better place' (2.4.13–14). This doesn't in itself echo the proverbial 'Home is home, though it be never so homely' (or the more modern 'East, west, home's best'), but that saying finds its way back into the play through the extension of the word 'home' from comfort to plainness.[27] Touchstone's prizing of home comforts seems also to influence his choice of marriage partner. Announcing his engagement to the rustic Audrey, he tells the Duke; 'A poor virgin sir, an ill-favoured thing sir, but mine own . . . Rich honesty dwells like a miser sir, in a poor house, as your pearl in your foul oyster' (5.4.57–61). Hovering behind the first of these statements is Erasmus' adage, 'What is one's own is beautiful', which he amplifies at some length: 'Even today there is a shrewd and common saying, "there's no such thing as an ugly sweetheart", because to him who loves them even homely things must seem very beautiful.'[28] Touchstone has a mastery of the language arts, not just old saws, but his homely wisdom on making the best of things is part of a pragmatic outlook on life that recommends accommodation over ambition. Jaques offers supercilious reflections on the world, but the play points homewards. Even clever, pretty, genteel Rosalind, tired of playing pastoral, says simply 'I would I were at home' (4.3.161).

Shakespeare's sayings do their work locally, and have local effects, tied to character and scene, but as some of the examples will have shown they also reverberate thematically through entire plays. The proverb play itself was a mid-sixteenth-century form, and it would probably have looked a bit antique by the 1590s. Shakespeare does, however, experiment once with the genre in *All's Well That Ends Well*, and, arguably, in *Measure for Measure*. As Helena puts it, plotting the bed-trick with her surrogate, Diana:

> All's well that ends well; still the fine's the crown.
> Whate'er the course, the end is the renown.
>
> (4.4.35–6)

The first line combines two proverbs recorded in Tilley and Whiting which also appear in Heywood's *Dialogue* and elsewhere in Shakespeare; the second line amplifies these.[29] But what do they mean for the play as a whole? It is Helena who is principally responsible for seeing that all ends well and that she gets her man, but the resistance she has to overcome is not only to her person but to the very state of marriage itself. Parolles supports Bertram's misogamist objections with another proverb: 'A young man that's married is a man that's marred' (2.3.294).[30] So the cards are quite heavily stacked against all ending well. With that in mind, the play's title seems deliberately challenging. It might be understood in the Machiavellian sense of the ends justifying the means, and Helena's comment on her own resourcefulness is a gesture in that direction: 'Our means will make us means' (5.1.34). Yet it also seems to anticipate the objections of nineteenth- and twentieth-century critics who described *All's*

Well as a 'problem play'. It's as though Shakespeare were saying that a play may have a beginning, a middle and an end, but it's the end that counts. Or perhaps we are simply required to forgive and forget, as the King does in this play and as Lear was to beg Cordelia a few years later (*AW* 5.3.9; *KL* 4.7.83).

It might be misleading to extrapolate from Shakespeare's use of popular sayings more general conclusions about types and categories, especially on the basis of the small selection discussed here. Yet certain themes or clusters do seem to emerge from an overview of this kind of discourse. Popular culture is constantly aware that life is hard, and its sayings operate as coping mechanisms, advising caution and offering consolation. Things may not always be as they seem: 'fair face, foul heart', as well as 'all that glitters is not gold'. Perhaps more crucially, things can be made better or worse: all's well that ends well if you make the best of a bad bargain, but what can't be cured must be endured. You can make or mar, you can mend *and* mar, and on occasion, marrying may be marring.[31] Many proverbs are drawn from the world of work, agricultural or domestic, and many focus on parts of the body – head, heart, hand, tongue and eye, especially – to suggest harmony or conflict between saying and doing, seeing and knowing. They are concerned with the passages of life, as well as the practicalities of living, and there are many reflections on time. But the subject that gathers many of these themes into its orbit, and which is undoubtedly central to popular culture, as we have already seen from Heywood, is marriage. So I want to turn now to two plays where marriage is important as an experience, not merely as a desired outcome, and where the proverbial has work to do in that context.

Proverbs in *The Taming of the Shrew* combine almost seamlessly with its ballad and folk-tale elements to make this early play arguably more deeply rooted in peasant life than any other of Shakespeare's works. Folklorists have found versions of the *Shrew* story from all over the world and counted about 400 different texts. The basic plot motif is as follows: the youngest of three sisters is a shrew. In order to teach her a lesson her husband shoots his dog and his horse and brings his wife to submission. He then makes a wager with the husbands of the other sisters as to which of them is most obedient. There are many variations on this basic motif, some of which are very sadistic. One version, printed in 1550, describes a 'taming' where the husband wraps his wife in a salted horse's hide and beats her with birch rods, which is presented as a 'merry jest'.[32] Other versions appear in ballad form: 'There was a wee cooper who lived in Fife, / Nickity, nackity, noo, noo, noo', one of these begins.[33] Jest and ballad are staples of oral tradition, and in the play itself they combine with a patter of proverbial expression to create a distinctively folk-ish environment. Petruchio tells Kate's father that 'little fire grows great with little wind' and Kate herself that his crest is 'A combless cock, so Kate will be my hen'. He promises that 'will you, nill you, I will marry you' and she tells a servant that 'You may be jogging whiles your boots are green'; the servant himself observes that 'winter tames man, woman, and beast' and that the marital home offers 'cold comfort'. Petruchio reflects on his scheme of taming with the words 'This is a way to kill a wife with kindness.'[34] Not only do master and servant speak in the same rustic idiom, but these expressions also conjure up a very rudimentary lifestyle, for all Petruchio's wealth: the need to keep warm, the proximity of the human and animal worlds.

But where is this play set that it should be so permeated by sayings of this sort? The induction places it firmly in Shakespeare's home county of Warwickshire, where a drunken tinker is deceived into thinking he is a great lord. The play itself is presented as an entertainment for him. Is it 'household stuff', he asks – to which the answer would be both yes and no. We are immediately whisked off to the entirely opposite world of Padua, a city that stands first for education (the play opens with Lucentio announcing that he is going to study at its famous university) and second for money (Padua is a near neighbour of Venice, hub of international trade between East and West). So marked is the discrepancy between the play's folk elements – its brutishness, even – and the sophisticated continental world of wealth and social prestige, that it seems almost to operate like an anamorphic picture. As far as education is concerned, one sister gets the soft option: home tutors, a bit of Ovid, 'music, instruments, and poetry' (1.1.93) – whatever she feels like. The other is sent to the school of hard knocks. But it is money, or property, that is probably the more important issue. Sly asks whether the play is 'household stuff', but in the play's antecedent, *The Taming of A Shrew*, Sander, one of the acting troupe, tells the Lord that 'you may have a "tragicall" or a "commodity" or what you will'.[35] Since this is the play of Shakespeare's that most obviously presents marriage in terms of commodity exchange, and comedies, we are always told, deal with marriage, this is a revealing slip, though (probably) not one of Shakespeare's own making. And this is where the proverbial reappears. The play's first scene stages a confrontation betwen Kate and her suitors where the air hums with traded sayings: 'comb your noddle with a three-legg'd stool', and 'it is best put finger in the eye' from Kate; and from the suitors 'Our cake's dough on both sides', 'There's small choice in rotten apples', 'Happy man be his dole. He that runs fastest gets the ring.' These men are supposed to be wealthy Italian merchants, but they speak in the language of Barton Heath market. This is indeed 'household stuff'.

The question of what conclusions we draw from this and what sense we make of the play as a whole remains something of a challenge. It is difficult for the twenty-first-century reader to avoid seeing *The Shrew* as a too-familiar tale of domestic violence within marriage. But its language of commodity exchange may be pointing to quite separate issues. Petruchio's own motives in wooing Kate seem ambiguous. He has no need to look for a fortune, for one thing, and his claim that he couldn't care less how ugly and bad-tempered the girl is provided she's rich sounds as though it's meant to ring hollow. When he asks Baptista very directly about his daughter in these terms, Gremio, one of the other suitors, tells him 'You are too blunt, go to it orderly' (2.1.45). But Gremio and Hortensio have already discussed Kate in marketplace idiom. While all the characters are fond of expressing themselves through popular sayings, what Petruchio seems to be doing is exposing the hypocrisy of people who also demand a speech decorum based on the pretence of romantic love when they in fact see marriage as a purely economic transaction. Petruchio, by contrast, is a Jack Nicholson figure, anarchic and predatory, though one who in Shakespeare's play is also blunt enough to call a spade a spade. That is what lies behind his stunningly demeaning assertion that Kate is 'My household stuff, my field, my barn, / My horse, my ox, my ass, my any thing' (3.2.229–30). Whether his relationship with Kate amounts to something we can respond to with any sympathy probably depends not so much on the notorious submission speech as on the end of the previous scene. Gremio is still grumbling about his cake being dough, and disappears, while Petruchio invites Kate to kiss him in the street: 'Come, my sweet Kate. / Better once than never, for never too late' (5.1.137–8). The conflation of 'Better late than never' with 'Never too late to mend' transforms two rather stale sayings into a moment of seized opportunity, promise, and emotional and sexual excitement. It is a brilliantly deft reworking of the proverbial, and a good deal hangs upon it.

To suggest that *Macbeth* is also about 'household stuff' might seem to be stretching a point, but the homeliness of the play has been greatly underrated.[36] It centres on a partnership between man and wife in a way that none of the other tragedies do. Alongside, and perhaps stemming from that relationship, is a subcurrent of domestic themes. Far from being a one-dimensional play of nightmarish violence, the pervasive sense of evil in *Macbeth* is constantly mitigated by our awareness of a better world – of fertility and fruitfulness, home comforts, feasting, sleep. The apparent ineptitude of Lady Macbeth's feigned reaction to the news of the murder – 'What! in our house?' is entirely in keeping with this. So too are 'the blanket of the dark', the 'procreant cradle', 'the ravelled sleeve of care', 'the wine of life', 'the timely inn', 'the sauce to meat', 'life's feast' and 'a woman's story at a winter's fire'. The emotional quality of *Macbeth* derives, to a greater degree than any other of Shakespeare's plays, from an intersection between the horrific and the homely, and proverbs play an important part in this. A.R. Braunmuller has pointed out in a well-chosen phrase that 'proverbs toll through important moments in Act 3 – "Men are but men"; "Fair face foul heart"; "And there's an end"; "Blood will have blood"'.[37] But perhaps the best-known reference to a proverb in the play is the one that is not articulated: Lady Macbeth's taunting her husband with cowardice and accusing him of 'Letting "I dare not" wait upon "I would," / Like the poor cat i' th' adage' (1.7.44–5). The adage in question appears in Heywood as 'The cat would eate fysshe, and wold not wet her feete' (1.869).[38] In fact, this timid creature, who sounds more like a household pet than a witch's familiar, unwittingly offers a premonition of the sea of blood that Macbeth will have to wade through and that will revisit his wife in nightmares. The 'adage' looks forward to the bitter resignation of 'I am in blood / Stepp'd in so far' (3.4.135–6), which itself echoes the proverbial 'Having wet his foot he cares not how deep he wades' and 'Over shoes over boots'.[39] This immersion in turn echoes the earlier one of the bloodstained hands, the futile washing, and Macbeth's imagining the 'multitudinous seas' made crimson with gore. They are both in deep, hand and foot.

To wash your hands of something is to get it over and done with by evading the consequences of your actions. This is what Macbeth hopelessly looks for in the soliloquy 'If it were done, when 'tis done', knowing that he can never be done with the consequences of his action. While his wife at first shuts her mind to the future, imagining that 'a little water clears us of this deed', she eventually falls back on the empty consolation of 'Things without all remedy / Should be without regard; what's done is done' (3.2.11–12). Proverbial in itself, this has some close relations in medical sayings such as 'What can't be cured must be endured' and 'Past cure past care'. They have a final echo in the pathos and terror of Lady Macbeth's own terminal illness, where she gropes for her husband's hand: 'Come, come, come, come, give me your hand. What's done cannot be undone. To bed, to bed, to bed' (5.1.63–5). The proverbial fabric of *Macbeth* reinforces our sense that the play is grounded in the experiences of everyday life. The fear it arouses comes from the suddenness with which the ordinary is precipitated into nightmare and from the realization that the nightmare is true and irreparable. 'Things done cannot be undone'[40] is the tragic crossing of the comedic proverb 'Never too late to mend'. The twist in *Macbeth* is that the dead end is accompanied by the horror and emptiness of repetition. The childless couple discover that blood breeds ('Blood will have blood', 3.4.121); that words and images return; that ghosts come back to haunt them. In all this they are perpetually suspended from the social comforts of friends and family, a point brought home to Macbeth in the banquet scene when he is unable to sit down with his guests. We are told by the Elizabethan playgoer, Simon Forman, that in early performances, as Macbeth attempted to give the company good cheer, the ghost of Banquo seated himself in his chair – an action that plays maliciously with the proverb 'An unbidden guest knows not where to sit.'[41] The action also makes a ghost of Macbeth himself. What he has done has unmade him. As his wife says, in a phrase that sounds proverbial, but isn't quite: 'Nought's had, all's spent' (3.2.4). No honour. No children. The empty house.

Shakespeare's sayings have many functions, but their ultimate effect is one of bringing it all back home. To give the last word to John Heywood: 'Homely matters homely terms do best express'.[42] It is certainly true that Shakespeare also worked in the more learned commonplace tradition, and that it is almost impossible to disengage his more bookish sayings from those of a largely oral provenance. But then that in itself is enough to show how vital a part his sayings have in Shakespeare's response to Elizabethan popular culture.

Chapter Eight

SHAKESPEARE AND POPULAR SONG

Stuart Gillespie

INTRODUCTION

W.H. Auden, perhaps the best-known twentieth-century commentator to have sustained an interest in Shakespeare's use of music, made these comments on Duke Orsino's song 'Come away, death':

> This is not the folk song that the Duke's request for 'that old and antique song we heard last night' would lead us to expect, but a sophisticated treatment of a folk theme. What began as a theme of courtly love for higher classes and progressed to folk ballads has now returned to a sophisticated form. This process often occurs with conventional material: ballads provide matter for epics, courtly love themes move through folk songs to pastorals, and in America hymns are transformed into spirituals.[1]

Auden's remarks remind us that popular songs and ballads often fail to originate with 'the people', and that they are often developed in a non-'popular' context. Nevertheless, some early modern English songs are definably more 'popular' than others, and some of these more popular kinds were strongly represented on the stage, though not necessarily in the form of full-scale performances from first line to last. By 'more popular kinds' I mean folk songs and to some extent street songs, though the latter – the type of thing Autolycus' pack contains – were usually composed by a particular writer, to an existing folk tune.[2] Folk songs were for the most part either ballads, three-man songs (set in simple three-part harmony), or catches (short rounds, like 'Three blind mice'). But the ballad form had also migrated to the street, so that 'ballad' usually meant 'broadside ballad'.[3] The songs performed in something like complete form within Shakespeare's plays are much more often art songs – freshly written pieces by a professional author, that author usually being Shakespeare himself – than popular or traditional ones. But I am also concerned in what follows with the much larger number of songs in Shakespeare which are sung in part, quoted, or alluded to in one way or another.[4] Here the popular or traditional song is much more pervasive; the very different characters of Falstaff, Mercutio, Sir Toby Belch, Hamlet and Lear's Fool are all among those who conspicuously echo contemporary ballad literature. One reason for this disproportion is that only 'called for' as opposed to impromptu songs are likely to be at all diligently performed, and characters do not usually call for popular songs when they have the chance to hear a professional performer (such as Feste).[5]

In many ways, however, songs from the popular end of the spectrum are better suited to the English Renaissance stage than art songs. In a period when a member of the higher social echelons would not have performed music in public, songs in plays were usually sung by secondary characters such as clowns and rustics, not by the characters of gentlefolk – with exceptions occurring when the setting is clearly a private one. Ophelia sings before an assortment of courtiers only because she is unhinged; Gertrude would never perform in so public a setting, though like other ladies she would be sufficiently accomplished to do so. The first song in Shakespeare to be assigned to a noble rather than a commoner or page is Balthasar's 'Sigh no more, ladies' in *Much Ado about Nothing*, a substantial distance into Shakespeare's playwriting career. Several other factors pulled a playwright in the same direction, including financial considerations. The differences between popular and art songs were strongly marked not only in terms of subject matter, rhythm and poetic style, but by the fact that folk songs and ballads needed no special instrumentalists or trained singers for their performance. Songs like Sir Toby's need be accompanied only by a cittern or pipe and tabor, so could be more freely written into a play. Aesthetic issues are intertwined with practical ones like these: considerable playwriting skill is required to

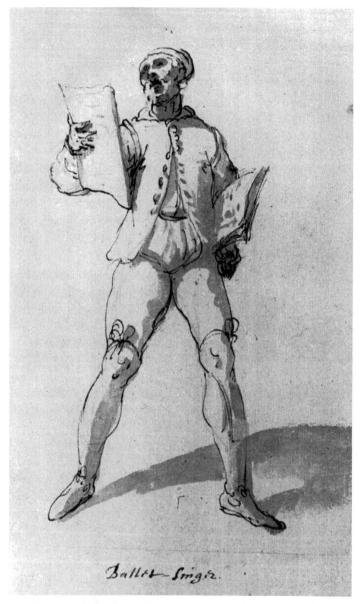

FIGURE 12   A ballad singer, by Inigo Jones.

integrate a trained singing-man into the action, and the reliance for example in *As You Like It* on Amiens, barely a character in his own right, is usually seen as a flaw. All in all there were many reasons why, if a playwright wanted vocal music, it was much less trouble to work in popular songs. Somewhat paradoxically, their relatively infrequent performance on stage probably results as much as anything else from the frequency with which they were encountered in everyday life: they were simply taken too much for granted to be considered worth paying to hear. Nevertheless there are, as we shall see, occasions in Shakespeare, as hardly ever in the drama of his contemporaries, when popular songs are of the most central importance to a scene and even to a play.

LOVE'S LABOURS LOST: ALLUDING TO POPULAR CULTURE

This discussion will follow the broad chronology of Shakespeare's work in its treatment of a few episodes significant in the present volume's terms for their manner of using song and for their use of particular songs. The music in the earliest plays is limited and largely conventional, but the end of *Love's Labours Lost*, where two paired songs are rather abruptly introduced (they are perhaps an afterthought, or in other words an alternative ending), is something of a new departure. This is the first point in Shakespeare's career at which the distinction between the popular and the sophisticated seems to come to the fore in connection with vocal music. I give the first of the pair together with the introduction they are accorded:

ARMADO   But, most esteemed greatness, will you hear the dialogue that the two learned men have compiled, in praise of the owl and the cuckoo? It should have followed in the end of our show.
KING   Call them forth quickly; we will do so.
ARMADO   Holla! Approach.

Enter all.

This side is Hiems, winter; this Ver, the spring – the one maintained by the owl, th'other by the cuckoo. Ver, begin.

THE SONG

VER.

When daisies pied and violets blue
   And lady-smocks all silver-white
And cuckoo-buds of yellow hue
   Do paint the meadows with delight,
The cuckoo then on every tree
   Mocks married men; for thus sings he:
      'Cuckoo!
Cuckoo, cuckoo!' – O, word of fear,
Unpleasing to a married ear.

When shepherds pipe on oaten straws
   And merry larks are ploughmen's clocks,
When turtles tread and rooks and daws,
   And maidens bleach their summer smocks,
The cuckoo then, on every tree,
   Mocks married men; for thus sings he:
      'Cuckoo!
Cuckoo, cuckoo!' – O, word of fear,
Unpleasing to a married ear.

(5.2.872–99)

This is, of course, no popular song, and it might easily be misleading to call it, as it has been called, Shakespeare's 'most rustic, simple, and countrified' piece of vocal music.[6] It is certainly Shakespeare's evocation of the everyday world, one which contrasts strongly with that of a banished duke and his court in Arcadia. This much can be agreed on as a description of the function of this passage, and to achieve this concluding contrast, it appears, a song or two was the quickest and most effective means. But taking the 'Spring' text with its ensuing counterpart, 'Winter', whose burden is 'While greasy Joan doth keel the pot', we have two songs which, in C.L. Barber's words, 'are not simply *of* the world they describe, not folk songs; they are art songs, consciously pastoral, sophisticated enjoyment of simplicity'.[7] While the métier of these lyrics may be rustic, and while 'Joan', 'Dick' and 'Tom' (in 'Winter') are names suggesting humble folk, the treatment is clearly in the courtly tradition. The 'oaten straws' (891)

FIGURE 13   A courtier and a rustic, from Robert Greene, *A Quip for an Upstart Courtier* (1592).

will probably first call to mind Spenser's *Shepherd's Calendar* for the modern reader; the 'turtles' are a standby for poets from the time of Chaucer, especially in the usefully rhyming form of 'turtledoves'. Maidens doubtless really did bleach their summer smocks, since Autolycus derives part of his income from filching such items (*WT* 4.2.23–4). But the 'debate' format implied in Armado's introduction recalls highly literary medieval debate poems (such as those on the holly versus the ivy), and there are specific literary associations for a 'cuckoo song' in the *reverdie*, the poem on nature's rejoicing at the return of spring. In other words, this is sophisticated allusion to popular culture, and by no means an example of The Thing Itself. The song appears to offer a perspective quite different from that of the play that precedes it, an effect that would have been heightened on stage as the clowns returned to perform it and close up the action.[8] But the degree of artifice and the distance from actual popular culture are scarcely less than in the posturings of the lords of Navarre.

TWELFTH NIGHT AND
DIFFERENCE OF DEGREE

A later comedy, *Twelfth Night*, presents a different picture. It does contain popular songs, if mostly in brief snatches. It also contains art songs. It is, of course, famous as containing one of Shakespeare's meditations on the nature and effects of music. Perhaps most interesting of all in the present context, it contains art songs which are redolent of popular songs, which is to say that J.M. Nosworthy's generalization needs to be qualified when he writes of the 'clear-cut distinction [the play] imposes between the higher order of song and the ballads and catches which make up Sir Toby's repertoire'.[9] But it is still broadly correct, and more-over differences of social standing in *Twelfth Night*, as between Orsino and Olivia on the one hand and the latter's unruly guests on the other, closely follow differences in musical taste and expression. Feste, whose profession is that of domestic minstrel, does not sing real popular songs for his masters, but imitations of them penned (as far as we know) by Shakespeare – 'Come away, death' and 'O mistress mine' – and his relation to the dramatic action is slight enough to show that Shakespeare has still not fully resolved the problem of integrating the singing-man into the play. But on another plane the work is permeated by the snatches of popular song from Sir Toby, and there is a catch in which Feste joins forces with Sir Andrew as well as his companion in mischief.

I shall focus on the remarkable scene 2.3. This, like another scene in *Hamlet* to which we will attend shortly, weaves song much more closely and more sustainedly into a dramatic episode than any of Shakespeare's contemporaries seems even to have attempted. Six songs are involved, only the first two of which were apparently intended to be sung in full:

> 'O Mistress mine'
> 'Hold thy peace'
> 'Three merry men be we'
> 'There dwelt a man in Babylon'
> 'O' the twelfth day of December'
> 'Farewell dear heart'

The first is performed by Feste after he has offered the carousing Sir Toby and Sir Andrew the choice of 'a love-song, or a song of good life' (2.3.36). A few moments later, at Sir Andrew's insistence, the clown begins and his two companions join in with the catch 'Hold thy peace'. The next three songs are hollered out impromptu and apparently fragmentarily by the increasingly drunken Sir Toby, eventually occasioning Malvolio's arrival and remonstrations. The last, 'Farewell dear heart', is turned into a duet in which Sir Toby and Feste jocularly apply the words of a song to their present situation ('Shall I bid him go' – 'O no, no, no, no, you dare not', 109–12), with particular reference to Malvolio, the better to annoy him.

The dates at which the first-known version of each song is recorded provide a quick indication of the kind of ancestry they possess.[10] The first and last can be assigned to no remoter date than 1600–1, the first being original with *Twelfth Night*, and the last being found in Robert Jones's *First Booke of Songes and Ayres* of 1600. The tune and general type of the first was traditional ('O mistress mine' is the start of many traditional English songs), while the last would have been familiar to members of Shakespeare's audience as a recent or current hit (Jones collected but does not claim to have authored it). But this pair are art songs, written by contemporaries, the first by Shakespeare, the second by persons unknown. The rest, on the other hand, are mostly known from at least as far back as the middle of the sixteenth century. These two kinds of song are presented very differently, and have a very different appeal. It is the second group, as popular songs, that we are concerned with here, but as far as the play is concerned its qualities are defined partly in relation to the other. This second, middle group of four traditional songs and ballads clearly belongs to a downmarket and old-fashioned, though much loved, body of material. Malvolio disdains them as 'coziers' [cobblers'] catches', appropriate for an 'ale-house' (3.2.90–1). But we know which side the audience will be on, even if its own usual attitude to such material is unlikely to have been naively uncritical (a point to which I shall return below). Such music had an entertainment potential that should not be underestimated, and one closely connected with its cultural valency. Bruce Smith writes elsewhere in the present volume that one of the functions of ballads in Shakespeare ('On the twelfth day of December' and

'Farewell dear heart' are the first lines of ballads, or at least of songs derived from ballads) is to help establish a sense of common culture, 'a commonality of memory that unifies the audience and imbricates them in the fictional world of the play'. Peter Seng has described the overall effect of Sir Toby's singing thus:

> Shakespeare's audience, knowing – and probably able to sing – the originals of his songs, must have derived considerable pleasure from sheer recognition as the drunken knight bawled out line after line with greater and greater gusto.

(Seng, p.104)

Throughout Shakespeare's work, in fact, the ballads that are sung and quoted are invariably the best known and most popular. As I have said, this scene in *Twelfth Night* integrates musical materials into a spoken play perhaps more closely than is to be found elsewhere on the English Renaissance stage. What is more, though, it turns popular songs at once into an immediately engaging part of the spectacle; into a plot device; and into a kind of touchstone – one effect of unifying the audience being to place Malvolio outside its pale. By this I do not mean that such songs are presented as a simple or unqualified positive (Sir Toby is, after all, drunk, and the catch is very far from being one of the best catches available). Yet the set of functions these songs perform could not be accomplished nearly so well by any other means.

Twelfth Night is haunted by song, and popular song is never far away, even, as Auden remarked, in the art songs. The play's parting shot is Feste's song of the wind and rain, a song which, though it may look traditional, we have no evidence existed before the play.[11] Shakespeare evidently wished it to have some of the characteristics of popular songs (such as regularity of rhythm), and thereby evoke them – an effect that would have been strengthened by using a familiar tune to accompany it, as was often the practice with newly written ballads and other songs. No detailed discussion can be offered here of strictly musical aspects of Shakespeare's songs; it should be noted in passing that since almost all were probably written with an existing folk tune in view, this is in itself an aspect of his use of popular culture. But the songs in *Twelfth Night* are all songs found, so to speak, in their rightful places. There is nothing untoward about a professional entertainer performing sophisticated vocal pieces or a drunken knight singing a catch: the degree of the character in the comedies, generally speaking, is in line with the genre of the song. The case is different in Shakespearean tragedy.

TRAGIC BALLADS: OPHELIA AND OTHERS

Shakespeare's willingness to disobey the conventions covering the use of music in tragedy is exemplified by his assignment of songs to Ophelia and other major characters of high social status. It is also reflected in his use of ballads, a form reviled not only by Puritans and other killjoys; Jonson's advice that 'a Poet should detest a Ballet maker' was widely heeded.[12] Jonson's remark is at bottom an expression of a craftsman's pride, but it can easily appear uncomfortably close to the deeply snobbish attitude of such a writer as Sir William Cornwallis, the essayist, who with considerable condescension confided to his readers in 1600:

> I haue not beene ashamed to aduenture mine eares with a ballad-singer, and they haue come home loaden to my liking, doubly satisfied, with profit, and with recreation. The profit, to see earthlings satisfied with such course stuffe, to heare vice rebuked, and to see the power of Vertue that pierceth the head of such a base Historian, and vile Auditory.
>
> The recreation to see how thoroughly the standers by are affected, what strange gestures come from them, what strayned stuffe from their Poet, what shift they make to stand to heare, what extremities he is driuen to for Rime, how they aduenture theyr purses, he his wits, how well both their paines are recompenced, they with a filthy noise, hee with a base reward.[13]

Not only did Shakespeare not disdain popular songs and ballads: he used them even in tragedy. The popular status of this material, though sometimes not obvious to modern readers and audiences, is just as crucial to their role in the tragedies as we have seen it to be in *Twelfth Night*. It is also something of which a contemporary audience would never have lost sight.

Mercutio has already been mentioned, and Lear's Fool and *Othello* will receive some attention shortly, but the tragedy commanding most attention here is *Hamlet*, a work which makes much more use of music than any other Shakespearean tragedy, and in which the music is very largely popular song. First, however, some observations I postponed above.

The popular culture of Shakespeare's time, far from simply 'possessing' popular songs as one of its constituents, stood or could stand in a sophisticated critical relation to them. Parodies and burlesques of traditional songs and ballads were common, and when Polixenes' servant describes Autolycus' ballads, most of the jokes are plainly old ones (about dildos, for example):

> He hath songs for man or woman, of all sizes: no milliner can so fit his customers with gloves: he has the prettiest love-songs for maids, so without bawdry (which is strange); with such delicate burdens of dildoes and fadings, jump her and thump her; and where some stretch-mouthed rascal would, as it were, mean mischief and break a foul gap into the matter, he makes the maid to answer 'Whoop, do me no harm, good man;' – puts him off, slights him, with 'Whoop, do me no harm, good man.'
>
> (*WT* 4.4.193–202)

There is, in fact, one quite major way in which Shakespeare seems to make direct use of the parody tradition. The 'ballad medley' was a nonsense miscellany of ballad lines of which we have examples for onstage singing by a fool ('medley' and 'motley' being frequent synonyms) from mid-sixteenth-century English drama. Lear's Fool appears to draw on this tradition at several points.[14] Fools and clowns have been in the background to much of this discussion so far, and the mixture of laughter and sympathy they call forth (onstage, at least) may form a sort of parallel to the mixture of satirical humour and fondness that popular songs seem to have elicited, or indeed may be partly occasioned by it. At any rate, Shakespeare seems quite well aware of the ambivalent effect old ballads may have.

These reflections are germane to Ophelia, the principal singer in *Hamlet*, whose final and most extensive scene (4.5) starts with her 'enter[ing] distracted' to the Queen. After discoursing distractedly with Claudius and

Gertrude she exits, and the action proceeds to her brother's appearance at the head of a band of armed followers, threatening the King. Ophelia re-enters to demonstrate to the anguished Laertes the loss not only of his father but now of his sister's sanity, and this scene eventually offers us our last sight of her alive. This is a second episode in which Shakespeare succeeds not just in making music a part of the drama rather than a mere interlude within it, but in making the music actively carry the role of the character, Ophelia, and with it, at this point, the play as a whole. Parts of five songs are normally sung (as opposed to spoken, as mere quotations) by Ophelia in 4.5.[15] They begin, in sequence, as follows:

> 'How should I your true love know'
> 'By Gis and by Saint Charity'
> 'They bore him barefac'd on the bier'
> 'For bonny sweet Robin is all my joy'
> 'And will a' not come again?'

Whether or not this scene represents Shakespeare's most powerful use of popular songs is a matter of opinion, but it does represent a most evocative use of, so to speak, the *idea* of popular song. As others have remarked, Ophelia is literally playing the fool here, one of the stage fool's principal activities being the singing of snatches of ballads (the only other characters in Shakespeare to sing as many are clowns like Sir Toby). 'As an "antike," she is simply doing what the appellation suggests: she is drawing on the ancient folk songs, folk plays, and remnants of pagan customs as part of her "act."'[16] The sad thing is, of course, that it is no act to her – her mental condition is far more parlous than that of professional fools, though the fool's lesser abnormality is relevant. Among the most characteristic features of the fool's or clown's repartee are its riddling, sometimes mysterious ambiguity – from simple sexual innuendo to the dark and deep tonal ambiguities of Lear's Fool – and its ambivalence, as when a fool (say Lear's again) pretends to one emotion while evidently feeling another. It is thus in the mode of the clown or fool that the richly opaque Ophelia of this scene manages, most of all through her songs, to suggest multilayered significance. Like a fool, she cannot be expected to explain, and will not abide anyone's question – or will weave it into another flight of fancy.

Which is perhaps just as well for her, because some of these songs ought to bring a blush to any maiden's cheek, being by no means suitable for polite company. It looks as though in her confused state she has remembered, not the songs of her adult experience as the privileged and sheltered daughter of a powerful courtier, but the songs she once heard from her nurse when young, or from servants. 'Bonny Robin' is almost certain to have been a well-known text deriving from a Robin Hood ballad; 'by Shakespeare's time these stories had already long undergone epic degeneration, and the name Maid Marion had become a by-word for promiscuity' (Seng, p.153), 'Robin' being a phallic term. While this is likely to be lost on an uninformed audience today, the sexual import of Ophelia's second song could not be:

> By Gis and by Saint Charity,
>   Alack and fie for shame,
> Young men will do't if they come to't –
>   By Cock, they are to blame.
> Quoth she, 'Before you tumbled me,
>   You promis'd me to wed.'
> He answers,
> 'So would I a done, by yonder sun,
>   An thou hadst not come to my bed.'

(4.5.58–66)

At one level, it seems plain, Ophelia is envisioning a nightmare world in which she has been the victim of Hamlet's betrayal. In this respect her singing, her songs, have the obvious function of reinforcing her characterization as a helpless, poignantly pathetic creature. And yet these are not the *only* meanings of these songs. Another meaning is that she suffers from sexual frustration. And the pervasive references to death, though they may at some level be proleptic of her own or Hamlet's demise, must more directly relate to her father's.

It might be agreed that Ophelia's songs are, in context, richly evocative, but does it really matter what she sings, or would virtually anything seem poignant and suggestive? In some cases the suggestiveness might be largely a matter of the simple discrepancy between who Ophelia is and what she is singing. But the first of her 'snatches of old lauds' (*Ham* 4.7.176), 'How should I your true love know', is more complex than the bawdy ditties just mentioned, and provides more answers to this question. It is manifestly a version of an old folk ballad. The source does not survive, but it can be surmised that like Ophelia's version the original was written in ballad metre and cast in the form of a dialogue with question and answer (hence perhaps a jig). The beginning of the narrative, which can be reconstructed from analogues and variants, tells of a lover who meets on the road a pilgrim returning from the shrine of Our Lady of Walsingham.[17] The lover's mistress has made a pilgrimage to the same destination but failed to return, and the lover asks a stranger he meets whether he has encountered her on the way. The stranger asks him to describe her. This attractive opening was developed and the story concluded in different ways within the nexus of variants, some pre-dating and others post-dating *Hamlet* (one is sometimes attributed to Sir Walter Ralegh). In giving Shakespeare's version I omit the brief interruptions of dialogue between Ophelia and the Queen:

> *How should I your true love know*
> > *From another one?*
> *By his cockle hat and staff*
> > *And his sandal shoon.*
> *He is dead and gone, lady,*
> > *He is dead and gone,*
> *At his head a grass-green turf,*
> > *At his heels a stone.*
> *White his shroud as the mountain snow -*
> > *Larded with sweet flowers*
> *Which bewept to the grave did not go*
> > *With true-love showers:*
>
> (4.5.23–6, 29–32, 36, 38–40)

Some commentators contend that the lost folk ballad behind Shakespeare's and all the other variants bore a much closer resemblance to Ophelia's version than to any of the other surviving texts, while others suggest that only the first four lines above belong to the 'Walsingham ballad' type, the rest to two other ballads no longer extant. However this may be, members of Shakespeare's audience would have been familiar with these lines or something like them. Perhaps, assuming 'single ballad' origins, only minimal changes would have been apparent in the *Hamlet* version. Most obviously, as Shakespeare permits himself to do elsewhere, the genders have probably been reversed. As outlined above, surviving analogues suggest that the lover left behind was originally male, the pilgrim female (pilgrims wore cockle shells in their hats to symbolize spiritual regeneration), whereas Ophelia is here cast in the former role, and Hamlet, whom she knows to have travelled far on a mysterious voyage, in the latter. The odd line 39, 'Which bewept to the grave did not go', with its 'not' sounding inauthentic because metrically out of place, probably reflects Ophelia's own addition of the negative.[18]

One or more popular songs have here been assimilated directly into the play, then. But, as in the cases of Ophelia's other songs, the effect goes far beyond that of creating an interlude in the action, or of providing evocative 'atmosphere'.[19] According to Seng, 'Ophelia's song is, *au fond*, far more meaningful than most critics have suspected; it has, indeed, an organic relationship to the rest of the play' (p.141). Yet there has been much disagreement as to exactly what that relationship is. Is the main referent (a) Polonius, (b) Prince Hamlet or (c) Hamlet Senior? Each of these three interpretations is possible, for such reasons as those following. (a) Commentators such as Caldecott and later Kittredge and Brooke suggested the 'not' was Ophelia's interpolation to make the line refer to Polonius' funeral.[20] Admittedly this is a love song, on the face of it as inappropriate for Ophelia to apply to her father as to Hamlet Senior; but Prince Hamlet is not yet dead. (b) The song first comes to Ophelia's mind not in connection with a death, but as an explanation of Hamlet's disappearance: he has gone on a pilgrimage – having reason to do penance. Coleridge, who in his lectures on Shakespeare first suggested the application to Prince Hamlet, suggested the connection in Ophelia's mind was via Polonius – that

this song like her others connects 'two thoughts that had never sub-
sisted in disjunction, the love for Hamlet and her filial love'.[21] (c) At the
point when Ophelia sings the first few lines, only Gertrude, Horatio
and an unnamed courtier are on stage. Whatever her mental condition, Ophelia is rather careful to whom she sings her songs, and
the question 'How should I your true love know?' can be seen as directed
slyly at Gertrude, who indeed seems to remonstrate with her for
it ('Nay, but, Ophelia –', 4.5.37). The line on the funeral also applies to
Hamlet Senior; that on the stone about the heels, whether alluding
to an unusually positioned memorial stone or some custom to prevent
a ghost walking, fits him better than Polonius, who can scarcely
have a memorial stone as yet, and whose ghost is not tempted to
perambulate.

Multiple meanings and suggestions of meanings, as we have said,
are only to be expected in songs sung by fools: a fundamental aspect of
their performance is to offer caps that may be worn if they seem to fit.
But there is at least one more layer, perhaps a deeper one. Whoever else
Ophelia's song refers to, it also refers to herself, and her relationship
with the dead man. The original song had its own logic; what did it
say? The singer learns from a stranger that the loved one's pilgrimage
has been halted for ever by death – a simple tragic note characteristic
of the folk ballad. In the song, the pilgrim is laid to earth by strangers,
without a true-love's tears. The absence of the true-love hints at the
singer's sense of guilt. Why guilt? Because the cause of the death, as of
the pilgrimage, was the singer's indifference.[22] One might almost say
the story of Hamlet and Ophelia follows the song's course; at the very
least, it expresses her inmost thoughts with an indirectness that alone
makes them articulable. In casting herself in the role of the indifferent
lover, Ophelia becomes in her own mind the type of a figure in an old
ballad. But she also becomes such a figure for us – especially, perhaps,
in our last image of her a couple of scenes later, when we hear of how
she tried to hang her garland on a willow, just like a lover in an old
song. The effect of turning Ophelia from individual unfortunate into a
type of human suffering is in no small part accomplished by associating

her with figures in ballads, and at the end with one ballad in particular, about a willow.

'A SONG OF WILLOW'

A couple of years after *Hamlet*, on 3 September 1604, a certain Symon Stafford, perhaps intending to capitalize on the popularity of the songs in the play, published 'A Ballad called *Tytles of Ballades or A newe medley beginning* ROBIN *is to the grene gone as I went to Walsingham*'. It looks as though Shakespeare not only used old ballads, but in some cases breathed sufficient new life into them to ensure their survival into the future. And he himself used one of Ophelia's ballads once more. Desdemona's reprise of what has now become known as the 'Willow' song has been much discussed, and here I merely offer some comments which seem to arise directly from matters considered so far. It is worth stressing that this is indisputably a ballad widely known to the Shakespearean audience; Shakespeare has selected certain verses from it, but again, only slight adjustments have been made to these parts.[23]

Once more, a 'real' individual – a family servant – is figured as a character in an old ballad. Barbara's death identifies her with the forsaken lover in the song:

> My mother had a maid called Barbary,
> She was in love, and he she loved proved mad
> And did forsake her. She had a song of 'willow',
> An old thing 'twas, but it expressed her fortune
> And she died singing it.

(4.3.24–8)

Old ballads reflect the way things are, or possibly *vice versa* (and at this point in *Othello*, we are about to be shown another example of this symbiosis). The adjective 'old' is mildly pejorative here: it is not that the song is venerable, but that it is familiar – not modish, not sophisticated or exciting; not much is to be expected of it. Nevertheless (perhaps on account of its very familiarity, which underwrites the authenticity of its feeling),

the maid found the ballad expressive of her condition. Desdemona finds
that it expresses her feelings too – or rather, it is more expressive of her
feelings than anything else:

> That song tonight
> Will not go from my mind. I have much to do
> But to go hang my head all at one side
> And sing it like poor Barbary.
>
> (28–31)

Once again, an old song allows the expression of feelings not otherwise
articulable. Desdemona will not admit to Emilia that Othello has rejected
her:

> EMILIA   Would you had never seen him!
> DESDEMONA   So would not I: my love doth so approve him
>   That even his stubbornness, his checks, his frowns
>   – Prithee unpin me – have grace and favour.
>
> (16–19)

Instead, a moment later the song of unrequited love does it for her:

> The poor soul sat sighing by a sycamore tree,
>   Sing all a green willow:
> Her hand on her bosom, her head on her knee,
>   Sing willow, willow, willow.
> The fresh streams ran by her and murmured her moans,
>   Sing willow, willow, willow:
> Her salt tears fell from her and softened the stones,
>   Sing willow, willow, willow . . .
> Sing all a green willow must be my garland.
> Let nobody blame him, his scorn I approve –
>
> (39–46, 51–2)

The last line here seems indeed to be taken from the original ballad (one
analogue contains the line 'Let nobody chyde her, her scornes I
approue'; Seng p.196), but Desdemona's troubled mind has promoted it
to the wrong point, as the rhyme shows, and her self-correction in the

next line – 'Nay, that's not next' (53) – tries to unsay it, adding a further twist to the pathos of self-control versus the longing to speak out. Desdemona's song even seems to reveal something she will not admit to herself, let alone to Emilia: that she knows or suspects the true cause of Othello's anger:

> I called my love false love; but what said he then?
>   Sing willow, willow, willow:
> If I court moe women, you'll couch with moe men.
>
> (54–6)

Desdemona could not say the word 'whore' (4.2.163), and would not be prepared in other circumstances to use the indecorous term 'couch'. She can, however, utter it in a song – but plainly, for this purpose the song must be an existing one, a text to repeat and not a new composition; 'an old thing'.

It seems universally agreed that Desdemona's singing is an example of Shakespeare's highest dramatic power. As if that were not enough, the 'willow' song had sufficient emotive charge to affect the rest of this extraordinary scene, the rest of this extraordinary play. Desdemona's request for her bedsheet to become her shroud has been related to the influence of the willow garland as a symbolic object in the ballad, and Bradley suggested that 'when Desdemona spoke her last words' – 'Nobody – I myself. Farewell' – 'perhaps that line of the ballad which she sang an hour before ['Let nobody blame him . . .'] was still busy in her brain'.[24] Emilia's recapitulation of Barbara's death ('She died singing it') in 5.2 draws on the same emotive energies. For all this, Shakespeare is indebted neither to the classics nor the Italians; not to his contemporaries, nor to the realms of professional writing; but to a song so familiar as to be barely noticeable any longer as a vehicle of tragic emotion, and which, whatever its ultimate origins, now belongs firmly to popular culture. One more apparent paradox seems worth stressing. Our initial expectation would be that popular songs go with comedy, art songs with tragedy. As far as this discussion has shown, in Shakespeare it would be much truer to say the opposite.

Chapter Nine

SHAKESPEARE'S RESIDUALS: THE CIRCULATION OF BALLADS IN CULTURAL MEMORY

Bruce R. Smith

When John Danter entered into the Stationers' Company register on 6 February 1594 his rights to 'a booke intituled *a Noble Roman Historye of TYTUS ANDRONICUS*' as well as 'the ballad thereof',[1] he was securing for himself what today's entertainment business knows as 'residuals'. The quarto that Danter went on to publish later that year presents itself on the title page as a repeat, in a different medium, of a stage performance: *The Most Lamentable Romaine Tragedie of Titus Andronicus: As it was Plaide by the Right Honourable the Earle of Darbie, Earle of Pembroke, and Earle of Sussex their Seruants* (STC 22328). Danter, Jonathan Bate argues, may have had in mind one quite specific performance by an amalgam of actors from these three companies just a month before Danter entered his copyright.[2] Each time the broadside ballad inspired by the play was purchased, Danter collected a fee. No copies of the 1594 printing survive, but at least seven reprintings of the ballad 'The Lamentable and Tragical History of Titus Andronicus' in the seventeenth century (the latest in 1700) testify to a continuing commercial viability that rivals that of the playscript, reprinted in 1600 and 1611 and included in the folios of Shakespeare's *Comedies, Histories, and Tragedies* in 1623, 1632, 1663 and 1685.[3] In the medium of broadside ballad, repeat performances would have been even closer to the theatre, as the purchaser got the text by heart and sang it, to the tune of 'Fortune My Foe', in the dramatic first person of Titus himself. Until 1642, of course, Shakespeare's company could continue to collect royalties on any repeat stage performances of the play. References to such revivals between 1594 and 1642 are nil, however – in sharp contrast to the many repeat performances, in different media, by purchasers of the quartos and broadsides. 'Titus Andronicus's Complaint', as the ballad came to be entitled, is far from unique in the Shakespeare residuals business. Thomas Percy in *Reliques of Ancient English Poetry* (1765) includes among 'Ballads That Illustrate Shakespeare' not only 'Titus' but broadsides that spin out narrative strands from *The Taming of the Shrew*, *The Merchant of Venice*, and *King Lear*. Those four ballads – and the ways they circulate in memory – constitute my subject here.

Residuals in the contemporary entertainment industry work in a similar way to Danter's exclusive deal with *Titus Andronicus*. *OED* cites no usage earlier than 1966 of *residual* as 'a royalty paid to an actor, musician, etc., for a repeat of a play, television commercial, etc.' (*OED*, 'residual', *n.*, 4), but as early as 1941 radio performers who recorded live programmes on the East Coast of the United States were being paid extra for rebroadcasts of the same shows on the West Coast a few hours later. In 1951 the first residuals were paid for movies shown on television. A series of strikes by the Screen Actors' Guild in the 1950s, 1960s and 1970s helped to establish the practice and expand it, so that today hundreds of millions of dollars in residuals are paid out each year to writers, directors and performers. As often as not residuals involve a transfer between media: films that become television broadcasts, soundtracks that become CDs, stage performances that become videotapes. In Los Angeles, you can find the Re$iduals (*sic*) Bar on Ventura Boulevard in Studio City. Founded, according to the establishment's website, by a group of writers, producers and directors, the bar features multiple VCR, DVD and CD players that presumably allow patrons to watch and hear repetitions of their own work while they spend some of their residuals on drink and food.

During the sixteenth and seventeenth centuries, in the absence of electromagnetic sound recording, moving pictures on celluloid, and digitized sound and images on videotape and DVD, printed ballads functioned as a way of perpetuating stage performances by transferring them into a different, less time-bound medium. Ballads did not *record* performances;

they *perpetuated* them. They enabled performances to happen again and again as new performers learned the words and took up the story. With respect to stage plays, ballads functioned as residuals in a more fundamental sense than royalty payments. The core idea of *residual* is, after all, *residuum*, something left over or left behind. The technical uses of the term in mathematics (*OED*, 'residual', *n.*, 1.a–b), statistics (1.c), geophysics (2.b) and geology (5), as well as the entertainment business (4), all depend on this 'remaindered' quality. Landscapes of the American Southwest show residuals in the form of buttes and mesas that have been left behind by erosion. In a similar way, ballads stand as what remains after stage performances are over and done with, what lingers like particles of dust when actors have melted into thin air, what racks are in fact left behind when the cloud-capped towers have dissolved. As evidence of what versifiers, singers and listeners found worthy of remembering and keeping alive, broadside ballads can be set alongside the memoranda of Shakespeare performances in Simon Forman's notebooks, John Manningham's diary, or Henry Jackson's letter to a friend.[4] None of these witnesses records the entirety of the play he saw on a given occasion; rather, each writer perpetuates the performance in the portions that struck him most. Forman, famously, forgot that Hermione's statue comes to life at the end of *The Winter's Tale* (unless it didn't in the version of the script he happened to see), but he devotes fully a third of his account of *Macbeth* to the Doctor who attends Lady Macbeth in her last illness. *Memorandum*: Forman himself was a self-licensed doctor.[5]

Understandably we want to seize on Forman, Manningham and Jackson as objective witnesses. What we get for all our grasping, however, is subjective memory. Ballads, I wish to argue, function in the same way as these prose accounts do, as documents of memory. Instead of personal memories, however, ballads offer us cultural memories of Shakespeare. Or rather they offer us both. In the case of ballads the cultural *is* the personal, since each performance involves acts of impersonation on the parts of both singers and listeners. The four narrative ballads collected in the Shakespeare section of *Reliques of Ancient English Poetry* are said by Percy to 'illustrate Shakespeare'. What they illustrate instead is cultural memory *after* Shakespeare. Ballads give us the *re-*, the *after*, in *residual*.

Before turning to Percy's four Shakespeare ballads, let us consider how ballads circulate within Shakespeare's own scripts as tokens of cultural memory.

* * *

Shakespeare's invocations of ballads call forth two qualities in particular: pastness and passion. On occasion songs get performed in their entirety in Shakespeare's scripts, especially in scripts written after Robert Armin brought his singing talents to the company in about 1599,[6] but more often than not ballads are sung or cited only in snatches. With respect to the present they serve as reference points to the past, as gestures towards experiences that the audience, like the protagonists, is presumed already to have had. Ballads establish a commonality of memory that unifies the audience and imbricates its members in the fictional world of the play. The midnight revels of *Twelfth Night* 2.3 offer a good example. In the midst of the carousing, Feste, played originally by Robert Armin, stops the show long enough to sing two verses of 'O mistress mine' (2.3.40–53). His performance inspires Sir Toby and Sir Andrew to join Feste and make up a trio. 'But shall we make the welkin dance indeed?' Sir Toby exclaims. 'Shall we rouse the night-owl in a catch that will draw three souls out of one weaver? Shall we do that?' (2.3.58–60). 'Hold thy peace, thou knave' rouses Maria as well as the night-owl. Although Shakespeare specifies the words to 'O Mistress Mine', the stage direction in the 1623 Folio for 'Hold thy peace' says only '*Catch sung*'.[7] *That* song, so the script implies, the actors and the audience know already. Why write out the words? Similarly with 'Three merry men be we' (2.3.77–8), 'There dwelt a man in Babylon, Lady, Lady' (2.3.79–80), and 'O' the twelfth day of December' (2.3.85): these songs are merely cued, not transcribed. The latter two probably derive from printed broadsides.[8]

Another group of characters full of ballads is Falstaff and his boon companions in Gloucestershire. Earlier in *2 Henry IV* Falstaff has blustered into Mistress Quickly's tavern with a drunken conflation of two ballads on his lips – 'When Arthur first in court . . . And was a worthy king' (2.4.33–4) – but he really comes into his element when he is sitting around in Justice Shallow's country garden along with Shallow, Silence, Davy and Bardolph. Snatches of six songs enliven their conversation in 5.3, the last of them a line or two from 'Robin Hood and the Jolly Pinder of Wakefield'. As Peter Seng observes (p.53), Silence's song, like Falstaff's mangling together of 'Sir Lancelot du Lac' and 'John Careless' in 2.3, 'evokes a world of the past, a world concerned with a kind of honor and *gentilesse* that the fat old knight and his cronies in Eastcheap and Gloucestershire are far from sharing'. Or is it nostalgia for the lost world of their youth that harmonizes the old men's exchanges? Either way, the ballads come across as ironic. The same holds true for Benedick, the confirmed bachelor, when he tries out his voice on 'The god of love, / That sits above, / And knows me, and knows me' (*MA* 5.2.24–6) – a hit song that was already enjoying lots of residuals in the form of parodies and moralizations.[9] For there to be irony there has to be knowledge, *prior* knowledge. The ballads in Shakespeare's plays possess an 'always-already' quality. They bring to presence something that exists somewhere else and will continue to exist there, long after the present moment has passed. It is the metonymy of singers' and listeners' bodies that effects the connection of an already existing past with the dramatic present – and assures that the dramatic present, in its turn, becomes part of that already existing past.

In *The Defence of Poesie* Sir Philip Sidney praises verse for exceeding prose 'in the knitting up of the memory'. Experts in memory, Sidney says, have likened that human faculty to a room in which each idea or element finds a place:

> they that have taught the Art of memory have shewed nothing so
> apt for it as a certaine roome divided into many places well and
> throughly knowne. Now, that hath the verse in effect perfectly, every
> word having his naturall seate, which seate must needes make the
> words remembred.[10]

Ballads passed down in oral tradition display this spatialized quality of memory in particularly striking ways. James H. Jones, drawing on anthropological fieldwork by Milman Parry and Albert B. Lord, has demonstrated how the quatrain structure and formulaic phrases of English and Scottish popular ballads help to fix the ballad in a singer's memory at the same time that they allow for improvisation.[11] David Buchan in *The Ballad and the Folk* confirms Jones's findings.[12] As texts designed for memorization, Shakespeare's scripts sometimes replicate the symmetrical structure of oral ballads like 'Edward' (Child no. 13),[13] in which the singer, rather than proceeding in linear fashion from a beginning to a middle to an end, moves depthwise towards a centre and then out again.[14] Even printed broadside ballads, as I tried to demonstrate in *The Acoustic World of Early Modern England* (pp.203–5), are designed as mnemonic devices. Replications of the designated tune serve to fix the words in the singer's mind; woodcuts give the singer visual reference points for the subject positions and sequence of events in the story.

In both oral and printed forms, ballads are implicated in memory. They reside in the body. Their residual traces are to be found, not only in the brain, but in diaphragm, lungs, mouth, ears – and heart. The last organ is precisely where Sidney locates his experience of the ballad of *Chevy Chase* (Child no. 162; Percy Book 1, no. 1): 'I never heard the olde song of *Percy* and *Douglas* that I found not my heart moved more then with a Trumpet; and yet is it sung but by some blinde Crouder, with no rougher voyce then rude stile' (*Defence of Poesie*, p.106). Rude, yes, but blind? Why should Sidney specify that the ballad-singer be blind? Homer is reputed to have been blind, of course, and singing ballads on the street or at markets and fairs was something that blind people could do to support themselves in early modern England, but Sidney's reference focuses attention on the power of ballads to subvert the certainty of vision. Sung ballads have the power to invade the very body of the listener. If Sidney is embarrassed about his fondness for the ballad of *Chevy Chase* – 'I have to confesse my own barbarousnes', he says before anything else (p.106) – it is because the ballad's primary appeal is not to his faculty of judgement but to his susceptibility to passion. As Thomas Wright explains in *The Passions of the Minde in Generall* (1604), passions find their natural seat in the heart just as understanding does in the brain:

> the very seate of all Passions, is the heart, both of men and beasts . . . for as the brayne fitteth best, for the softnesse and moysture, to receiue the formes and prints of obiects for vnderstanding; euen so the heart endued with most fiery spirits, fitteth best for affecting.[15]

The passions stand in an uneasy relationship to the rational soul. Reason ought to direct the passions, but the passions have a friendlier working relationship with the senses. The passions can prevent reason from knowing the truth about objects that the body, through the senses, sees, hears, touches, tastes, and smells:

> indeed the Passions, not vnfitly may be compared to greene spectacles, which make all things resemble the colour of greene; euen so, he that loueth, hateth, or by any other passion is vehemently possessed, iudgeth all things that occur in fauour of that passion, to be good and agreeable with reason.[16]

A few sentences later it is not green spectacles that the passions impose but a blindfold.

Passions give Shakespeare's characters their cue to sing. Ophelia in *Hamlet* 4.3 presents the extreme case of a protagonist who exists as much – or more – in song as in speech. Before Ophelia comes on stage singing fragments of a song that sounds like 'Walsingham',[17] the ever-rational Horatio tries to prepare Gertrude for what she is about to see and hear:

> Her speech is nothing,
> Yet the unshaped use of it doth move
> The hearers to collection. They aim at it,
> And botch the words up fit to their own thoughts
>
> (4.5.7–10)

Ophelia's songs speed up the centrifugal gyre from reason towards passion, frustrating the rationalist's impulse towards 'collection'. The fragments of ballads that Edgar sings as Tom o' Bedlam in *Lear* 3.4 are impelled by this same centrifugal force. 'Childe Rowland to the dark tower came, / His word was still "Fie, foh, and fum, / I smell the blood of a British man"' (178–80): in Edgar's parting lines to the audience in 3.4 Lear becomes a phenomenon of blood, smell and phatic cries, even as his present suffering is enfolded into a future that is history for the audience. If Geoffrey of Monmouth is right that Lear was the tenth Celtic king after Brutus (placing Lear's reign in the ninth century BCE), then Roland of Roncevalles (eighth century CE) would post-date Lear by a millennium. In Tom o'Bedlam's singing Lear becomes an entity the audience already knows, indeed has always known. What resides as memory in Tom's song, as in all of Shakespeare's quoted ballads, is passion, passion that wells up from a past that unites actors and audiences across the platform's edge.[18] Ballads in Shakespeare's plays help to establish a sense of common culture. The ground for that common culture is not chronological knowledge but *feeling*.

* * *

The ballad of *Chevy Chase* may be an occasion for apologetic nostalgia for Sidney, but for Thomas Percy it figures in an enterprise of high serious-ness. In *Reliques of Ancient English Poetry* (1765) Percy attempts to doc-ument an age of 'minstrelsy' that does for British culture what Homer and Virgil did for classical culture.[19] In this endeavour ballads figure as forms of epic. Precedent for such claims is to be found in the three-volume *Collection of Old Ballads* published in 1723–5. According to the anonymous compiler of that anthology:

> the very Prince of Poets, old *Homer*, if we may trust ancient Records, was nothing more than a blind *Ballad-singer*, who writ Songs of the Siege of Troy, and the Adventures of *Ulysses*; and playing the Tunes upon his Harp, sung from Door to Door, till at his Death somebody thought fit to collect all his Ballads, and by a little connecting 'em, gave us the *Iliad* and *Odysses*, which since that Time have been so much admired.[20]

Like Homer, the editor claims, the writers of the old British ballads were 'the greatest and most polite Wits of their Age'; their language was 'the purest that was used in their Days'. Indeed, Sidney's commendation of *Chevy Chase* 'is in a much ruder Stile than the Ballad it self'.[21] The edi-tor's claims were extravagant enough to invite ridicule, or so his prefaces to Volumes Two and Three imply. Percy may be more tactful, but his pro-ject proceeds from the same assumption: as relics of a vanished heroic age, ballads figure as the source for contemporary British literary cul-ture. The fact that Percy should devote one of the collection's nine books to Shakespeare stands as testimony not only to Shakespeare's cultural capital in the eighteenth century but to Shakespeare's importance as an intermediary between the age of minstrelsy and the age of reason. Percy carefully designed the engravings that embellish the first edition of *Reliques*.[22] The image for Volume I, Book II, 'Ballads That Illustrate Shakespeare', captures Shakespeare's chronological position precisely (see Figure 14). As minstrels sing, Shakespeare listens (note the cocked head), marvels at what he hears (note the expressive left hand), and *writes* (note the quill in the right hand). On a podium between the minstrels

𝔄 𝔫 𝔠 𝔦 𝔢 𝔫 𝔱

SONGS AND BALLADS,

&*c.*

SERIES THE FIRST.
BOOK II.

BALLADS THAT ILLUSTRATE SHAKESPEARE.

FIGURE 14   Title page from Thomas Percy, *Reliques of Ancient English Poetry* (1765).

and Shakespeare rest the writings that figured in the eighteenth century, and continue to figure today, as prime exhibits in the museum of British culture. In Percy's scheme, ballads are not residuals of Shakespeare; Shakespeare is a residual of ballads.

'A Lamentable Song of the death of King Leare and his three Davghters' presents a crucial test for Percy's chronological argument. The ballad made its first surviving appearance in print in what purports to be the third edition of Richard Johnson's *The Golden Garland of Princely pleasures and delicate Delights* (1620), an anthology that includes commercially produced ballads as well as ballads with connections to oral tradition. The subtitle describes the collection as '*the Histories of many of the Kings, Queenes, Princes, Lords, Ladies, Knights, and Gentle worthies of the Kingdome*'. Possibly because Lear's story is the oldest, Lear's ballad comes first. Despite the thoroughly commercial character of Johnson's book, the early eighteenth-century editor of *A Collection of Old Ballads* includes 'Lear' and insists on its antiquity. 'I cannot be certain directly to the Time when this Ballad was written', he declares, 'but that it was some Years before the Play of *Shakespear*, appears from several Circumstances, which to mention would swell my Introduction too far beyond its usual length.'[23] What those 'several Circumstances' might be remains a mystery. Of external proofs there are, in fact, none. Samuel Johnson makes the best possible case for the ballad's priority in his edition of Shakespeare's plays, published the same year as Percy's *Reliques*, but his reasons are limited to internal details – what is *not* included in the ballad as well as what is. The story, except for the subplot involving Edmund, is taken originally from Geoffrey of Monmouth, so Johnson reports, 'but perhaps more immediately from an old historical ballad'.[24] Most unusually, Johnson incorporates most of this possible source (sixteen of the ballad's twenty-three stanzas) in his commentary. In the 1773 edition the missing stanzas, in which Lear questions his daughters, are likewise supplied. Johnson's logic betrays how fervently – how passionately – he wants the ballad to be the play's authentic source:

> My reason for believing that the play was posteriour to the ballad rather than the ballad to the play, is, that the ballad has nothing

of Shakespeare's nocturnal tempest, which is too striking to have been omitted, and that it follows the chronicle; it has the rudiments of the play, but none of its amplifications: it first hinted Lear's madness, but did not array it in circumstances. The writer of the ballad added something to the history, which is a proof that he would have added more, if more had occurred to his mind, and more must have occurred if he had seen Shakespeare.[25]

Like Johnson, Percy notes in the ballad 'the hint of Lear's madness, which the old chronicles do not mention', as well as the daughters' cruelty and the circumstances of Lear's death. Finally, however, Percy is less willing than Johnson to make such internal evidence definitive: 'this the Reader must weigh and judge for himself', he warns.[26] Passion in the form of nationalist nostalgia is no less prominent than pastness in the eighteenth century's attraction to 'ancient English poetry'.

What Percy chose to include among ballads that illustrate Shakespeare is, by our standards, quite a diverse lot. In addition to the ballads that retell plot elements of *Titus*, *Shrew*, *Merchant* and *Lear*, Percy reproduces (a) narrative ballads that receive momentary mention in Shakespeare's scripts – 'Adam Bell, Clym of the Clough, and William of Cloudesly' alluded to in *Much Ado*; 'King Cophetua and the Beggar-Maid', *LLL* 1.2, *RJ* 2.2, and *2H4* 5.3; 'Sir Lancelot du Lake', *2H4* 2.4; 'There dwelt a man in Babylon', *TN* 2.3; (b) one dialogue song – 'Take Thy Old Cloak About Thee', a stanza of which is sung by Iago in *Oth* 2.2; and (c) no fewer than seven texts that we would classify as songs or lyric poems – the supposed original of the gravedigger's song in *Ham* 5.1; 'Where griping griefs the hart would wound' from *Romeo* 4.5; the expanded version of Desdemona's 'Willow Song' in the broadside version 'A Lover's Complaint'; Marlowe's 'The Passionate Shepherd' and Ralegh's 'The Nymph's Reply' from *Merry Wives* 3.1; 'Take, oh take, those lips away' from *Measure for Measure* 4.1; and 'Crabbed age and youth / Cannot live together' from *The Passionate Pilgrim* – not to mention (d) a pastiche of Percy's own invention that turns song fragments from Shakespeare's plays into a lovers-reunited ballad with the title 'The Friar of Orders Gray'. Percy submitted his 'little TALE . . . to the Reader's candour'.[27] At least one such reader, the scholarly ballad editor Joseph Ritson, found the exercise unforgivably fatuous.[28]

The 'promiscuous' quality of Percy's choices – the adjective is Percy's own[29] – serves as a reminder that in Percy's time 'ballad' still carried its sixteenth- and seventeenth-century sense of 'a light, simple song of *any* kind' (*OED*, 'ballad', 2; my emphasis). The notion of a ballad as 'a simple spirited poem in short stanzas . . . in which some popular story is graphically *narrated*' (*OED* 5, my emphasis) dates only from the late eighteenth century. 'Ancient Songs and Ballads' is the running title in Percy's *Reliques*. The miscellaneous quality of Autolycus' repertory – 'When daffodils begin to peer', 'But shall I go mourn for that, my dear', 'Jog on, jog on, the footpath way', 'Lawn as white as driven snow', 'Get you hence, for I must go', 'Will you buy any tape', along with the broadside ballads about prodigies that fill his pack (all in *WT* 4.4) – are very much in the spirit of Percy's collection. It takes attendance at only a few poetry readings these days to demonstrate that the formalist distinction between narrative poetry and lyric poetry does not ring true to experience. Poets, when they read their work to an audience, are always supplying stories into which their poems can be fitted, just as readers who encounter lyric poems in printed isolation from other poems by the same writer *tell* the poems to themselves. In effect, readers insert the poems they encounter into their own life stories. A good argument could be made that lyrics as well as narrative ballads can function as residuals, that the 'Willow Song' captures something as essential to *Othello* as the events that actually transpire in the play.[30] Even as I concentrate on four of the narrative ballads in Percy that perpetuate Shakespeare's stories, I would argue that the drift of cultural memory is towards those moments of suspended action and intense feeling that, since the Romantics, we have come to call 'lyric'.

* * *

Hard as Johnson laboured to establish the priority of 'A Lamentable Song of the death of King Leare and his three Davghters', it seems patently clear today that all four of Percy's ballads 'illustrating' *Titus, Shrew, Merchant* and *Lear* functioned in their own day as commercially produced residuals. All four ballads perpetuate prior theatrical performances.

What gets perpetuated in each case? What aspects of the theatrical production make it into the ballad? What are the *residua*, and where in human consciousness do they reside? Answers to these questions will help us chart the ways in which these four plays circulated in cultural memory down through the eighteenth century. In the process, we can learn to appreciate how ballads offer themselves as neglected documents in the history of the cultural institution known as 'Shakespeare'. I propose to take up the four ballads in the order of the plays' likely first performances: *Titus* (1589–94), *Shrew* (1593–4), *Merchant* (1594–6) and *Lear* (1605–6).

Of the four ballads, the one with the demonstrably closest connection to a Shakespeare script is 'Titus'. Danter's joint entry in the Stationers' Register invites us to consider the ballad as an instance of media transfer, from play into ballad. What that transfer entails, most remarkably, is a shift from the play's multiple speakers to the ballad's one:

> You Noble minds, and famous Martial Wights,
> That in defence of Native Countries fights,
> Give ear to me that ten years fought for *Rome*,
> Yet reap'd disgrace at my returning home

(stanza 1)

The 'me' who is installed here sings all thirty of the ballad's stanzas – including the penultimate stanza, in which the singing 'I' takes his own life. No less emphatically present in all thirty stanzas is the 'you' who appears in the ballad's very first word. The entire transaction becomes an intimate exchange between this solitary singing 'I' and the listening 'you'. Characters in plays, Bert O. States observes, don't just feed each other lines; they feed each other *character*. Even such seemingly stand-alone protagonists as Hamlet need other characters for their very existence.[31] In the ballad of 'Titus' this existential situation is extreme: other than 'I', the only other physically present entity is 'you'. Indeed, the impulse behind the ballad is to turn that listening 'you' into the singing 'I'. The ballad's title in some later printings, 'Titus Andronicus's Complaint', suggests the connection of Titus with the speakers in *A Mirror for Magistrates*, ghosts who come back from the dead to recount the circumstances of their own deaths. Yet another connection is with convicts, whose scaffold confessions took the form of a balladized 'complaint'.[32] What resides amid the many reprintings of 'Titus Andronicus's Complaint' between 1594 and 1700 is intense first-person suffering – suffering that becomes the listener's own.

Bullough and Bate have detailed the coincidences and the minor differences between events dramatized in the play and narrated in the ballad.[33] Alike as the incidents are, the ballad has its own distinctive ways of *structuring* them, of putting them into memory. In keeping with the centralized design of most oral ballads, the ballad of 'Titus' moves in towards a central event, the violation of Lavinia in stanzas 13–15, and then out again, balancing the story of Titus' conquests in the first four stanzas (1–4) with the story of Titus' revenge in the last four (9–12).[34] The movement towards the centre and out again happens via two kinds of links: 'then'/'and when' and 'yet'/'but'. The first stanza's 'Yet reap'd disgrace' finds its first echo in the stanza introducing Lavinia's rape: 'But now behold what wounded most my mind' (13). The 'but' links continue, as new atrocities are added to Titus' pain: Titus' first sight of his mutilated daughter (17) and the return of his severed hand along with the heads of his two surviving sons (23). In the course of this sequence, 'Yet . . . when . . . and so . . . then . . . but now', the singer keeps turning obsessively to certain parts of the human body: blood, tears, tongue, hand. As with Marcus' grotesque blazon of Lavinia's bleeding, handless, tongueless body in 2.3 of the play, the ballad focuses blood, tears, tongue and hand on Lavinia's body before finding radiations in Titus' 'tears of blood' (17), his wish that 'the hand that fought for Countryes / In cradle rockt had first been strucken lame' (26), his 'bleeding heart' (22), the 'bootless hand' that the Emperor returns to him (23), the implicit hand that effects bloody revenges on the oppressors (27–30), perhaps even the blood that thickens the meat pies:

> I cut their throats, my daughter held the pan
> Betwixt her stumps, wherein the blood it ran:
> And then I ground their bones to powder small
> And made a paste for Pies straight therewithal
>
> (stanza 27)

Blood, tears, tongue and hand figure in the ballad's concern with 'writing' grief. As Lavinia writes the identity of her attackers in a plot of sand, so Titus 'with my tears writ in the dust my woes' (24). The downward motion of Titus' tears in the first half of stanza 24 finds its counterpart in the arrows he shoots towards heaven in the second half – arrows that Percy connects with Psalm 64: 3: 'They shoot out their arrowes, even bitter words.'[35] Writing in 'Titus Andronicus's Complaint' happens through the suffering body of the ballad's 'I', through blood, tears, tongue, hand. Memory traces of Shakespeare's play are written, not on paper, but on the singer's body, and, through that aural amanuensis, on the listener's body. These body-based memories circulated in early modern culture as widely as – perhaps more widely than – the printed script of Shakespeare's play. Just as play and ballad first saw print in 1594, so the appearance of the First Folio in 1623 was followed the next year by a new entry for the ballad of 'Titus' in the Stationers' Register and by new printings in 1625 and 1628/9. Publication of the Third Folio in 1663 coincided with the illustrated reissue of the ballad (Wing L252A) from which I have been quoting. A further reissue of the 'Titus' ballad (Wing L252B) reached the streets at about the time the Fourth Folio appeared in booksellers' shops in 1685. In the meantime the ballad of 'Titus' circulated in a form somewhere in between ballad and book, through its inclusion in Richard Johnson's *Golden Garland*, perhaps in as many as thirteen editions if the title page to the 1690 reprinting (Wing J804A) can be believed. The two copies of the broadside that Pepys acquired (STC11796.5, *c.*1625, and Wing L254A, 1658/9) ended up in two different thematic sections of his collection, the earlier one under 'devotion & morality', the later under 'history – true and fabulous'.[36] Circulation in the more private form of manuscript can be witnessed in the early eighteenth-century chapbook that combines the ballad and a prose narrative that has sometimes been taken as a source for Shakespeare's play but is more likely a pastiche of play and ballad.[37] The ballad's not particularly prominent place in the Shakespeare section of Percy's *Reliques* (item 11 of 16), and Percy's doubts about Shakespeare's authorship of the play in the first place,[38] indicate a forgetting of the ballad's hold on cultural memory in the seventeenth century and the ascendance of a literary sensibility that found 'A Lamentable Song of the death of King Leare and his three Davghters' more suitable for learned commentary.

'The Frolicksome Duke: Or, The Tinker's good Fortune' (Wing F2236A, *c.*1690) does for the frame plot of *The Taming of the Shrew* what ballads about scolding women do for the main plot of Petruchio's taming of Kate.[39] In both cases, the ballads would seem to affirm conventional ways of thinking about class and gender. But 'The Frolicksome Duke' has much more subversive potential than the ballads about scolds. The opening stanza establishes a 'you' that is outside the story, someone looking on and laughing:

> Now as fame does report, a young duke keeps a court,
> One that pleases his fancy with frolicksome sport:
> Now amongst all the rest, here is one I protest,
> Which make you to smile when you hear the true j[e]st.[40]

The true jest, however, turns out to involve a double perspective. The wealth of incidental details – the star-emblazoned clothing put upon the tinker (5), the golden-canopied chair of state in which he is seated (7), the specifically Spanish wines ('Rich canary with sherry, and tent [= tinto] superfine') that make him 'seven times drunker then ever before' (8) – can either be laughed at from without on the scoffer's part, or luxuriously enjoyed from within on the tinker's part. The tinker does not remain the third-person butt of the joke. In the course of the ballad he is given a voice, an *internal* voice: 'For he said to himself, *Where is Joan my sweet wife? / Sure she never did see me so fine in her life*' (5). That voice comes into its own towards the end, when the sobered-up tinker is brought back to the court and exchanges speeches with the Duke who has tricked him. The Duke hails him as '*a jolly bold blade*' and offers to become '*thy good friend, / Nay, and* Joan *thy sweet wife shall my dutchess attend*' (11). The last stanza is the tinker's, as he rejoices in the 'good Fortune' of the ballad's subtitle. The residual in this version of Shakespeare's frame plot is a dream come true – a residual that may in its own way be a comment on the wish-fulfilling gender politics of the play's main plot.

The comic double perspective of 'The Frolicksome Duke' – the 'not I' who becomes 'I' in the course of the ballad – is especially complicated in 'A new Song, shewing the crueltie of Gernutus a Iew'. The section in which Pepys pasted down this particular broadside, as with one of his two copies of 'Titus Andronicus', was the section reserved for 'devotion

& morality'.[41] Perhaps Pepys took his cue from the emphatically moral-
ized conclusion to the ballad:

> Good people that do heare this song
> for trueth I dare well say,
> That many a wretch as ill as he,
> doth liue now at this day.
>
> That seeketh nothing but the spoyle
> of many a wealthy man:
> And for to trap the Innocent,
> deuiseth what they can.
> From whom, the Lord deliuer me,
> and euery Christian too:
> And send to them like sentence eke
> that meaneth so to doe.[42]

The 'I' who sings these final stanzas emerges quite unexpectedly out of
the various incarnations of 'I' who sing earlier in the ballad. The most
persistent of these dramatic 'I's' is none other than Gernutus the Jew of
Venice. He commands thirty-one lines against the Merchant's mere six.
The first of two woodcuts that accompany the 1620 printing of the ballad establishes the Jew's dominant position (see Figure 15). Wearing a
hat that was fashionable in early Stuart England but recalls as well the
conical hats that Jews wore in medieval iconography, Gernutus is surrounded by pots, *chamber* pots, of his filthy lucre. The connection of lucre
with faeces is made explicit in comparisons of Gernutus' life to that of 'a
Barrow-hog' that does no one any good till it is slain (3) or 'a filthy heape
of Dung' that does no one any good 'till it be spread abroade' (4). The
Jew's emergence into first-personhood comes via a third-person invocation of the poor who are the ultimate victims of his usury:

> His heart doth thinke on many a wile,
> how to deceiue the poore:
> His mouth is almost ful of mucke,
> yet still he gapes for more

(stanza 6)

A new Song, shewing the crueltie of Gernutus a Iew, who lending to a Marchant a hundred Crownes, would haue a pound of his flesh, because he could not pay him at the day appoynted. To the tune of, Blacke and Yellow.

In Venice towne not long agoe,
a cruell Iew did dwell,
Which lined all on Vsurie,
as Italian writes tell.

Gernutus called was the Iew,
which neuer thought to die,
Nor neuer yet did any good,
to them in streetes that lie.

His life was like a Barrow-hog,
that liueth many a day:
Yet neuer once doth any good,
until men will him slay.

Or like a filthy heape of Dung,
that lyeth in a whoard,
Which neuer can doe any good,
till it be spread abroad.

So fares it with the Vsurer,
he can not sleepe in rest:
For feare the theefe will him pursue,
to plucke him from his nest.

His heart doth thinke on many a wile,
how to deceiue the poore:
His mouth is almost ful of mucke,
yet still he gapes for more.

His wife must lend a Shilling,
for euery weeke a penny,
Yet bring a pledge that's double worth,
if that you will haue any.

And see likewise you keepe your day,
or else you loose it all:
This was the liuing of the Wife,
her Cow she did it call.

Within that Citie not that time,
a Marchant of great fame,
Which being distressed in his need,
vnto Gernutus came.

Desiring him to stand his friend,
for twelue month and a day,
To lend to him an hundred Crownes,
and he for it would pay

Whatsoeuer he would demaund of him,
and pledges he should haue.
No (quoth the Iew with flearing lookes)
Sir aske what you will haue.

No penny for the lone of it,
for one yeare you shall pay:
You may doe me as good a turne,
before my dying day:

But we will haue a merry iest,
for to be talked long:
You shall make me a Band (quoth he)
that shall be large and strong.

And this shall be the forfeyture,
of your owne Flesh a pound:
If you agree, make you the Band,
and here is a hundred Crownes.

With right good-will the Marchant sayd,
and so the Band was made.
When twelue month and a day drew on,
that backe it should be payd,

The Marchants Ships were all at Seas,
and Mony came not in:
Which way to take, or what to doe,
to thinke he both begin.

And to Gernutus straight he comes,
with cap and bended knee:
And sayd to him, of curtesie.
I pray you beare with mee.

My day is come, and I haue not
the Mony for to pay:
And litle good the forfeyture
will doe you, I dare say.

With all my heart, Gernutus sayd,
commaund it to your minde,
In things of bigger waight then this
you shall me ready finde.

He goes his way, the day once past
Gernutus doth not slacke,
To get a Sergiant presently,
and clapt him on the backe:

And layed him into Prison strong,
and sued his Band withall.
And when the iudgement day was come,
for iudgement he did call.

The Marchants friendes came thither fast,
with many a weeping eye,
For other meanes they could not find,
but he that day must die.

FIGURE 15 *A new Song, shewing the crueltie of Gernutus a Iew* (1620).

What the singer and the listener confront in Part One of the ballad are, in effect, two subject positions. Implicitly they are invited to identify with the poor, but most of the words they actually sing and hear as 'I' come out of the mouth of Gernutus. Deceptive heart and gaping mouth are, indeed, the body parts that epitomize the Jew and characterize his speech acts, as he entices the Merchant to sign the bond for a pound of flesh. There is a suggestive metonymy between the physicality of the 'band' and the physicality of the Merchant's body: 'You shall make me a Band', says the Jew, 'that shall be large and strong' (13). That physicality becomes ever more substantial as the money falls due and the 'band' gets tightened. The Merchant sings his six first-person lines, begging for mercy 'with cap [in hand] and bended knee' (17). To the Merchant's face the Jew promises leniency. But as soon as the day is done, the Jew works behind the Merchant's back and begins his physical torture:

> He goes his way, the day once past
> > *Gernutus* doth not slacke,
> To get a Sergiant presently,
> > and clapt him on the backe:
>
> And layed him into Prison strong,
> > and sued his Band withal
> > > (stanzas 20-1)

Part Two turns the tables as a Judge transforms first-person utterance into two-person dialogue. In the woodcut the Judge appears as a king with crown and sceptre, accompanied by two other figures who establish the 'us'-against-'him' situation that isolates the Jew, and, in the course of the verses, deprives him of his vocal power (see Figure 16). But not before the Jew's singing 'I' has refused all counter-offers – 'A pound of flesh is my desire, / and that shall be my hire' (25) – and come within inches of realizing his designs on the Merchant's body. Take the flesh, the Judge orders, from such a place as will let the Merchant live. No, sings the Jew, 'For I will haue my pound of flesh / from vnder his right side' (27). The Jew, 'with whetted blade in hand', is just on the point of 'spoiling' the Merchant's blood (29) when the Judge intervenes a second time: in claiming the pound

The Second part of the Iewes crueltie, setting foorth the
mercifulnesse of the Iudge towardes the Marchant.
To the tune of Blacke and yellow.

Some offred for his hundred Crownes,
fiue hundred for to pay;
And some a thousand, two, or three;
yet still he did denay.

And at the last, Ten thousand Crownes
they offred him to saue:
Gernutus said, I will no Gold,
my forfeite I will haue.

A pound of flesh is my desire,
and that shall be my hyre.
Then quoth the Iudge, yet good my friend,
let me of you desire,

To take the flesh from such a place,
as yet you hurt him liue:
Else fiue hundred an hundred Crownes,
to thee here will I giue.

No, no, (quoth he) no iudgement here,
for this it shalbe tride,
For I a will haue my pound of flesh
from vnder his right side.

It grieued all the companie,
his crueltie to see:
For neither friend nor foe could helpe,
but he must spoyled bee,

The blood ... running ... vp is,
with ... blood in hand,
To spoyle the blood of Innocent,
by tyrants of his Band.

And as he was about to strike,
in him the death to ...
Stay, quoth the Iudge, thy crueltie,
I charge thee to do so,

With needes thou wilt thy forfeit haue,
which is of flesh a pound:
See that thou shed no drop of blood,
nor yet the man confound.

For if thou doe, like murderer,
thou here shalt hanged bee:
Likewise of flesh see that thou cut,
no more then longes to thee.

For if thou take either more or lesse,
to the value of a Mite,
Thou shalt be hanged presently,
as is both law and right.

Gernutus now wext franticke man,
and wotes not what to say:
Quoth he at last, ten thousand Crownes
I will that he shall pay.

And so I graunt to set him free.
The Iudge doth answere make,
You shall not haue a penny giuen,
your forfeyture now take.

At the last he doth demaund,
but for to haue his owne.
No quoth the Iudge, doe as you lift,
thy Iudgement shalbe showne.

Either take your pound of flesh, quoth he,
or cancell me your Band:
O cruell Iudge, then quoth the Iew,
that doth against me stand.

And so with griping grieued minde,
he biddeth them farewell:
All the people praysed the Lord,
that euer this heard tell.

Good people that doe heare this song,
for trueth I dare well say,
That many a wretch as ill as he,
doth liue now at this day.

That seeketh nothing but the spoyle
of many a wealthy mans
And for to trap the Innocent,
deuiseth what they can.

From whom, the Lord deliuer me,
and euery Christian too:
And send to them like sentence eke,
that meaneth so to doe.

FINIS.

Imprinted at London for T.P.

FIGURE 16   *The Ballad of Gernutus, part two (1620).*

of flesh the Jew must shed no drop of blood (31). The almost mutilated body of the Merchant haunts the ballad of 'Gernutus the Jew of Venice' no less than the multilated body of Lavinia haunts the ballad of 'Titus'.

Numerous details link 'Gernutus' to Shakespeare's *The Merchant of Venice* – Bullough declares, despite the late publication date of 1620, that the ballad 'is probably pre-Shakespearian'[43] – but it is the Jew's subjectivity, his first-person presence, that connects the ballad most closely to Shakespeare's play. More than the deceptive heart, what sticks in memory is the Jew's gaping mouth, the mouth full of muck that would eat the Merchant's carved flesh, the mouth that sings most of the ballad's first-person lines, the mouth that has the last first-person word. Such memories present a crisis of sorts for 'I'. Singer and listener are asked to be both Jew and Christian. Despite the emergence in the last four stanzas of a detached, omniscient 'I' who draws all Christians together into a group behind the woodcut's Judge, Gernutus shares with Shylock a dramatic immediacy that refuses to go away. The crisis of 'I' is perhaps registered in the ballad's several uses of the ethical dative. 'You shall make me a Band', the Jew tells the Merchant (12). 'Either take your pound of flesh', the Judge tells the Jew, 'or cancell me your Band' (37). The phrase is reminiscent of the way Shylock introduces the story of Laban's sheep: 'The skilful shepherd pill'd me certain wands' (*MV* 1.3.79). In both situations, the speaker inserts himself as a reflexive presence in an action that belongs in fact to someone else. In terms of the narrative, the Merchant's body occupies that dative position: it is the recipient of actions performed by both the Jew's speaking 'I' and the Judge's. The ballad of 'the crueltie of Gernutus a Iew', like *The Merchant of Venice*, creates a situation in which 'I' is implicated in bodily practices that inspire fascination no less than abhorrence. Pepys's consignment of the ballad to 'devotion & morality' would seem to deny, and thus forget, any such claims on the singer's and listener's imaginations.

No modern editor takes seriously Samuel Johnson's claim that the ballad of 'Leare' preceded the play. Neither Geoffrey Bullough in *Narrative and Dramatic Sources of Shakespeare* nor R.A. Foakes in the Arden 3 edition of *Lear* finds the ballad worthy of a single mention. At the same time, it is hard to credit Percy's suggestion that the ballad and

Shakespeare's play might both derive from the earlier play of *Leir*, printed in 1605 but probably acted at least a decade earlier.[44] Like
Shakespeare's play, the ballad defies the historical sources in the matter
of Lear's and Cordelia's deaths. *The True chronicle Historie of King Leir and
his three daughters*, to give the older play its full title, ends, like the chronicles, with the old king regaining his kingdom. Leir's closing couplet,
thanking the King of France and Cordella for the victory they have
helped him achieve, sounds a note of triumph: 'Come, sonne and daughter, who did me advaunce, / Repose with me awhile, and then for
Fraunce'.[45] The ballad, like Shakespeare's play, ends in despair, as
Cordelia is killed in battle and Lear dies in a swoon over her body:

> But when he heard *Cordels* dead,
>   who dyed indeed for loue
> Of her deare father, in whose cause
>   she did this battell mooue
> He swounding fell vpon her brest
>   from whence he neuer parted,
> But on her bosome left his life,
>   that was so truely hearted.[46]

What's more, the ballad intimates Lear's madness and sets up cosmic sympathy between his state of mind and the state of nature. Cast out by both
Ragan and Gonorell, Leir considers seeking out the banished Cordela:

> But doubting to repaire to her,
>   whom he had banisht so:
> Grew franticke mad, for in his minde,
>   he bore the wounds of woe.
>
> Which made him rend his milk white locks
>   and tresses from his head:
> And all with blood bestaine his cheekes,
>   with age and honour spred:
> To hils, and woods, and watry founts,
>   he made, his hourely moane:

> Till hills and woods, and sencelesse things,
> did seeme to sigh and groane
>
> (stanzas 17–18)

As with 'Titus Andronicus's Complaint', the ballad of 'King Lear' dis-
tils from the play the subjectivity of the sufferer, and locates that suffering in certain parts of the body: the rent hair, the stained cheeks, above
all the daughter's breast on which the father expires. Visual as those
details might seem, the residuals of Lear's story happen through sound,
through the singer's taking on Lear's personhood and giving it voice.
Percy misses this quality of aural inwardness when he silently changes
'thus have you heard the fall of pride, / And disobedient sin' (23) to 'thus
have you *seen*' (my italics).[47] By the time the ballad of 'Leare' had been
reprinted in the thirteenth edition of Richard Johnson's *Golden Garland*
in 1690, Nahum Tate's version of Shakespeare's play (1681), with its
happy ending, had taken over the stage. Samuel Johnson's preference for
Tate's ending represents a cultural forgetting of just the sort that over-
took the ballad of Titus in the eighteenth century. 'Since all *reasonable*
beings naturally love justice', Johnson concludes in his notes to *Lear*, 'I
cannot easily be persuaded, that the observation of justice makes a play
worse.'[48] In confessing that he was 'so shocked' by Cordelia's death that
he could not bear rereading the last scene until he edited the play,
Johnson refuses the passion, the *unreasonable* passion, that the ballad of
'Leare' perpetuated for nearly a century.

* * *

As residuals of Shakespeare's plays, the four ballads of Titus
Andronicus, the tinker who becomes a duke's friend, the Jew of Venice
and King Lear perpetuate three aspects of performance in particular:
passion, body and first-person subjectivity. The passion in each case may
be different – physical suffering in Titus, luxurious abandon in the tinker,
bloody-mindedness in Gernutus, mental anguish in Lear; but the ballads
ask singers and listeners to *feel* what they sing and hear. To worry too

much whether this or that episode in the play's plot finds its way into the ballad is to miss the point. Memory of the plays is written in, on, and through the human body, in the diaphragm, lungs, tongue, teeth, and lips of the singer, in the ears, heart, and fantasy of the listener. Perhaps it is this physicality of perception that makes ballads so attentive to body parts: Titus' hands, the tinker's gullet, Gernutus' mouth, Lear's hair. What the ballads do above all else is turn the *actors'* story into *my* story. In *The Tragedy of King Lear*, for example, the actor playing the title role establishes his identity in the first scene, not in soliloquy, but in speeches exchanged with (in this order) Gloucester, Goneril, Regan, Cordelia, Kent, Albany, Burgundy and France. Later in the play the Fool emerges as no less necessary to Lear's dramatic existence. Meanwhile, Edmund and Edgar stake claims to the play's story, with only their father Gloucester providing a tenuous link to Lear. By comparison, 'A Lamentable Song of the death of King Leare and his three Davghters' is astonishingly concentrated. Ragan and Gonorell sing for one stanza each, Cordela for half a stanza; otherwise, first-person experience in the ballad is altogether Lear's – and the singer's and the listener's. Ballads turn the diffuse inter-personality of the theatre into first-personality, even as learning to sing the ballad or just hearing it interpolates the consumer into a cultural group whose identity involves a common memory of the ballad.

In his commentary on *King Lear*, Samuel Johnson draws together three distinct kinds of texts: scholarly and theoretical writings by the likes of Thomas Warton and Joseph Addison; Nahum Tate's script for the stage; and the ballad of 'Leare'. Two of these sorts of texts remain familiar to students of early modern theatre today; the third sort, ballads, has been largely forgotten. With scholarly argumentation and theatre history we know the nature of the evidence and what we can do with it; with ballads we don't quite know where to begin. In this essay I have tried to make such a beginning, by suggesting that ballads preserved distinctive kinds of knowledge about Shakespeare's plays as they circulated in cultural memory during the seventeenth and eighteenth centuries. Instead of two parallel tracks of inquiry in Shakespeare studies, one that pursues philology, bibliography, social history, political history, and another that pursues performance history, we need a third track that takes popular culture seriously and finds in that culture ways of knowing that the other tracks neglect. Works of materialist criticism like Michael Bristol's *Big-Time Shakespeare* have taught us to think about Shakespeare's legacy in political and economic terms, as 'cultural capital'.[49] To that materialist understanding of residuals I wish to add a phenomenological understanding that attends to affect and memory. The scholarly tradition in Shakespeare studies can be said to have started with the 1623 Folio and continued with the labours of Warton, Johnson and their many successors. Performance history is already present in Johnson's discussion of Tate's ethically reconceived *King Lear*. With respect to popular culture, Peter Burke has suggested a rift between 'the great tradition' and 'the little tradition' that, in England, began in the 1620s,[50] at just the point when ballads on subjects from Shakespeare's plays began to appear in large numbers. That rift between high culture and low has continued in our own day, even as the 1990s witnessed an unprecedented number of big-time residuals in films like Julie Taymor's *Titus* and Gil Jungen's updating of *Shrew* in *Ten Things I Hate About You*.[51] Shakespeare's residuals began 400 years before that, with ballads. It is a curious coincidence, to say the least, that films offer the same kind of intensely personal experience that ballads do, in a medium that is no less socially inclusive and crassly commercial.

NOTES

INTRODUCTION: SHAKESPEARE AND ELIZABETHAN POPULAR CULTURE

1. See *Shakespeare: The Critical Heritage*, ed. Brian Vickers, 6 vols (London, 1975), vol. 3, p.190.
2. This was particularly evident in Germany: see Johann Gottfried Herder, 'Extract from a Correspondence on Ossian and the Songs of Ancient Peoples' and 'Shakespeare' in *German Aesthetic and Literary Criticism*, ed. H.B. Nisbet (Cambridge, 1985), pp.154–76. Herder thought that both Homer and Shakespeare were transmitting a kind of folk poetry which he regarded as the original language of the human race: see Simon Williams, *Shakespeare on the German Stage: 1586–1914* (Cambridge, 1990), p.20. See also David Hopkins, '"The English Homer": Shakespeare, Longinus, and English "Neo-classicism"', in *Shakespeare and the Classics*, ed. Charles Martindale and A.B. Taylor (Cambridge, 2004), pp.261–76.
3. Jonathan Dollimore, *Radical Tragedy: Religion, Ideology and Power in the Drama of Shakespeare and his Contemporaries*, 3rd edn (Basingstoke, 2004), p.xvii.
4. C.L. Barber, *Shakespeare's Festive Comedy: A Study of Dramatic Form and Its Relation to Social Custom* (Princeton NJ, 1959).
5. Peter Burke, *Popular Culture in Early Modern Europe* (London, 1978); Robert Weimann, *Shakespeare and the Popular Tradition in the Theater: Studies in the Social Dimension of Dramatic Form and Function* (Baltimore MD, 1978); a representative (and influential) article would be Natalie Zemon Davis, 'The Reasons of Misrule: Youth Groups and Charivaris in Sixteenth-Century France', *Past and Present*, 50 (1971), 41–75.
6. Mikhail Bakhtin, *Rabelais and his World*, trans. Hélène Iswolsky (Cambridge MA, 1968). For Bakhtin's influence see Neil Rhodes, *Elizabethan Grotesque* (London, 1980); Michael D. Bristol, *Carnival and Theater: Plebeian Culture and the Structure of Authority in Renaissance England* (New York, 1985); Peter Stallybrass, *The Politics and Poetics of Transgression* (London, 1986).
7. For these see the items in the Select Bibliography, below, by Michael D. Bristol, Mary Ellen Lamb, François Laroque, Annabel Patterson, and Garrett Sullivan and Linda Woodbridge.

8. Burke, *Popular Culture*, p.277.

9. Burke, *Popular Culture*, p.277.

10. For one of the discussions see François Laroque, 'Shakespeare's "Battle of Carnival and Lent": The Falstaff Scenes Reconsidered (*1 & 2 Henry IV*)', in *Shakespeare and Carnival: After Bakhtin*, ed. Ronald Knowles (Basingstoke, 1998), pp.83–96.

11. William Harrison, *The Description of England*, ed. Georges Edelen (Washington, 1994), p.118; see also Keith Wrightson, *English Society 1580–1680* (London, 1993), pp.18–23.

12. Sir Thomas Smith, *De Republica Anglorum*, ed. Mary Dewar (Cambridge, 1982), pp.73–6. The book was written in the early 1560s, though not published until 1583.

13. See Christopher Brooks, 'Professions, Ideology and the Middling Sort in the Late Sixteenth and Early Seventeenth Centuries', in *The Middling Sort of People: Culture, Society and Politics in England, 1550–1880*, ed. Jonathan Barry and Christopher Brooks (Basingstoke, 1994), pp.113–40, esp. pp.126–8.

14. On *Coriolanus* and the Midlands Rising of 1607 see Annabel Patterson, *Shakespeare and the Popular Voice* (Oxford, 1989), pp.135–46, and on civic values in the play see Cathy Shrank, 'Civility and the City in *Coriolanus*', *Shakespeare Quarterly*, 54 (2003), 406–23. Instances of the term 'popular' in Shakespeare are *Cor* 2.1.212, 2.3.101, 3.1.105, 5.2.39; *H5* 4.1.38; *Tem* 1.2.92.

15. For a detailed account of this episode see Katherine Duncan-Jones, *Ungentle Shakespeare: Scenes from his Life* (London, 2001), pp.93–6.

16. See Tim Harris, 'Problematising Popular Culture', in *Popular Culture in England, c. 1500–1850*, ed. Harris (London, 1995), pp.1–27, at p.10.

17. On folk drama see E.K. Chambers, *The English Folk Play* (Oxford, 1933), and Weimann, *Shakespeare and the Popular Tradition*, pp.15–48.

18. On jest books and rogue literature see Garrett Sullivan and Linda Woodbridge, 'Popular Culture in Print', in *The Cambridge Companion to English Literature 1500–1600*, ed. Arthur F. Kinney (Cambridge, 2000), pp.265–86; on almanacs see Bernard Capp, *Astrology and the Popular Press: English Almanacs 1500–1800* (London, 1979).

19. H.S. Bennett, *English Books and Readers 1475 to 1557*, 2nd edn (Cambridge, 1969), p.149.

20. For these attacks on romance as well as a revaluation of the genre in the Renaissance see Alex Davis, *Chivalry and Romance in the English Renaissance* (Cambridge, 2003), pp.10, 12.

21. The best survey of the field remains Paul Salzman, *English Prose Fiction, 1558–1700* (Oxford, 1985).

22. On literacy see David Cressy, *Literacy and the Social Order: Reading and Writing in Tudor and Stuart England* (Cambridge, 1980); Keith Thomas, 'The Meaning of Literacy in Early Modern England', in *The Written Word: Literacy in Transition*, ed. Gerd Baumann (Oxford, 1986), pp.97–131.

23. See Adam Fox, *Oral and Literate Culture in England 1500–1700* (Oxford, 2000), pp.19–36.

24. See Bruce Smith, *The Acoustic World of Early Modern England: Attending to the O-Factor* (Chicago IL, 1999), p.169.

25. See Fox, *Oral and Literate Culture*, pp.37–40, 50.

26. As Helen Cooper points out: see below, pp.19–20.

27. Barry Reay, *Popular Cultures in England 1550–1750* (London, 1998), p.59.

28. Reay, *Popular Cultures*, p.56.

29. As does Michael D. Bristol, 'Theater and Popular Culture', in *A New History of Early English Drama*, ed. John D. Cox and David Scott Kastan (New York, 1997), pp.231–48.

30. Sarah Annes Brown, '"There is no End but Addition": The Later Reception of Shakespeare's Classicism', in *Shakespeare and the Classics* (note 2), pp.277–93, at p.277.

31. See *A Midsummer Night's Dream*, ed. Harold F. Brooks (London, 1979), pp.32–3. Golding's Ovid features specifically, as also do Seneca's *Medea* and *Oedipus*, in Brooks's explication of Titania's speech.

32. Patricia Parker, '(Peter) Quince: Love Potions, Carpenter's Coigns and Athenian Weddings', *Shakespeare Survey*, 56 (2003), 39–54.

33. For the 'name-only' case see Merritt Y. Hughes, 'A Classical *vs.* A Social Approach to Shakspere's Autolycus', *Shakespeare Association Bulletin*, 15 (1940), 219–26; quotation from p.223. Hughes argues that Shakespeare may have learned more on Autolycus from Renaissance mythography.

34. For this case see Mary Ellen Lamb, 'Ovid and *The Winter's Tale*: Conflicting Views toward Art', in *Shakespeare and Dramatic Tradition: Essays in Honor of S.F. Johnson*, ed. W.R. Elton and William B. Long (Newark DE, 1998), pp.69–87, with useful retrospective bibliography pro and contra at p.84, n.2.

35. Geoffrey Bullough, *Narrative and Dramatic Sources of Shakespeare*, 8 vols (London, 1957–75).

36. Anne Barton, 'The Wild Man in the Forest', *Comparative Criticism*, 18 (1996), 21–54. This outstanding investigation of the subject down to the Renaissance, to which we are indebted for our account, supplies further detail on *Timon* at pp.47–50, on *Mucedorus* and *James IV* at pp.46–7.

37. François Laroque, 'Popular Festivity', in *The Cambridge Companion to Shakespearean Comedy*, ed. Alexander Leggatt (Cambridge, 2002), pp.64–78.

38. Ben Jonson, *Bartholomew Fair*, ed. E.A. Horsman (Manchester, 1960), 2.4.9–18.

39. Mary Ellen Lamb, 'The Red Crosse Knight, St. George, and the Appropriation of Popular Culture', *Spenser Studies*, 18 (2003), 185–208, at p.185.

40. Diane Purkiss, *Troublesome Things: A History of Fairies and Fairy Stories* (London, 2000), p.86.

1: SHAKESPEARE AND THE MYSTERY PLAYS

1. The story is quoted from *Records of Early English Drama: Cumberland, Westmorland and Gloucestershire*, ed. Audrey Douglas and Peter Greenfield (Toronto, 1986), p.219.

2. 'Corpus Christi play' was by the sixteenth century a generic term, not necessarily indicating performance on the feast of Corpus Christi; Chester's cycle, for instance, was acted at Whitsun, and later moved to Midsummer. The term 'mystery play' is often also connected with the 'mysteries' or crafts specific to the guilds that in many towns sponsored and acted the plays.

3. The phrase is a key one in Bruce R. Smith, *Ancient Scripts and Modern Experience on the English Stage, 1500–1700* (Princeton NJ, 1988).

4. Aristotle, *Poetics*, 1450b (the end of section 6 in the most widely accessible translation by S.H. Butcher); on the academic interest in Greek drama, see the listings in Alfred Harbage's *Annals of English Drama 975–1700*, rev. S. Schoenbaum, 3rd edn rev. Sylvia Stoler Wagonheim (London, 1989).

5. Gail McMurray Gibson, in *The Theater of Devotion: East Anglian Drama and Society in the Late Middle Ages* (Chicago IL, 1989), uses the term about medieval drama generally.

6. *The Complete Plays of John Bale*, ed. Peter Happé, 2 vols (Cambridge, 1985–6), vol. 1, pp.8–9.

7. From his *Treatise against Dicing, Dancing, Plays and Interludes*, quoted in E.K. Chambers, *The Elizabethan Stage*, 4 vols (Oxford, 1923), vol. 4, pp.198–9.

8. Michael O'Connell argues forcefully for this as the basis of Reformist objections in *The Idolatrous Eye: Iconoclasm and Theater in Early Modern England* (New York, 2000).

9. *Vertue's Commonwealth by Henry Crosse*, ed. Alexander B. Grosart (Manchester, 1878), pp.112–13.

10. Given the word's clear attestation in the dramatic sense only from three centuries later, it seems unlikely that Crosse could have intended a pun on 'mystery', though the wide currency of the French *mystère* (and of 'mystery' in its professional guild sense) makes a pun not altogether impossible: see note 2, above.

11. David Mills, 'The Chester Cycle', in *The Cambridge Companion to Medieval English Theatre*, ed. Richard Beadle (Cambridge, 1994), pp.109–33, at p.110.

12. Information comes from the *Records of Early English Drama* project volumes: E.K. Chambers, *The Mediaeval Stage*, 2 vols (Oxford, 1903), vol. 2, pp. 329–406; Harold C. Gardiner, SJ, *Mysteries' End: An Investigation of the Last Days of the Medieval Religious Stage* (New Haven CT, 1946), pp. 72, 86–7, 92; *Non-Cycle Plays and Fragments*, ed. Norman Davis, EETS s.s. 1 (London, 1970); and *The Creacion of the World*, ed. and trans. Paula Neuss (New York, 1983). There is also some evidence for a late Corpus Christi play in Lancaster: see Chambers, vol. 2, p. 375. Thomas Heywood describes the Kendal play as still continuing in his 1612 *Apology for Actors*, but there is no documentary support.

13. Chambers, *Mediaeval Stage*, vol. 2, p. 382; the later play was performed at Ely House some time between 1613 and 1622.

14. Emrys Jones's phrase for the impression made by popular entertainments of this kind; *The Origins of Shakespeare* (Oxford, 1977), p. 51.

15. Jones, *Origins*, pp. 31–5, 84; and for an indication of what progress has been made, see Stuart Gillespie, *Shakespeare's Books: A Dictionary of Shakespeare's Sources* (London, 2001), s.v. 'Mystery Plays' (pp. 376–83).

16. Just how extreme such views of the plays could be is shown by the withering scorn that greeted Thomas Sharpe when he published the Coventry *Pageant of the Shearmen and Taylors* early in the nineteenth century. The *Monthly Review* noted: 'There is no intrinsic merit in this wretched and doggerel piece to render its publication at all necessary' (quoted from *The Coventry Corpus Christi Plays*, ed. Pamela M. King and Clifford Davidson (Kalamazoo MI, 2000), p. 56).

17. The magisterial *New History of Early English Drama*, ed. John D. Cox and David Scott Kastan (New York, 1997) accordingly gives fifteen and a half pages to the cycle plays, fifteen of them to urban hierarchies and policies of exclusion, the remaining half to claiming that their theology was largely irrelevant either to their promotion or their suppression (pp. 77–92, 135).

18. On terminology, see John Orrell, 'The Theaters', in Cox and Kastan, *New History*, pp. 103–4.

19. On the assimilation of supposedly classical theatre design to more familiar native structures, see Smith, *Ancient Scripts*, pp. 59–97.

20. Quoted by Meg Twycross in Beadle, *Cambridge Companion*, pp. 46–7.

21. The York Mercers' pageant had such painting, and it may well have been more widespread: see Beadle, *Cambridge Companion*, p. 94, and Orrell, 'Theaters', p. 106.

22. See Jones, *Origins*, p. 34, on the earlier recognition of the parallel. Something of the effect that could be obtained by a day-long performance was given by Adrian Noble's 1989 RSC production of *The Plantagenets*.

23. As Martin Stevens puts it, 'Perhaps the greatest cultural contribution that the *theatrum mundi* of the Middle Ages made to the native dramatic tradition

is the introduction of universal time, space, and action'. 'From *Mappa mundi* to *Theatrum mundi*: The World on Stage in Early English Drama', in *From Page to Performance: Essays in Early English Drama*, ed. John A. Alford (East Lansing MI, 1995), pp.25–49, at p.44.

24. On the relationship between stage and audience, see in particular Anne Barton, *Shakespeare and the Idea of the Play* (1962; repr. Harmondsworth, 1967).

25. *An Apology for Poetry*, ed. Geoffrey Shepherd, rev. R.W. Maslen (Manchester, 2002), p.112.

26. For example, The Lollard *Tretise of Miraclis Playinge*, ed. Clifford Davidson (rev. edn, Kalamazoo MI, 1993), raises objections on those grounds, as does Philip Stubbes in his *Anatomie of Abuses*, ed. Margaret Jane Kidnie (Tempe AZ, 2002), pp.198–206.

27. In *The Late Medieval Religious Plays of Bodleian MSS Digby 133 and E Museo 160*, ed. Donald C. Baker, John L. Murphy and Louis B. Hall, EETS 283 (Oxford, 1982), pp.24–95; it is a saint's play, not biblically based. The Digby plays were written before 1500 and copied slightly later, but there is evidence that they may have been acted at Chelmsford as late as 1562. See John Coldewey, 'The Digby Plays and the Chelmsford Records', *Research Opportunities in Renaissance Drama*, 18 (1975), 103–21.

28. *Apology*, ed. Shepherd, p.110. On the different forms of staging, see e.g. Robert Weimann, *Shakespeare and the Popular Tradition in the Theater: Studies in the Social Dimension of Dramatic Form and Function*, ed. Robert Schwartz (Baltimore MD, 1978), pp.73–85.

29. See Meg Twycross in Beadle, *Cambridge Companion*, p.62, on 'split-screen' action and locational shifts; and David Mills, 'The Chester Cycle' (note 11, above), pp.120–1, on temporal elisions.

30. The texts of all the surviving cycles are headed with some form of this statement; it is not clear whether they were in all cases part of the spoken text.

31. On Peele's part in *Titus*, see for instance Brian Vickers, *Shakespeare, Co-Author* (Oxford, 2002), pp.148–243.

32. *A Comedy concernynge thre lawes*, in Happé, *Complete Plays*, vol. 2, p.68; written in 1538, it was printed in 1548 on the continent, in 1562 in London. God is given an entry in the stage directions: he was not represented just as an offstage voice.

33. *The N-Town Play: Cotton MS Vespasian D.8*, ed. Stephen Spector, EETS s.s. 11–12 (Oxford, 1991): *The Fall of Man*, line 194 (vol. 1, p.30).

34. Editions forthcoming; see also Helen Cooper, 'Guy of Warwick, Upstart Crows and Mounting Sparrows', in *Shakespeare, Marlowe, Jonson: New Directions in Biography*, ed. J.R. Mulryne and Takashi Kozuka (London, 2004), pp.119–38.

35. See *The Foure PP*, lines 823–36, for 'the devyll that kept the gate' in 'the play of Corpus Cristi' at Coventry: *The Plays of John Heywood*, ed. Richard Axton and Peter Happé (Cambridge, 1991), p.132. The original play does not survive.

36. In the opening play of the Chester cycle: *The Chester Mystery Cycle*, ed. R.M. Lumiansky and David Mills, EETS s.s. 3 (London, 1974), lines 102ff.

37. See William Tydeman, *The Theatre in the Middle Ages* (Cambridge, 1978), pp.176–7; *The Staging of Religious Drama in the Middle Ages: Texts and Documents in English Translation*, ed. Peter Meredith and John E. Tailby (Kalamazoo MI, 1983), esp. ch. 4.

38. *Records of Early English Drama: Chester*, ed. Lawrence M. Clopper (Toronto, 1979), p.124.

39. For the particular extravagance of the Coventry Herod, see *The Pageant of the Shearmen and Taylors*, line 728, S.D. (*Coventry Corpus Christi Play*, ed. King and Davidson); and for the porter, see note 35 above.

40. See Geoffrey Bullough, *Narrative and Dramatic Sources of Shakespeare*, 8 vols (London, 1957–75), vol. 1, pp.10–11, 50–4, for Shakespeare's use of Gower's version of the story for the ending of the play. *Apollonius* is also likely to underlie the opening frame story, of Egeus' account of his loss of his wife, and the change of the location of the main action to Ephesus, where Apollonius and his wife are reunited.

41. Jones, *Origins*, p.51.

42. *Mac* 4.2, *H5* 3.3.38, 41; and see Gillespie, *Shakespeare's Books*, *s.v.* 'Mystery Plays'.

43. *N-Town* 'Burial', especially the stage direction at line 121 for laying the body of Christ 'in oure Ladys lappe' (ed. Spector, vol. 1, p.342); Digby, 'Christ's Burial' (ed. Baker, p.155). Other cycles have Joseph and Nicodemus take down the body but do not specify the Virgin's receiving of it, even though she is still onstage. The Passion section of the Coventry cycle does not survive. For the veneration of the Pity, see the regrets expressed by the Long Melford recusant David Martin (?1527–1615) quoted in Kathleen Kamerick, *Popular Piety and Art in the Late Middle Ages* (New York, 2002), p.69.

44. See Jones, *Origins*, esp. pp. 54–74; and William Tydeman, 'An Introduction to Medieval English Theatre', in Beadle, *Cambridge Companion*, p.35.

45. It is triggered by a comparison with Christ in Holinshed's account: see Jones, *Origins*, p.54.

46. From John 18.11, used as the first line of a speech from Christ in the Chester, N-Town and Towneley cycles; Chester, N-Town and York all make reference to torches either in the speeches or stage directions.

47. *Oedipus*, trans. Alexander Neville, in *Seneca his Tenne Tragedies edited by Thomas Newton (1581)*, intro. T.S. Eliot (London, 1927), vol. 1, pp.225–6.

48. York *Crucifixion*, in *The York Plays*, ed. Richard Beadle (London, 1982), pp.318, 122–6.
49. Though see further Pauline Kiernan's *Shakespeare's Theory of Drama* (Cambridge, 1996).
50. King and Davidson, *Coventry Plays*, p.48.

2: SHAKESPEARE AND POPULAR FESTIVITY

1. Useful historical surveys of the status and survival of popular festivals in sixteenth-century England and beyond include David Cressy, *Bonfires and Bells: National Memory and the Protestant Calendar in Elizabethan and Stuart England* (London, 1989); Eamon Duffy, *The Stripping of the Altars: Traditional Religion in England c. 1400–c. 1580* (London, 1992); and Christopher Hill, *Society and Puritanism in Pre-Revolutionary England* (2nd edn, New York, 1967).
2. For recent studies, see in particular for Shakespeare, François Laroque, *Shakespeare's Festive World: Elizabethan Seasonal Entertainment and the Professional Stage* (Cambridge, 1993); Pamela Allen Brown, *Better a Shrew than a Sheep: Women, Drama, and the Culture of Jest in Early Modern England* (Ithaca NY, 2003); and *Shakespeare and Carnival: After Bakhtin*, ed. Ronald Knowles (London, 1998).
3. See for some of the history of Shakespeare as 'child of nature' E.A.J. Honigmann, *Myriad-minded Shakespeare: Essays chiefly on the Tragedies and Problem Comedies* (Basingstoke, 1989), pp.189–90; for the family lawsuits Park Honan, *Shakespeare: A Life* (Oxford, 1998), pp.25–42; and for the possible public shaming of Shakespeare, Leah S. Marcus, 'Who Was Will Peter? Or, a Plea for Literary History', *Shakespeare Studies*, 25 (1997), 211–28, at pp.222–6.
4. C.L. Barber, *Shakespeare's Festive Comedy: A Study of Dramatic Form and its Relation to Social Custom* (1959; repr. Cleveland OH, 1963), pp.3, 193.
5. In Barber's reading, however, Shakespeare doesn't quite succeed – hence audiences' frequent failure to accept the prince's repudiation of Falstaff, pp.217–21. See also David Ruiter, *Shakespeare's Festive History: Feasting, Festivity, Fasting and Lent in the Second Henriad* (Aldershot, 2003).
6. See Cressy, *Bonfires and Bells*, pp.18–19.
7. See in particular, Duffy, *Stripping of the Altars*, and Hill, *Society and Puritanism*, for their discussions of how official English attitudes towards popular festivity altered along with ecclesiastical and royal policy towards more specifically liturgical rituals.
8. Philip Stubbes, *The Anatomie of Abuses*, ed. Margaret Jane Kidnie (Tempe AZ, 2002), pp.214–15.
9. See Cressy, *Bonfires and Bells*, pp.16–17.

10. *The Political Works of James I*, ed. C.H. McIlwain (Cambridge MA, 1918), p.27.

11. Jonson's *Bartholomew Fair* and *The Tale of a Tub* obviously constitute exceptions to this generalization.

12. Of course not all contemporaries who held such opinions were Puritans, though many were. See Jonas A. Barish, *The Antitheatrical Prejudice* (Berkeley CA, 1981), pp.80–117.

13. See Peter Milward, *Shakespeare's Religious Background* (Bloomington IN, 1973), and Ian Wilson, *Shakespeare, the Evidence: Unlocking the Mysteries of the Man and His Work* (New York, 1993).

14. Mikhail Bakhtin, *Rabelais and his World*, trans. Hélène Iswolsky (Cambridge MA, 1968), p.255.

15. Michael D. Bristol, *Carnival and Theater: Plebeian Culture and the Structure of Authority in Renaissance England* (New York, 1985), p.13.

16. Natalie Zemon Davis, *Society and Culture in Early Modern France* (Stanford CA, 1975).

17. For a more extended argument about *King Lear* at court on St Stephen's Day, see Leah S. Marcus, *Puzzling Shakespeare: Local Reading and Its Discontents* (Berkeley CA, 1988), pp.148–59.

18. Marcus, *Puzzling Shakespeare*, pp.148–54.

19. Naomi Conn Liebler, *Shakespeare's Festive Tragedy: The Ritual Foundations of Genre* (London, 1995), pp.25–6.

20. Stubbes, *Anatomie*, p.209.

21. See Leah S. Marcus, *The Politics of Mirth: Jonson, Herrick, Milton, Marvell and the Defense of Old Holiday Pastimes* (Chicago IL, 1986), pp.159–60.

22. For more literary allusions and liturgical echoes, see Marcus, *The Politics of Mirth*, pp.156–65.

23. On Skimmington and related rituals, see D.E. Underdown, 'The Taming of the Scold: The Enforcement of Patriarchal Authority in Early Modern England', in *Order and Disorder in Early Modern England*, ed. Anthony Fletcher and John Stevenson (Cambridge, 1985), pp.116–36; David Underdown, *Revel, Riot, and Rebellion: Popular Politics and Culture in England 1603–1660* (Oxford, 1985), pp.102–11; and Buchanan Sharp, *In Contempt of All Authority: Rural Artisans and Riot in the West of England, 1586–1660* (Berkeley CA, 1980).

24. See Barber, *Shakespeare's Festive Comedy*, pp.205–21; Laroque, *Shakespeare's Festive World*, pp.188–267; and Jeanne Addison Roberts, *Shakespeare's English Comedy: 'The Merry Wives of Windsor' in Context* (Lincoln NE, 1979), pp.78–83.

25. See Brown, *Better a Shrew*, pp.33–55, and Leah S. Marcus, *Unediting the Renaissance: Shakespeare, Marlowe, Milton* (London, 1996), pp.88–97.

26. Michael D. Bristol, *Big-Time Shakespeare* (London, 1996), pp.180–92. See also Robert Hornback, 'Emblems of Folly in the First *Othello*: Renaissance

Blackface, Moor's Coat, and "Muckender"', *Comparative Drama*, 35 (2001),
69–99, and Pamela Allen Brown, '*Othello* and Italophobia' in *Shakespeare
and Intertextuality: The Transition of Cultures between Italy and England in the
Early Modern Period*, ed. Michele Marrapodi (Rome, 2000), pp.179–92.

3: SHAKESPEARE'S CLOWNS

1. David Wiles, *Shakespeare's Clown: Actor and Text in the Elizabethan Playhouse*
(Cambridge, 1987), pp.57–8.
2. *The Defence of Poesie* (London, 1595), sig. I1r-v.
3. *The Pilgrimage to Parnassus with the Two Parts of the Return From Parnassus*,
ed. W.D. Macray (Oxford, 1896), p.22.
4. George Whetstone, *The Right Excellent and Famous Historye, of Promos and
Cassandra* (London, 1578), Dedication.
5. Wiles, *Shakespeare's Clown*, p.61. On the word 'clown' generally, see Wiles,
pp.61–72, and Mary Thomas Crane, 'Linguistic Change, Theatrical Practice
and Ideologies of Status in *As You Like It*', *English Literary Renaissance*, 27
(1997), 361–92.
6. *Popular Culture in England, c.1500–1850*, ed. Tim Harris (London, 1995),
pp.4–5.
7. Thomas Fuller, *A History of the Worthies of England* (London, 1662), sig.
Fff4r. An alternative account relates that Tarlton trained as an apprentice.
See the introduction to *Tarlton's Jests: and, News Out of Purgatory*, ed. James
Orchard Halliwell (London, 1844), which gives a full account of Tarlton's
life and reputation which I have drawn on here. Despite their titles, these
works were not actually authored by Tarlton, but are jest-book compilations
produced after his death.
8. Fuller, *History of the Worthies*, sig. Fff4r.
9. Wiles, *Shakespeare's Clown*, pp.136–44.
10. John Southworth, *Fools and Jesters at the English Court: Studies in the Social
Dimension of Dramatic Form and Function* (Stroud, 1998), p.1.
11. See Wiles, *Shakespeare's Clown*, pp.20–2; C.L. Barber, *Shakespeare's Festive
Comedy* (Princeton NJ, 1959), pp.24–30; and Robert Weimann, *Shakespeare and
the Popular Tradition in the Theater: Studies in the Social Dimension of Dramatic
Form and Function*, ed. Robert Schwartz (Baltimore MD, 1978), pp.20–8.
12. See *A Hundred Merry Tales, and Other English Jestbooks of the Fifteenth and
Sixteenth Centuries*, ed. P.M. Zall (Lincoln NE, 1963).
13. Linda Woodbridge, 'Jest Books, the Literature of Roguery and the Vagrant
Poor in Renaissance England', *English Literary Renaissance*, 33 (2003),
201–10, at p.206.

14. See *The Tragicall Historie of Hamlet Prince of Denmark* (London, 1603), sig. F2^{r-v}. The grammar of this passage is hopelessly confused, but the joke seems to be about the staleness of the clown's humour – so dead that it can be copied down *before* the play is viewed.

15. BL MS Sloane 1489, fo. 20. See also *Tarlton's Jests*, p.xxxi, where it is noted that this anecdote also appears in Vaughan's *Golden Fleece* (1626).

16. On such effects see the interesting pages in William Empson, *The Structure of Complex Words* (London, 1979), pp.105–57.

17. Appendix IV of Harold F. Brooks's Arden edition of the play (London, 1979) contains a correctly punctuated version of Quince's speech.

18. See Weimann, *Shakespeare and the Popular Tradition*; see also his *Author's Pen and Actor's Voice: Playing and Writing in Shakespeare's Theatre* (Cambridge, 2000).

19. Brooks's note.

20. Mary Ellen Lamb, 'Taken by the Fairies: Fairy Practices and the Production of Popular Culture in *A Midsummer Night's Dream*', *Shakespeare Quarterly*, 51 (2000), 277–312, at p.281. See also Wendy Wall, 'Why Does Puck Sweep? Shakespearean Fairies and the Politics of Cleaning', in Wall, *Staging Domesticity: Household Work and English Identity in Early Modern Drama* (Cambridge, 2002), pp.94–126.

21. David Wallace, *Chaucerian Polity: Absolutist Lineages and Associational Forms in England and Italy* (Stanford CA, 1997), pp.120–2.

22. See Clifford Davidson, '"What Hempen Home-spuns have we Swagg'ring Here?" Amateur Actors in *A Midsummer Night's Dream* and the Coventry Civic Plays and Pageants', *Shakespeare Studies*, 19 (1987), 87–99.

23. A much more positive account of popular culture in the play is offered by Michael D. Bristol, *Carnival and Theatre: Plebeian Culture and the Structures of Authority in Renaissance England* (New York, 1985), pp.172–8.

24. Terms used to describe what is planned for Christopher Sly (Induction, 1.34–43).

25. Elizabeth I, quoted in Susan Frye, *Elizabeth I: The Competition for Representation* (New York, 1993), p.9.

26. Peter Burke, *Popular Culture in Early Modern Europe* (New York, 1978), p.3.

27. Enid Welsford's *The Fool: His Social and Literary History* (London, 1935) distinguishes between clown and fool, but uses the terms in a different way from this essay, and sometimes interchangeably; see pp.273–86.

28. Richard Helgerson, *Forms of Nationhood: The Elizabethan Writing of England* (Berkeley CA, 1992), pp.245, 266.

29. Wiles, *Shakespeare's Clown*, pp.116–35

30. Quoted in J.H.P. Pafford's Arden edition (London, 1963), p.xxii.

31. Wiles, *Shakespeare's Clown*, p.129.

32. See David Scott Kastan, '"The King Hath Many Marching in his Coats," or, What did you do in the War, Daddy?' in David Scott Kastan, *Shakespeare after Theory* (New York, 1999), pp.129–47, and his introduction to the Arden edition of *1H4* (London, 2002).

33. See Stephen Greenblatt, 'Invisible Bullets', in Stephen Greenblatt, *Shakespearean Negotiations: The Circulation of Social Energy in Renaissance England* (Oxford, 1988), pp.47–50. Greenblatt's is of course the seminal text in discussions of the 'theatricality of power' in Renaissance England.

34. See Kastan, 'Is There a Class in This (Shakespearean) Text?' in *Shakespeare after Theory*, pp.149–64.

4: SHAKESPEARE AND POPULAR ROMANCE

1. See *The Spirit of Medieval English Popular Romance*, ed. Ad Putter and Jane Gilbert (London, 2000), and *Pulp Fictions of Medieval England: Essays in Popular Romance*, ed. Nicola McDonald (Manchester, 2004).

2. Paul Strohm, 'The Origin and Meaning of Middle English *Romance*', *Genre*, 10 (1977), 1–28.

3. Cited in Strohm, 'Origin and Meaning', p.2.

4. Tessa Watt, *Cheap Print and Popular Piety, 1550–1640* (Cambridge, 1991), p.5, and Roger Chartier, *The Cultural Uses of Print in Early Modern France*, trans. Lydia G. Cochrane (Princeton NJ, 1987), p.3, both warn against such assumptions.

5. See Carol M. Meale, 'Caxton, de Worde, and the Publication of Romance in Late Medieval England', *The Library*, 14 (1992), 283–98; A.S.G. Edwards, 'William Copland and the Identity of Printed Middle English Romance', in *The Matter of Identity in Medieval Romance*, ed. Philippa Hardman (Cambridge, 2002), pp.139–47; and Ronald S. Crane, *The Vogue of Medieval Chivalric Romance During the English Renaissance* (Menasha WI, 1919).

6. Watt, *Cheap Print*, p.262, and Margaret Spufford, *Small Books and Pleasant Histories: Popular Fiction and its Readership in Seventeenth-Century England* (Cambridge, 1981), pp.50–1, 225–7.

7. Watt, *Cheap Print*, p.269. *Sir Eglamour* may have suggested the use of this name in *The Two Gentlemen of Verona*, and *Robert the Devil* is a possible source for *King Lear* (see Donna B. Hamilton, 'Some Romance Sources for *King Lear*: Robert of Sicily and Robert the Devil', *Studies in Philology*, 71 (1974), 173–91).

8. George Puttenham, *The Arte of English Poesie*, ed. Gladys Doidge Willcock and Alice Walker (Cambridge, 1970), pp.83–4.

9. Watt, *Cheap Print*, Table 4, pp.270–1.

10. Robert Langham, *A Letter*, ed. R.J.P. Kuin, MRTS 2 (Leiden, 1983), p.53.

11. Henry Parrot, *The Mastive, Or Young-Whelpe of the Old-Dogge. Epigrams and Satyrs* (London, 1615), sigs. H4^v–I1^r.

12. *The Works of Thomas Nashe*, ed. Ronald B. McKerrow, 5 vols (Oxford, 1958), vol. 1, p.26.

13. Puttenham, *English Poesie*, p.42.

14. H.R.D. Anders, *Shakespeare's Books: A Dissertation on Shakespeare's Reading and the Immediate Sources of his Works* (Berlin, 1904), pp.158–63, outlines Shakespeare's possible reading in the genre.

15. See respectively Ronald S. Crane, 'The Vogue of *Guy of Warwick* from the Close of the Middle Ages to the Romantic Revival', *PMLA*, 30 (1915), 125–94, at p.135, and Velma Bourgeois Richmond, *The Legend of Guy of Warwick* (London, 1996), p.184.

16. Aubrey, *Brief Lives*, ed. Richard Barber (Woodbridge, 1982), p.285, reports Shakespeare's killing of a calf 'in a high style'. This is discussed by Katherine Duncan-Jones in *Ungentle Shakespeare: Scenes from his Life* (London, 2001), p.15.

17. Performances of these plays are recorded in *Henslowe's Diary*, ed. R.A. Foakes, 2nd edn (Cambridge, 2002), p.20 (for *Huon*), pp.58–9 (for *Uther Pendragon*) and pp.89–90, 324 (for *King Arthur*). See also the list compiled by Michael L. Hays, 'A Bibliography of Dramatic Adaptations of Medieval Romances and Renaissance Chivalric Romances First Available in English through 1616', *Research Opportunities in Renaissance Drama*, 28 (1985), 87–109. The French romance *Huon of Bordeaux* (translated into English in 1533–42) is the source for the figure (and name) of Oberon in *A Midsummer Night's Dream*: see Geoffrey Bullough, *Narrative and Dramatic Sources of Shakespeare*, 8 vols (London, 1957–75), vol. 1, pp.370–1, 390.

18. Sydney Anglo, 'The *British History* in Early Tudor Propaganda', *Bulletin of the John Rylands Library*, 44 (1961), 17–48, at p.38.

19. Bullough, *Narrative and Dramatic Sources*, vol. 3, pp.79–80.

20. Introduction to Arden 3 *1H6*, ed. Burns (London, 2000), p.39.

21. See, for example, David Scott Kastan's introduction to Arden 3 (London, 2002), pp.14–16.

22. Keith Thomas, *Religion and the Decline of Magic: Studies in Popular Beliefs in Sixteenth and Seventeenth Century England* (London, 1971), ch. 13.

23. Holinshed, *The Mirror for Magistrates*, 2nd edn (1587), vol. 3, p.521 (as per note in Arden 3), and Bullough, *Narrative and Dramatic Sources*, vol. 4, p.201.

24. Bullough, *Narrative and Dramatic Sources*, vol. 4, p.165.

25. Terence Hawkes, 'The Fool's "Prophecy" in *King Lear*', *Notes and Queries*, 7 (1960), 331–2.

26. A Shakespearean neologism, glossed by *OED* as 'confused, incoherent, non-sensical, rubbishy'.

27. Howard Dobin, *Merlin's Disciples: Prophecy, Poetry and Power in Renaissance England* (Stanford CA, 1990), p.38.

28. A better understanding of Glendower's significance is shown by the Earl of Westmorland, in his description of the Welsh leader as 'irregular and wild' (i.e. lawless) (1.1.40), by King Henry's reference to 'that great magician, damned Glendower' (1.3.83), and by Mortimer and Worcester's rebuke to Hotspur for his insult to Glendower (3.1.161–85). Political prophecies figured in the historical rebellions by Owain Glyndŵr against Henry IV and by Rhys ap Gruffydd against Henry VIII, and the Moldwarp prophecy was deployed in the historical Percy revolt (Thomas, *Religion*, pp.398–9).

29. See A.R. Humphrey's note in Arden 2 (London, 1981).

30. Leo Salingar identifies in *King Lear* an interest in romance themes such as fathers and daughters, and separated and reunited families; he further remarks that the play's 'oscillations between hope and dismay' chime with 'the stage traditions of romance'. See his essay 'Romance in *King Lear*', in Salingar, *Dramatic Form in Shakespeare and the Jacobeans* (Cambridge, 1986), pp.91–106, at p.105.

31. Bullough, *Narrative and Dramatic Sources*, vol. 7, pp.271–3.

32. The authenticity of the prophecy has been debated because it does not appear in the Quarto text of the play. See Joseph Wittreich, *'Image of that Horror': History, Prophecy and Apocalypse in 'King Lear'* (San Marino CA, 1984), pp.55–6, and Sheldon P. Zitner, 'The Fool's Prophecy', *Shakespeare Quarterly*, 18 (1967), 76–80.

33. David Scott Kastan, Introduction to Arden 3 *IH4* (London, 2002), p.35.

34. *The Works of Thomas Deloney*, ed. Francis Oscar Mann (Oxford, 1912), pp.323–6.

35. The activities of this society are described by one of its members, Richard Mulcaster, in his *Positions . . . for the training up of children* (1581); see Charles Bowie Millican, 'Spenser and the Arthurian Legend', *Review of English Studies*, 6 (1930), 167–74, at pp.167–8.

36. As is pointed out by H.R. Woudhuysen, Introduction to Arden 3 *LLL* (Walton-on-Thames, 1998), pp.41, 52.

37. See Henry Thomas, *Spanish and Portuguese Romances of Chivalry* (Cambridge, 1920), ch. 7; Mary Patchell, *The 'Palmerin' Romances in Elizabethan Prose Fiction* (New York, 1947); John J. O'Connor, *'Amadis de Gaule' and its Influence on Elizabethan Literature* (New Brunswick NJ, 1970); and Anthony Munday, *The Ancient, Famous and Honourable History of Amadis de Gaule*, ed. Helen Moore (Aldershot, 2004).

38. This book of the romance has also been adduced as a possible source for *The Winter's Tale*, potentially contributing the name of Florizel and influencing the depiction of Hermione's revivified statue. See E.A.J. Honigmann,

'Secondary Sources of *The Winter's Tale*', *Philological Quarterly*, 34 (1955), 27–38, at pp.30–3; and Stuart Gillespie, *Shakespeare's Books: A Dictionary of Shakespeare Sources* (London, 2001), p.15. Among Shakespeareans there is ongoing debate about whether the playwright possessed a direct knowledge of the Spanish romances.

39. *The Romance of Sir Beves of Hamtoun*, ed. Eugen Kölbing, EETS extra series 46, 48, 65 (London, 1885, 1886, 1894), p.75.

40. Quotations from the fifteenth-century manuscript (Chetham Library, Manchester, MS 8009) designated 'M' in Kölbing, p.75.

41. Shakespeare's familiarity with the legend of Roland, like that of Arthur, is derived primarily from its reiteration in historical narratives. In *1H6* Alençon recalls Froissart's judgement that 'England all Olivers and Rolands bred' during the reign of Edward III (1.2.30); Oliver is Roland's companion in the *Chanson de Roland*. As Edward Burns points out in the Arden 3 note *ad loc.*, this is an accurate reflection of the original, as translated into English by Lord Berners in 1523–5. Roland M. Smith, 'King Lear and the Merlin Tradition', *Modern Language Quarterly*, 7 (1946), 153–74, offers an alternative suggestion that Edgar's allusion may be to the old ballad of 'Child Rowland and Burd Ellen', and refer to a tradition of Arthur's having a son named Rowland.

42. The defeat of Ascopart becomes a prominent feature of the seventeenth-century Bevis chapbook tradition; see Jennifer Loney Fellows, *'Sir Beves of Hampton': Study and Edition*, 5 vols (unpublished Ph.D. dissertation, University of Cambridge, 1979), vol. 1, p.112. This would be in keeping with the character of both references discussed here.

43. Laurie Maguire, *Shakespearean Suspect Texts: The 'Bad' Quartos and their Contexts* (Cambridge, 1996), pp.237–8.

44. *The First Part of the Contention (1594)*, ed. William Montgomery (Oxford, 1985), l.879.

45. Cranmer's prophecy is greeted with awe by Henry: 'Thou speakest wonders' (5.4.55), he remarks, which chimes with Uter's exclamation in *The Birth of Merlin*, 'Thou speakst of wonders Merlin' (4.5.125). See Gordon McMullan's introduction to the Arden 3 *Henry VIII* (London, 2001), pp.179–80, for a discussion of the view put forward by Joanna Udall that *The Birth of Merlin* may have influenced the play. The line is, therefore, potentially a third Shakespearean reference to Merlin's prophecies. Whatever the nature of the relationship between the two plays, it is clear that the evocation of Elizabethan wonders with which the play ends contrasts favourably with the wondrous 'vanities' of the Field of the Cloth of Gold with which it opens.

46. *The Romance of Guy of Warwick*, ed. Julius Zupitza, EETS extra series 25–6 (London, 1875–6), pp.290–8.

47. See Richmond, *Guy of Warwick*, pp.183–9, and Crane, 'The Vogue of *Guy of Warwick*', p.135.

48. Colbrand's proverbial strength is also invoked by the Bastard in *King John* in order to mock his half-brother Robert's unimposing appearance (1.1.223–5). According to E.A.J. Honigmann, editor of the play for Arden 2 (London, 1954, pp.xxi–xxii), *King John* may also display some influence from the medieval romance of Richard Cœur de Lion, another popular romance printed in the early Tudor period.

5: SHAKESPEARE AND ELIZABETHAN POPULAR FICTION

1. Robert Greene, *Greenes Groatsworth of Wit* (1592), in Greene, *Life and Complete Works in Prose and Verse*, ed. Alexander B. Grosart, 15 vols (London, 1881–6), vol. 12, p.144. It should be noted that some scholars now claim for Henry Chettle the primary authorship of the *Groatsworth*: see D. Allen Carroll's edition for Medieval and Renaissance Texts and Studies (Binghamton NY, 1994). Carroll's evidence pointing to Chettle's role is filtered through dubious arguments about the psychology of plagiarism, but consistent with Chettle's having played a significant role as editor; he does not, however, prove the main author was not Greene.

2. See C.S. Lewis's negative judgement of *Euphues* in *English Literature in the Sixteenth Century, excluding Drama* (Oxford, 1954), esp. pp.313–15.

3. Nashe speaks of an artisan audience for Greene's work: 'he was a daintie slaue to content the taile of a Tearme, and stuffe Seruing mens pockets'. Nashe, *Strange Newes*, in *The Works of Thomas Nashe*, ed. Ronald B. McKerrow, 5 vols (Oxford, 1966), vol. 1, p.329.

4. For discussion of the contemporary reading public see Margaret Spufford, *Small Books and Pleasant Histories: Popular Fiction and its Readership in Seventeenth-Century England* (London, 1981), pp.19–37, and Adam Fox, *Oral and Literate Culture in England, 1500–1700* (Oxford, 2000), pp.16–18.

5. Austen Saker, *Narbonvs: The Laberynth of Libertie* (London, 1580); Emanuel Forde, *The Most Plesant History of Ornatvs and Artesia* (London, 1595).

6. Geoffrey Bullough, *Narrative and Dramatic Sources of Shakespeare*, 8 vols (London, 1957–75); Stuart Gillespie, *Shakespeare's Books: A Dictionary of Shakespeare Sources* (London, 2001); Kenneth Muir, *The Sources of Shakespeare's Plays* (London, 1977).

7. Thomas Lodge, *Rosalind*, ed. Donald Beecher (Ottawa, 1997), pp.168–9. All subsequent references are to this edition.

8. Robert Greene, *Pandosto*, in *The Descent of Euphues: Three Elizabethan Romance Stories*, ed. James Winny (Cambridge, 1957), p.89. All subsequent references are to this edition.

9. Richard Johnson, *The Renowned History of the Seven Champions of Christendom* (London, 1872), p.iii.

10. *The Seven Champions of Christendom*, ed. Arthur Burrell (London, 1912), p.5.

11. Richard Johnson, *The Most Famous History of the Seven Champions of Christendome* (London, 1608), sig. D1^v. All subsequent references are to this edition.

12. See Friedrich Brie, 'Eine neue Quelle zu "Cymbeline"?', *Jahrbuch der Deutschen Shakespeare-Gesellschaft*, 44 (1908), 167–70, who first commented on the relationship.

13. Richard Johnson, *The Most Pleasant History of Tom a Lincolne* (London, 1631), sig. E4^{r-v}. All subsequent references are to this edition.

14. Thomas Lodge, *Wit's Misery and the Worlds Madnesse* (London, 1596), sig. H4^v.

15. Richard Hirsch, in his 1978 edition of the work, says he is 'inclined to believe that *Tom a Lincolne* is indebted to *Hamlet*' but does not deal with the more obvious arguments for Johnson as a source for Shakespeare. *The Most Pleasant History of Tom a Lincolne*, ed. Hirsch (Columbia SC, 1978), p.xiv.

16. Thomas Nashe, *The Anatomie of Absurditie*, in *Works*, ed. McKerrow, vol. 1, p.12.

17. See David Margolies, '*Euphues* and *Mamillia*: Misogyny Transformed by "the Homer of Women"', in *Elizabethan Literature and Transformation*, ed. Sabine Coelsch-Foisner (Tübingen, 1999).

18. W.C., *The Aduentures of Ladie Egeria* (?1585).

19. *The Historie of the Damnable Life and Deserued Death of Doctor Iohn Faustus* (London, 1592), trans. 'P.F.'. Faustus borrows from a Jewish money lender and gives him his leg as a pledge, which, after a time, the money lender throws away. When Faustus comes to redeem the leg, the money lender is forced to pay him an additional sum.

6: SHAKESPEARE, GHOSTS AND POPULAR FOLKLORE

1. Stephen Greenblatt, *Hamlet in Purgatory* (Princeton NJ, 2001).

2. F.W. Moorman, 'The Pre-Shakespearean Ghost', *Modern Language Review*, 1 (1906), 86–95, and 'Shakespeare's Ghosts', *Modern Language Review*, 1 (1906), 192–201. Dover Wilson and May Yardley, eds, *Of Ghostes and*

Spirites walking by Nyght, 1572 (Oxford, 1929), and J. Dover Wilson, *What Happens in Hamlet* (Cambridge, 1935), ch.3.

3. Robert West, *The Invisible World: A Study of Pneumatology in Elizabethan Drama* (New York, 1969); Katharine M. Briggs, *The Anatomy of Puck: An Examination of Fairy Beliefs among Shakespeare's Contemporaries and Successors* (London, 1959). The phrase quoted in the next sentence is from Briggs p.119.

4. The ballad tells of a mother who kills her twin babies; when she returns home they greet her at the door. See Francis J. Child, ed., *The English and Scottish Popular Ballads*, 5 vols (1882–98; repr. New York, 1957), vol. 1, p.220.

5. See further D. Felton, *Haunted Greece and Rome: Ghost Stories from Classical Antiquity* (Austin TX, 1999), pp.1–10.

6. *Popular Culture in England, c.1500–1850*, ed. Tim Harris (London, 1995); Miri Rubin, *Corpus Christi: the Eucharist in Late Medieval Culture* (Cambridge, 1991); Roger Chartier, 'Popular Culture: A Concept Revisited', *Intellectual History Newsletter*, 15 (1993), 3–13. See also Adam Fox, *Oral and Literate Culture in England 1500–1700* (Oxford, 2000).

7. Mary Ellen Lamb, 'Taken by the Fairies: Fairy Practices and the Production of Popular Culture in *A Midsummer Night's Dream*', *Shakespeare Quarterly*, 51 (2000), 277–312; 'Old Wives' Tales, George Peele, and Narrative Abjection', *Critical Survey*, 14 (2002), 28–43. For a different interpretation that engages with similar questions, see Wendy Wall, 'Why does Puck Sweep? Shakespearean Fairies and the Politics of Cleaning', in *Staging Domesticity: Household Work and English Identity in Ealry Modern Drama* (Cambridge, 2002), pp.94–126.

8. Barry Reay, *Popular Cultures in England 1550–1750* (London, 1998), p.3.

9. For silent or repetitious ghosts, see 'Adam Bell', in *Scottish Fairy and Folktales*, ed. Douglas, p.201, reproduced in *A Dictionary of British Folktales in the English Language*, ed. Katharine M. Briggs, Part B: *Folk Legends*, 4 vols (London, 1971), vol. 1, pp.415–17. Briggs gives many other instances: see for example pp.427–8.

10. See for example Angela Bourke, 'Fairies and Anorexia: Nuala Ni Dhomhnaill's "Amazing Grass"', *Proceedings of the Harvard Celtic Colloquium*, 13 (1993), pp.25–38, at p.32. Further examples are found in the stories 'The Dance of Death', 'The Fair Maid of Clifton' and 'The Ghost of Gairnside' (Briggs, *Folktales*, pp.433–4, 449–50, 461–5).

11. For 'chesting' and other funeral feasts, see Claire Gittings, *Death, Burial and the Individual in Early Modern England* (London, 1988), pp.158–9. See also Ralph Houlbrooke, *Death, Religion and the Family in England 1480–1750* (Oxford, 1998).

12. See Nancy Caciola, 'Wraiths, Revenants and Ritual in Medieval Culture', *Past and Present*, 152 (1996), 3–45.

13. *Hamlet*, ed. G.R. Hibbard (Oxford, 1987), p.181; *Hamlet*, ed. Harold Jenkins (London, 1982), p.211.

14. Briggs, *Folktales*, supplies an account of tales about goblins.

15. For links between fairies and revenants, see Diane Purkiss, *Troublesome Things: A History of Fairies and Fairy Stories* (London, 2000), pp.86–7 and note.

16. On the most famous of these, John Darrell, see Keith Thomas, *Religion and the Decline of Magic: Studies in Popular Beliefs in Sixteenth and Seventeenth Century England* (London, 1971), pp.576–80.

17. Briggs, *Folktales*, p.443, cites Aubrey's *Miscellanies* on this subject.

18. See Felton (note 5, above), and Plato, *Phaedo*, 81: 'If when it [the soul] departs the body it is defiled and impure, because it was always with the body, and cared for it and loved it . . . such a soul is weighed down by this, and is dragged back into the visible world, through fear of the invisible.' *Phaedo*, ed. and trans. David Gallop (Oxford, 1999), translation adapted.

19. *Comus*, ll. 476–9, in *The Poems of John Milton*, edited by John Carey and Alastair Fowler (London, 1968).

20. On the long death in the early modern period see Gittings, *Death, Burial and the Individual*, pp. 114ff., and Houlbrooke, *Death, Religion and the Family*, p.291.

21. 'The Saga of Grettir the Strong', in *Medieval Ghost Stories: An Anthology of Miracles, Marvels and Prodigies*, ed. Andrew Joynes (Woodbridge, 2001), pp.114–19, and T.F. Thistleton-Dyer, *Domestic Folk-lore* (London, 1881), p.118.

22. On the *aoros* see Purkiss, *Troublesome Things*, ch. 1.

23. On ghosts and clothes see Jean-Claude Schmitt, *Ghosts in the Middle Ages: The Living and the Dead in Medieval Society*, trans. Teresa Lavender Fagan (Chicago IL, 1998), pp.201–4. For overviews of early modern ghosts see R.C. Finucane, *Ghosts: Appearances of the Dead and Cultural Transformation* (New York, 1996), pp.90–152, and Stephen Wilson, *The Magical Universe: Everyday Ritual and Magic in Pre-Modern Europe* (London, 2000), pp.289–310. Both of these are compendious rather than analytic. By contrast, *Ghosts: Deconstruction, Psychoanalysis, History*, ed. Peter Buse and Andrew Stott (Basingstoke, 1999), is analytic, but not historically inflected at all.

24. *Depositions from York Castle*, ed. James Raine (London, 1860), p.161.

25. Nathaniel Thompson, *The True Domestick Intelligence, or News both from the City and the Country*, no. 74 (16–19 March 1680). This story was much debated: see also from the same year *Currant Intelligence*, no. 4 (27 March–3 April) and *The Protestant (Domestick) Intelligence*, no. 75 (23 March).

26. Richard Baxter, *The Certainty of the World of Spirits*, ch.2, p.25, sig. C4^v.

27. *Hamlet*, Hibbard, p.282n.

28. John Webster, *The Displaying of Supposed Witchcraft* (London, 1677), p.303.

29. Mabel Balfour, 'Legends of the Cars', *Folklore*, II, 403–9, reproduced in Briggs, *Dictionary of British Folktales*, Part B, vol. 1, pp.453–4. For a similar story, see 'The Cruel Mother', in Child (n.4), vol. 1, p.220.

7: SHAKESPEARE'S SAYINGS

1. On *veredicta* see Michael Clanchy, *From Memory to Written Record: England, 1066–1307* (2nd edn, Oxford, 1992), p.207; on 'sentence' see *Oth* 1.3.211–16 and below, pp.157, 162–3.

2. See Adam Fox, *Oral and Literate Culture in England 1500–1700* (Oxford, 2000), esp. p.50.

3. James Howell, *Paroimiographia: Proverbs, or; Old Sayed Saws and Adages* (London, 1659), p.2.

4. For the importance of these qualities see Erasmus, *Collected Works*, vol. 31: *Adages*, trans. Margaret Mann Phillips (Toronto, 1982), p.4; Mary Thomas Crane, *Framing Authority: Sayings, Self, and Society in Sixteenth-Century England* (Princeton NJ, 1993), p.8.

5. The standard reference work is Morris Palmer Tilley, *A Dictionary of the Proverbs in England in the Sixteenth and Seventeenth Centuries* (Ann Arbor MI, 1950), which has 11 780 entries. I have also used Bartlett Jere Whiting with Helen Wescott Whiting, *Proverbs, Sentences, and Proverbial Phrases from English Writings mainly before 1500* (Cambridge MA, 1968); *The Oxford Dictionary of English Proverbs*, ed. F.P. Wilson (3rd edn, Oxford, 1970); and R.W. Dent, *Shakespeare's Proverbial Language: An Index* (Berkeley CA, 1981).

6. On Shakespeare's reworking of commonplaces, see Neil Rhodes, *Shakespeare and the Origins of English* (Oxford, 2004), pp.149–88. The present essay aims to complement that discussion by dealing with expressions of a popular character. It is arguable that this is an impossible distinction to make, but I intend 'popular' to refer here to proverbial and quasi-proverbial expressions used in everyday speech (though by people of all social classes) rather than in academic contexts.

7. See Ann Moss, *Printed Commonplace Books and the Structuring of Renaissance Thought* (Oxford, 1996).

8. The full title of Heywood's work is *A dialogue conteinyng the nomber in effect of all the proverbes in the englishe*. On 'the orality of popular print' see Barry Reay, *Popular Cultures in England 1550–1750* (London, 1998), p.59, and above, Introduction, p.1.

9. *Shakespeare's Plays in Quarto*, ed. Michael B. Allen and Kenneth Muir (Berkeley CA, 1981), sig. C2^{r-v}. On the use of quotation marks in printed texts of Shakespeare see Margreta de Grazia, 'Shakespeare in Quotation Marks', in *The Appropriation of Shakespeare*, ed. Jean I. Marsden (New York,

1991), pp.57–71; on the representation of speech in print more generally see D.F. McKenzie, 'Speech – Manuscript – Print', in *Making Meaning: 'Printers of the Mind' and Other Essays*, ed. Peter D. McDonald and Michael F. Suarez, SJ (Amherst MA, 2002), pp.237–58.

10. On Bruegel's use of proverbs see Mark A. Meadow, 'On the Structure of Knowledge in Bruegel's Netherlandish Proverbs', *Volkskundig Bulletin*, 18 (1992), 141–69; Ethan Matt Kavaler, *Pieter Bruegel: Parables of Order and Enterprise* (Cambridge, 1999), esp. pp.209–11, 225–40. (To describe Bruegel himself simply as a 'popular' artist, however, would be misleading.)

11. *John Heywood's A Dialogue of Proverbs*, ed. Rudolph E. Habenicht (Berkeley CA, 1963), 1.1745; compare *KL* 4.1.49, ''Tis the time's plague when madmen lead the blind.' Subsequent brief references to Heywood's *Dialogue* appear in the main text.

12. *MW* 4.5.6–78; *Luc* 244. Another passage in *MW* may be directly linked to Bruegel: see *The Merry Wives of Windsor*, ed. David Crane (Cambridge, 1997), p.72.

13. See Paula Neuss, 'The Sixteenth-Century English "Proverb" Play', *Comparative Drama*, 18 (1984), 1–17.

14. The first edition of the adages, *Adagiorum Collectanea*, appeared in 1500, followed by a series of expanded editions up to 1536, the year of Erasmus' death. See also Erika Rummel, 'The Reception of Erasmus's *Adages* in Sixteenth-Century England', *Renaissance and Reformation*, 18 (1994), 19–30.

15. Erasmus, *Adages*, pp.9, 14, 161–2, 5.

16. 1.2.4 (*Cor* 4.7.54); 1.3.28 (*Ham* 3.1.61); 3.6.85 (*TGV* 2.4.27–8; also *TS* 1.2.184 and *Mac* 4.1.149); 1.5.59 (*LLL* 5.1.65–6; also *TN* 1.3.78).

17. *The Adages of Erasmus*, selected by William Barker (Toronto, 2001), p.275 (3.4.2); see also 3.4.96.

18. Heywood, *Dialogue of Proverbs*, 1.141 (*3H6* 4.8.60–1); 1.670 (*AYL* 3.2.118–20); 1.716 (*TS* Ind. 1.37–8); 1.1496 (*LLL* 5.2.285).

19. *The Proverbs, Epigrams, and Miscellanies of John Heywood*, ed. John S. Farmer (London, 1906), p.107; *CE* 2.2.48; *MW* 5.5.125; *AYL* 3.2.398.

20. Emrys Jones, *The Origins of Shakespeare* (Oxford, 1977), p.21.

21. Surprisingly little has been written on the subject. The best accounts remain the two essays by F.P. Wilson, 'Shakespeare and the Diction of Common Life' and 'Shakespeare's Proverbial Wisdom' in *Shakespearian and Other Studies*, ed. Helen Gardner (Oxford, 1969), pp.100–29, 143–75. Hilda Hulme, *Explorations in Shakespeare's Language* (London, 1977), pp.39–88, is principally a philological study; Marjorie Donker, *Shakespeare's Proverbial Themes* (Westport CT, 1992), focuses particularly on *Hamlet* and *Romeo and Juliet*. There are some articles on individual proverbs but no more general account of how Shakespeare uses popular sayings.

240   SHAKESPEARE AND ELIZABETHAN POPULAR CULTURE

22. The source is 'Insanire paret certa ratione modoque', Horace, *Satires*, 2.3.271.

23. Cf. 'He that touches pitch shall be defouled', Whiting, *Proverbs, Sentences*, P236, and Ecclesiastes 13:1.

24. Samuel Palmer, *Moral Essays on Some of the Most Curious and Significant English, Scotch and Foreign Proverbs* (London, 1710), p.iii; Proverbs 1: 8. Hal quotes Proverbs 1: 20 at *1H4* 1.2.85–6: 'wisdom cries out in the streets and no man regards it'.

25. *Tit* 4.3.58, 66; Dent, *Shakespeare's Proverbial Language*, M1114. The accompanying text reads 'Whatever I do, I never succeed; I am always pissing at the moon'; Piero Bianconi, *The Complete Paintings of Bruegel* (London, 1969), p.91.

26. Tilley, *Proverbs In England*, A146; *MV* 2.7.65 (where 'glitters' is 'glisters', as also in Heywood, *Dialogue of Proverbs*, 1.668).

27. Wilson, *Oxford Proverbs*, H534; see also Heywood's 'And home is homely, though it be poore in syght', *Dialogue of Proverbs*, 1.218.

28. Erasmus, *Adages*, in *Collected Works*, pp.158–9 (1.2.15).

29. Tilley, *Proverbs In England*, E116, A154; Whiting, *Proverbs, Sentences*, E83; Heywood, *Dialogue of Proverbs*, 1.616; *2H6* 5.2.28; *TC* 4.5.224.

30. On proverbs in *AW* and on misogamy more generally in sixteenth- and seventeenth-century drama see R.L. Booth, '"Married and Marred": the Misogamist in English Renaissance Comedy', unpublished Ph.D. dissertation, University of London, 2003.

31. See Dent, *Shakespeare's Proverbial Language*, M48, M701, M875.1.

32. Joannes Bramis, *Here begynneth a merry ieste of a shrewde and curste wyfe, lapped in morelles skin, for her good behauyour* (London, 1580), STC 14521.

33. For a text see *The Taming of the Shrew*, ed. Brian Morris (London, 1981), p.314.

34. 2.1.134 (Tilley, *Proverbs in England*, W424; W448a); 2.1.224 (Tilley C526); 2.1.264 (Tilley W401); 3.2.209 (Tilley B536); 4.1.20 (Tilley A64); 4.1.28 (Tilley C542); 4.1.195 (Tilley K51).

35. *The Taming of a Shrew*, ed. Stephen Roy Miller (Cambridge, 1998), 1.57–8.

36. One exception is Sarah Wintle and René Weis, '*Macbeth* and the Barren Sceptre', *Essays in Criticism*, 41 (1991), 128–46, which discusses an adjacent theme.

37. *Macbeth*, ed. A.R. Braunmuller (Cambridge, 1997), p.47.

38. See Tilley, *Proverbs in England*, C144, and Martin Orkin, 'The Poor Cat's Adage and other Elizabethan Proverbs in Elizabethan Grammar-School Education', in *A Reader in the Language of Shakespearean Drama*, ed. Vivian Salmon and Edwina Burness (Amsterdam, 1987), pp.489–98.

39. For other examples see Wilson, 'Shakespeare's Proverbial Wisdom', p.154; also Dent, *Shakespeare's Proverbial Language*, S379, F565.1.

40. Compare Heywood, *Dialogue of Proverbs*, 2.629–31: 'True (quoth Ales) things done, can not be vndoone, / Be they done in due tyme, to late, or to soone. / But better late then never to repent this.'

41. See A.L. Rowse, *Simon Forman: Sex and Society in Shakespeare's Age* (London, 1974); Tilley, *Proverbs in England*, G476. Fox, *Oral and Literate Culture*, p.125, cites a version as 'An unbydden ghost knowes not where to sytt'. This is probably a misreading of 'ghest 'for 'ghost', but it is wonderfully suggestive in the context of *Macbeth*.

42. Farmer, *Proverbs, Epigrams, and Miscellanies*, p.108.

8 : SHAKESPEARE AND POPULAR SONG

1. W.H. Auden, *Lectures on Shakespeare*, reconstructed and edited by Arthur Kirsch (Princeton NJ, 2000), p.156. It is sometimes argued that the reason the song does not conform to Orsino's previous description is that it is a non-Shakespearean interpolation; this does not affect Auden's point.

2. Airs and madrigals, while they make numerous appearances in the drama of Shakespeare and his contemporaries, are beyond the scope of this discussion: both words and music for the former were normally penned by a composer, while the latter appear mainly in domestic performances, such as masques.

3. For further taxonomy see John H. Long, *Shakespeare's Use of Music: A Study of the Music and its Performance in the Original Production of Seven Comedies* (Gainesville FL, 1961), pp.1–2, and for ballads Natascha Würzbach, *The Rise of the English Street Ballad, 1550–1650*, translated by Gayna Walls (Cambridge, 1990), p.4.

4. Texts of all songs performed in the plays are supplied by Ross W. Duffin, *Shakespeare's Songbook* (New York, 2004). Texts of songs only quoted in spoken form in the plays (or of which only a line or two is sung – often the distinction is uncertain) are available in several compilations, usually selectively, starting with Thomas Percy's *Reliques of Ancient English Poetry* of 1765 and finishing with Duffin; on Percy's collection see further Bruce Smith's essay in the present volume.

5. The terminology of 'called for' versus impromptu songs is Auden's, in 'Music in Shakespeare', pp.500–27 in *The Dyer's Hand and Other Essays* (London, 1963).

6. Theodore Spenser, *Shakespeare and the Nature of Man* (New York, 1942), p. 90.

7. C.L. Barber, *Shakespeare's Festive Comedy: A Study of Dramatic Form and its Relation to Social Custom* (Princeton NJ, 1959), p.113.

8. The singers ('*Enter all*') appear to be Holofernes, Nathaniel, Moth, Costard, Dull and Jacquenetta: see Long, *Music in Seven Comedies*, p.73.

9. J.M. Nosworthy, 'Music and Its Function in the Romances of Shakespeare', *Shakespeare Survey*, 11 (1958), 60–9, at p.63.

10. For full details of the background to all these songs see Peter J. Seng's still essential study, *The Vocal Songs in the Plays of Shakespeare* (Cambridge MA, 1967), pp.94–108. This work is subsequently cited by page number in the main text.

11. See Duffin, *Shakespeare's Songbook*, p.449. Shakespeare alludes to what appears to be his own song later, in *King Lear* (3.2.74–7).

12. Jonson's advice is found in his Conversations with Drummond of Hawthornden; *Ben Jonson*, ed. C.H. Herford and Percy and Evelyn Simpson, 9 vols (Oxford, 1925–50), vol. 1, p.145. Further attacks on 'Ballet makers' are assembled by G.A. Thompson, *The Elizabethan Criticism of Poetry* (Menasha WI, 1914), and Würzbach, *English Street Ballad*, pp.242–52.

13. Sir William Cornwallis, 'Of the Observation and Use of Things', *Essayes* (London, 1600), sig. I7ᵛ.

14. On this tradition and its relation to Shakespeare see John H. Long, 'The Ballad Medley and the Fool', *Studies in Philology*, 67 (1970), 505–16.

15. For fuller discussion of musical aspects of Ophelia's songs see John H. Long, *Shakespeare's Use of Music: The Histories and Tragedies* (Gainesville FL, 1971), pp.122–9; for the musical settings, see F.W. Sternfeld, *Music in Shakespearean Tragedy* (London, 1963), pp.67–78.

16. Long, *Histories and Tragedies*, p.127.

17. My understanding on these points, as throughout this discussion of Ophelia's first song, is based on the comprehensive account in Seng, *The Vocal Songs*, pp.131–42. Seng prints two analogues and several other texts belonging to what is known as the 'Walsingham' ballad genre.

18. Pope and other early editors excised the 'not', but 'we must rather suppose it a deliberate interpolation by the singer, who recalls and so emphasizes that the pattern celebrated in the song is contradicted by the instance in her mind' – *Hamlet*, ed. Harold Jenkins (London, 1982), pp.349–50n. It appears in all F and Q texts and is retained in most modern editions. For a review of discussion see Lucy Bate, 'Which Did or Did Not Go to the Grave?', *Shakespeare Quarterly*, 17 (1966), 163–5, who concludes: 'the whole force of the lyric depends on that "not"' (164).

19. Nosworthy, 'Music and Its Function', p.63, makes the different but no less unsatisfactory suggestion that the purpose of all Ophelia's songs is practical – to convey her mad condition by a means which reduces strain on the boy actor playing her part.

20. See Bate 'Which Did or Did Not', p.164, on this point, and for Kittredge, *Hamlet*, ed. G. Kittredge (Boston MA, 1939), p.257.

21. *S.T. Coleridge's Shakespearean Criticism*, ed. Thomas M. Raysor, 2 vols (Harvard MA, 1930), vol. 1, p.33.

22. Although only implicit here, this element is further confirmed by related ballads such as 'Gentle Herdsman', in Percy's collection, in which a lover is
killed by a lady's scorn; the lady repents too late and embarks on a pilgrimage to Walsingham. This point is made by H.R.D. Anders, *Shakespeare's
Books: A Dissertation on Shakespeare's Reading and the Immediate Sources of his
Works* (Berlin, 1904), p.186.

23. These are summarized in, for example, Ernest Brennecke Jr, '"Nay, That's
Not Next!"', *Shakespeare Quarterly*, 4 (1953), 35–8.

24. Long, *Histories and Tragedies*, p.159; A.C. Bradley, *Shakespearean Tragedy*
(London, 1974), p.168.

9: SHAKESPEARE'S RESIDUALS: THE CIRCULATION OF BALLADS IN CULTURAL MEMORY

1. *A Transcript of the Registers of the Company of Stationers of London:
1554–1640 A.D.*, ed. Edward Arber, 5 vols (London, 1875), vol. 2, p.644.

2. William Shakespeare, *Titus Andronicus*, Arden 3, ed. Jonathan Bate (London,
1995), pp.73–7.

3. Hyder E. Rollins, *An Analytical Index to the Ballad-Entries (1557–1709) in the
Registers of the Company of Stationers of London* (Chapel Hill NC, 1924), contains four entries for a ballad of Titus Andronicus, including Danter's (1594,
1624, 1656, 1675). Surviving sheets of two pre-1642 printings (STC
24092.3, c.1625, and STC 24092.7, 1628–9) are included in Alfred W. Pollard
and G.R. Redgrave, *A Short-Title Catalogue of Books Printed in England, Scotland,
& Ireland and of English Books Printed Abroad, 1475–1640*, 3 vols (London,
1977–91). Five reissues (L252A, 1658–64; L252, 1674–5; L252B, 1684–6;
L253, ?1690; and L254, ?1700) are included in Donald Wing, *Short-Title
Catalogue of Books Printed in England, Scotland, Ireland, Wales, and British
America*, 3 vols (New York, 1972–88). In addition, the ballad was included in
Richard Johnson's anthology *The Golden Garland of Princely pleasures and deli-
cate Delights* (1620). All told, the SR entries and the associated printings, plus
the inclusion in Johnson's anthology, add up to at least nine editions before
1700. During the same period the playscript was printed seven times.

4. These and other eye-witness accounts are collected in William Shakespeare,
The Norton Shakespeare, ed. Stephen Greenblatt, Walter Cohen, Jean E.
Howard and Katharine Eisaman Maus (New York, 1997), pp.3334–7. I dis-
cuss the workings of memory in these documents in 'E/loco/com/motion',
in *From Script to Stage in Early Modern England*, ed. Peter Holland and
Stephen Orgel (Basingstoke, 2005), pp.131–50.

5. On Forman see Barbara Traister, *The Notorious Astrological Physician of London: Works and Days of Simon Forman* (Chicago IL, 2001).

6. David Wiles, *Shakespeare's Clown: Actor and Text in the Elizabethan Playhouse* (Cambridge, 1987), pp.144–58.

7. William Shakespeare, *Comedies, Histories, and Tragedies* (London, 1623), sig. Y5.

8. See Peter J. Seng, *The Vocal Songs in the Plays of Shakespeare: A Critical History* (Cambridge MA, 1967), pp.102–3.

9. See Seng, *Vocal Songs*, pp.62–3; Bruce R. Smith, *The Acoustic World of Early Modern England: Attending to the O-Factor* (Chicago IL, 1999), pp.196–8.

10. Philip Sidney, *The Defence of Poesie*, in *Defence of Poesie, Astrophil and Stella, and Other Writings*, ed. Elizabeth Porges Watson (London, 1997), pp.109–10; subsequent references in text.

11. James H. Jones, 'Commonplace and Memorisation in the Oral Tradition of the English and Scottish Popular Ballads', *Journal of American Folklore*, 74 (1961), 97–112.

12. David Buchan, *The Ballad and the Folk* (London, 1972), pp.51–61.

13. *The English and Scottish Popular Ballads*, ed. F.J. Child, 5 vols (1882–98; repr. New York, 1965).

14. Bruce R. Smith, 'Parolles' Recitations: Oral and Literate Structures in Shakespeare's Plays', *Renaissance Papers 1989* (Southeastern Renaissance Conference, 1989), 75–88.

15. Thomas Wright, *The Passions of the Minde in Generall* (London, 1604), sig. D1.

16. Wright, *Passions*, sig. E1ᵛ.

17. Seng, *The Vocal Songs*, p.137; see Stuart Gillespie's discussion of this song, above, pp.187–90.

18. In addition to these instances from *TN, 2H4, MA, Ham* and *KL*, there are 'ballad moments' and 'ballad clusters' to be found in *TS* 4.1, *RJ* 2.2 and 2.4, *LLL* 1.2, *MW* 5.5, *Oth* 4.3, *AW* 1.3 and *WT* 4.3, 4.4.

19. Nick Groom, *The Making of Percy's Reliques* (Oxford, 1999), pp.19–60; Bertram H. Davis, *Thomas Percy: A Scholar-Critic in the Age of Johnson* (Philadelphia PA, 1989), pp.82–119, 154–7.

20. *A Collection of Old Ballads. Corrected from the best and most Ancient COPIES Extant. With Introductions Historical and Critical or Humorous*, 3 vols (London, 1723–5), vol. 1, sig. A3ʳ⁻ᵛ.

21. *A Collection of Old Ballads*, vol. 2, sig. A5ᵛ.

22. See Nick Groom, Introduction to Thomas Percy, *Reliques of Ancient English Poetry*, 3 vols (1765; repr. London, 1996), vol. 1, pp.46–9.

23. *A Collection of Old Ballads*, vol. 2, sig. B6ᵛ.

24. *The Yale Edition of the Works of Samuel Johnson*, vol. 8: *Johnson on Shakespeare*, ed. Arthur Sherbo (New Haven CT, 1968), p.705.

25. *Johnson on Shakespeare*, p.205.
26. Thomas Percy, *Reliques of Ancient English Poetry*, 2 vols (London, 1765), vol. 2, p.211.
27. Percy, *Reliques*, vol. 2, p.225.
28. Joseph Ritson, *Ancient Songs and Ballads* (1790), rev. W. Carew Hazlitt (London, 1877), p.iv.
29. As is pointed our by Groom, *The Making of Percy's Reliques*, p.134.
30. See further Bruce R. Smith, 'Female Impersonation in Early Modern Ballads', in *Women Players in England, 1500–1660*, ed. Pamela Brown and Peter A. Parolin (Aldershot, 2005), pp.284–301.
31. Bert O. States, Hamlet *and the Concept of Character* (Baltimore MD, 1992), p.7.
32. Katharine Craig, 'Shakespeare's *A Lover's Complaint* and Early Modern Criminal Confession', *Shakespeare Quarterly*, 53 (2002), 437–59.
33. Geoffrey Bullough, *Narrative and Dramatic Sources of Shakespeare*, 8 vols (London, 1957–75), vol. 6, pp.11–12; *Titus*, ed. Bate, pp.83–5.
34. Anon., 'The Lamentable and Tragical History of *Titus Andronicus*' (London, 1658–9). Further references and quotations are cited in the text by stanza number.
35. Percy, *Reliques*, vol. 1, p.208.
36. *Catalogue of the Pepys Library at Magdalene College, Cambridge*, ed. Robert Latham, 7 vols (Cambridge, 1978–94), vol. 2, 1:3; *The Pepys Ballads*, ed. W. Gregory Day, facsimile edn, 5 vols (Cambridge, 1987), vol. 1, p.86; vol. 2, pp.184–5.
37. Bullough, vol. 6, pp.11–12.
38. Percy writes: 'not to mention that the stile is less figurative than his others generally are, this tragedy is mentioned with discredit in the Induction to Ben Jonson's BARTHOLOMEW-FAIR', *Reliques*, vol. 1, p.204.
39. William Shakespeare, *The Taming of the Shrew: Texts and Contexts*, ed. Frances Dolan (Boston MA, 1996), pp.208–18.
40. Anon., 'The Frolicksome Duke: Or, The Tinker's good Fortune' (London, [*c*.1690]), stanza 1. Further references and quotations are cited in the text by stanza number.
41. Day, *Pepys Ballads*, vol. 1, pp.144–5.
42. Anon., 'A new song, shewing the crueltie of Gernutus a Iew' (London, 1620), stanzas 35–41. Subsequent references in the text by stanza number.
43. Bullough, *Narrative and Dramatic Sources*, vol. 1, p.449.
44. Percy, *Reliques*, vol. 1, p.211. Percy knew about the earlier play but had not seen it before he published the first edition of *Reliques*.
45. Bullough, *Narrative and Dramatic Sources*, vol. 7, p.402.

46. Anon., 'A Lamentable Song of the death of King LEARE and his three DAVGHTERS', in Richard Johnson, *The Golden Garland of Princely pleasures and delicate Delights* (London, 1620), stanza 22. Subsequent references in the text by stanza number.
47. Percy, *Reliques*, vol. 2, p.219.
48. Johnson, *Works*, vol. 8, p.704; my emphasis.
49. Michael Bristol, *Big-Time Shakespeare* (London, 1996), pp.88–117.
50. Peter Burke, *Popular Culture in Early Modern Europe* (1978; rev. edn Aldershot, 1994), pp.277–8.
51. Essays considering this phenomenon are to be found in *Shakespeare, Film, Fin de Siècle*, ed. Mark Thornton Burnett and Ramona Wray (New York, 2000).

SELECT BIBLIOGRAPHY

WORKS ON MEDIEVAL AND EARLY MODERN POPULAR CULTURE

Bakhtin, Mikhail, *Rabelais and his World*, trans. Hélène Iswolsky (Cambridge MA, 1968)

Barry, Jonathan, and Brooks, Christopher, eds, *The Middling Sort of People: Culture, Society and Politics in England, 1550–1880* (Basingstoke, 1994)

Beadle, Richard, ed., *The Cambridge Companion to Medieval Drama* (Cambridge, 1994)

Bristol, Michael D., *Carnival and Theatre: Plebeian Culture and the Structure of Authority in Renaissance England* (New York, 1985)

——— 'Theater and Popular Culture', in *A New History of Early English Drama*, ed. John D. Cox and David Scott Kastan (New York, 1997), pp.231–48

——— 'Everyday Custom and Popular Culture', in *A Companion to Renaissance Drama*, ed. Arthur F. Kinney (Oxford, 2002), pp.121–34

Brown, Pamela Allen, *Better a Shrew than a Sheep: Women, Drama, and the Culture of Jest in Early Modern England* (Ithaca NY, 2003)

Buchan, David, *The Ballad and the Folk* (London, 1972)

Burke, Peter, *Popular Culture in Early Modern Europe* (London, 1978)

Chambers, E.K., *The English Folk Play* (Oxford, 1933)

Child, F.J., ed., *The English and Scottish Popular Ballads*, 5 vols (1882–98; repr. New York, 1965)

Clopper, Lawrence M., *Drama, Play and Game: English Festive Culture in the Medieval and Early Modern Period* (Chicago IL, 2001)

Crane, Ronald S., *The Vogue of Medieval Chivalric Romance during the English Renaissance* (Menasha WI, 1919)

Cressy, David, *Literacy and the Social Order: Reading and Writing in Tudor and Stuart England* (Cambridge, 1980)

——— *Bonfires and Bells: National Memory and the Protestant Calendar in Elizabethan and Stuart England* (London, 1989)

Davis, Alex, *Chivalry and Romance in the English Renaissance* (Cambridge, 2003)

Davis, Natalie Zemon, 'The Reasons of Misrule: Youth Groups and Charivaris in Sixteenth-Century France', *Past and Present*, 50 (1971), 41–75

——— *Society and Culture in Early Modern France* (Stanford CA, 1975)

Duffy, Eamon, *The Stripping of the Altars: Traditional Religion in England, c.1400–c.1580* (London, 1992)

Edwards, Kathryn A., ed., *Werewolves, Witches and Wandering Spirits: Traditional Belief and Folklore in Early Modern Europe* (Kirksville MO, 2002)

Finucane, R.C., *Ghosts: Appearances of the Dead and Cultural Transformation* (New York, 1996)

Firth, C.H., 'Ballads and Broadsides', in *Shakespeare's England: An Account of the Life and Manners of his Age*, 2 vols (Oxford, 1916), pp.511–38

Fletcher, Antony, and Stevenson, John, eds, *Order and Disorder in Early Modern England* (Cambridge, 1985)

Fox, Adam, *Oral and Literate Culture in England 1500–1700* (Oxford, 2000)

Gardiner, Harold C., SJ, *Mysteries' End: An Investigation of the Last Days of the Medieval Religious Stage* (New Haven CT, 1946)

Harris, Tim, ed., *Popular Culture in England, c.1500–1850* (London, 1995)

Hays, Michael L., 'A Bibliography of Dramatic Adaptations of Medieval Romances and Renaissance Chivalric Romances first available in English through 1616', *Research Opportunities in Renaissance Drama*, 28 (1985), 87–109

Heffernan, Thomas J., *The Popular Literature of Medieval England* (Knoxville TN, 1985)

Jones, James H., 'Commonplace and Memorisation in the Oral Tradition of the English and Scottish Popular Ballads', *Journal of American Folklore*, 74 (1961), 97–112

Marcus, Leah S., *The Politics of Mirth: Jonson, Herrick, Milton, Marvell and the Defense of Old Holiday Pastimes* (Chicago IL, 1986)

Margolies, David, *Novel and Society in Elizabethan England* (London, 1985)

Purkiss, Diane, *The Witch in History* (London, 1996)

—— *Troublesome Things: A History of Fairies and Fairy Stories* (London, 2000)

Putter, Ad, and Gilbert, Jane, eds, *The Spirit of Medieval English Popular Romance* (London, 2000)

Reay, Barry, *Popular Cultures in England, 1550–1750* (New York, 1998)

Rhodes, Neil, *Elizabethan Grotesque* (London, 1980)

Richmond, Velma Bourgeois, *The Legend of Guy of Warwick* (New York, 1996)

Smith, Bruce, *The Acoustic World of Early Modern England: Attending to the O-Factor* (Chicago IL, 1999)

Southworth, John, *Fools and Jesters at the English Court* (Stroud, 1998)

Spufford, Margaret, *Small Books and Pleasant Histories: Popular Fiction and its Readership in Seventeenth-Century England* (London, 1981)

Sullivan, Garrett, and Woodbridge, Linda, 'Popular Culture in Print', in *The Cambridge Companion to English Literature 1500–1600*, ed. Arthur F. Kinney (Cambridge, 2000), pp.265–86

Thomas, Keith, *Religion and the Decline of Magic: Studies in Popular Beliefs in Sixteenth and Seventeenth Century England* (London, 1971)

'The Meaning of Literacy in Early Modern England', in *The Written Word: Literacy in Transition*, ed. Gerd Baumann (Oxford, 1986), pp.97–131

Tilley, Morris Palmer, *A Dictionary of the Proverbs in England in the Sixteenth and Seventeenth Centuries* (Ann Arbor MI, 1950)

Underdown, David, *Revel, Riot, and Rebellion: Popular Politics and Culture in England, 1603–1660* (Oxford, 1985)

Watt, Tessa, *Cheap Print and Popular Piety, 1550–1640* (Cambridge, 1991)

Welsford, Enid, *The Fool: His Social and Literary History* (London, 1935)

Wilson, Stephen, *The Magical Universe: Everyday Ritual and Magic in Pre-Modern Europe* (London, 2000)

Wrightson, Keith, *English Society 1580–1680* (London, 1993)

Würzbach, Natascha, *The Rise of the English Street Ballad, 1550–1650*, trans. Gayna Walls (Cambridge, 1990)

WORKS ON SHAKESPEARE

Barber, C.L., *Shakespeare's Festive Comedy: A Study of Dramatic Form and its Relation to Social Custom* (Princeton NJ, 1959)

Bate, Jonathan, 'Shakespeare's Foolosophy', in *Shakespeare Performed: Essays in Honour of R.A. Foakes*, ed. Grace Ioppolo (Newark DE, 2000), pp.17–32

Davidson, Clifford, '"What hempen home-spuns have we swagg'ring here?" Amateur Actors in *A Midsummer Night's Dream* and the Coventry Civic Plays and Pageants', *Shakespeare Studies*, 19 (1987), 87–99

Dent, R.W., *Shakespeare's Proverbial Language: An Index* (Berkeley CA, 1981)

Duffin, Ross W., *Shakespeare's Songbook* (New York, 2004)

Gillespie, Stuart, *Shakespeare's Books: A Dictionary of Shakespeare Sources* (London, 2001)

Knowles, Ronald, ed., *Shakespeare and Carnival: After Bakhtin* (Basingstoke, 1998)

Lamb, Mary Ellen, 'Taken by the Fairies: Fairy Practices and the Production of Popular Culture in *A Midsummer Night's Dream*', *Shakespeare Quarterly*, 51 (2000), 277–312

―― *The Production of Popular Culture in Shakespeare, Spenser and Jonson* (London, 2004)

Laroque, François, *Shakespeare's Festive World: Elizabethan Seasonal Entertainment and the Professional Stage* (Cambridge, 1991)

Liebler, Naomi Conn, *Shakespeare's Festive Tragedy: The Ritual Foundations of Genre* (London, 1995)

Noble, Richmond, *Shakespeare's Use of Song, with the Text of the Principal Songs* (Oxford, 1923)

Patterson, Annabel, *Shakespeare and the Popular Voice* (Oxford, 1989)

Ruiter, David, *Shakespeare's Festive History: Feasting, Festivity, Fasting and Lent in the Second Henriad* (Aldershot, 2003)

Seng, Peter J., *The Vocal Songs in the Plays of Shakespeare: A Critical History* (Cambridge MA, 1967)

Smith, Bruce, 'Parolles' Recitations: Oral and Literate Structures in Shakespeare's Plays', in *Renaissance Papers 1989* (Columbia SC, 1989), pp.75–88

Wall, Wendy, 'Why does Puck Sweep? Shakespearean Fairies and the Politics of Cleaning', in Wall, *Staging Domesticity: Household Work and English Identity in Early Modern Drama* (Cambridge, 2002), pp.94–126

Weimann, Robert, *Shakespeare and the Popular Tradition in the Theater: Studies in the Social Dimension of Dramatic Form and Function*, ed. Robert Schwartz (Baltimore MD, 1978)

Wiles, David, *Shakespeare's Clown: Actor and Text in the Elizabethan Playhouse* (Cambridge, 1987)

Wilson, F.P., 'Shakespeare and the Diction of Common Life' and 'Shakespeare's Proverbial Wisdom', in *Shakespearian and Other Studies*, ed. Helen Gardner (Oxford, 1969), pp.100–29, 143–75

INDEX

Addison, Joseph 216
The Adventures of Lady Egeria 133
Akenside, Mark 2
alliteration 9, 155–6
almanacs 8
Amadis de Gaule 102–4
angels 32, 138
aphorism 155
Apollonius of Tyre 34
archery 101
Arthurian material 92–102,
      109–11, 122
Aristotle 20, 25, 31, 33
ark, Noah's 30, 33
Armin, Robert 67, 72, 83–5, 196
    Fool upon Fool 72
Ascham, Roger 8
Ash Wednesday 47
Atkinson, Anna 152
Attic tragedy 20
Auden, W.H. 174, 182

Bakhtin, Mikhail 3–7, 50
Balaam and the ass 32
Bale, John 21, 31
ballads
    popular ballads 1, 4, 9–11, 17,
        80, 86, 93–5, 100, 136, 138,
        141, 157, 169, chapter 8,
        chapter 9;
    ballad melodies: 'Fortune my
        foe' 193, 'Why let the stricken
        deer go weep' 68;
    individual popular ballads:
    'Chevy Chase' 4, 198, 200

'The Cruel Mother' 138
'Edward' 198
Robin Hood ballads 186
'The Unquiet Grave' 137–8
Walsingham ballad 187–9, 199
broadside ballads 9, 11, 16, 72,
      93–5, 100–1, 175, 181–4
    chapter 9;
individual broadside ballads:
'Adam Bell, Clym of the Clough,
    and William Cloudesly' 203
'The Frolicksome Duke' 207–8,
    215–16
'Gernutus' 208–13, 215–16
'John Careless' 197
'King Cophetua and the Beggar-
    Maid' 203
'King Leare and his three
    Daughters' 202–4, 207, 214–16
'A Lover's Complaint' 203
'Sir Lancelot du Lake' 100, 197, 203
'Titus Andronicus' 193–9, 205–8,
    213, 215–16
'Tytles of Ballades' 190
See also Percy, Thomas *Reliques of
    Ancient English Poetry*
ballad medley 184
Barber, C.L. 3, 46–8, 54, 57, 178
Barton, Anne 15
Bate, Jonathan 193, 206
bear-baiting 7, 108
beating the bounds 43
Beaumont, Francis
    The Knight of the Burning Pestle 103
Bennett, H.S. 8

Benoît de Sainte-Maure
    Roman de Troie 93
Bergomask 80
Bevis of Hampton 93–4, 105–8,
    111
Bible 1, 8, 18, 21, 36, 158
    Ecclesiastes 63
    1 James 63
    Luke 158–9
    Matthew 158
    Proverbs 162
    Psalms 207
blackface 65–6
Blackfriars theatre 83
bonfires 43, 59
Bowman, John, of Greenhill 152
Boxing Day *see* St Stephen's Day
Bradley, A.C. 192
Braunmuller, A.R. 171
Breton, Nicholas
    Crossing of Proverbs 164
    Soothing of Proverbs 164
A Brief Resolution
Briggs, Katharine 137–8
Bristol, Michael 50, 65, 217
Brown, Sarah Annes 12
Bruegel, Pieter 158, 164–5
Buchan, David 198
Bullough, Geoffrey 14, 97, 116, 206,
    213
Bunyan, John 95
Burgersh of Lincoln, Bishop 152
Burke, Peter 3–4, 11, 82, 217
Burns, Edward 97
Burrell, Arthur 122

cakes and ale 42, 87, 108
Calvinism 18
Candlemas 52
cant terms 100
carols 43, 55, 62

carnival 3, 5, 47, 64, 95, 108
Carnival and Lent 5, 47
Cartmel, old man of 18–20, 22–4
catches 175, 180, 182
Catholicism 5, 21, 25, 45, 48, 50,
    137–8
Caxton, William
    Brut 100
Chamberlain's Men 83–5
Le Chanson de Roland 106
chapbooks 11, 101
Charles I, King of England 49, 54
Chartier, Roger 139
Chaucer, Geoffrey 122, 179
    The Knight's Tale 92
Chrétien de Troyes
    Erec et Enide 99
Christmas 42–3, 48–9, 52–3, 58,
    94
Cicero 25, 28, 156
cliché 157
clowns and clowning 1, 7, 10,
    chapter 3, 184
Coleridge, Samuel Taylor 188
convicts' confessions 205
Cornwallis, Sir William 183
corpses revealing murderers 17,
    153
Corpus Christi, Feast of 20
Corpus Christi Plays *see* Mystery Plays
Cox, Captain 94
Cranmer, Thomas 108
cross-dressing 50, 65–6
Crosse, Henry 21–2
Crucifixion 19, 28, 32, 38
culture, concept of 7

dance 43, 68, 80
Dante Alighieri 28
Danter, John 193, 205
Davis, Natalie Zemon 51

Deloney, Thomas
    A Garland of Good Will 101
devils/demons 28, 32, 53, 59,
        137,147
Dionysus, Festival of 7
Dobin, Howard 99
Don Quixote 104
Donne, John 40
Dorne, John 93
dragons 59, 98
ducking 65
Dugdale, William 26
    The Antiquities of Warwickshire
        95
dumbshow 39

Easter Sunday 137
eclogue 116
Elizabeth I, Queen of England 8, 23,
        74, 94, 100, 108, 109
Epiphany 52
Erasmus 84, 160, 166
    Adagia 159
'Evil May Day' 43
exorcism 148

Fabyan, Robert
    New Chronicles 100, 108
fairies 17, 31, 61, 80, 147, 149, 151–2
Fall, the 27–8
Field of the Cloth of Gold 107
Fletcher, John
    Henry VIII collaboration 108–9
Flood (Genesis) 30
Foakes, R.A. 106, 213
folklore *see* chapter six
folk songs *see* popular song
folk tales
    'The Flying Childer' 153
    'Shrew' story 168–9
fools 7, 65, 75, 83, 101, 116, 184

Forde, Emanuel
    Ornatus and Artesia 133
Forman, Simon 172, 195
formulaic phrasing 92, 155, 197
Fox, Adam 10
Fuller, Thomas 70, 72
Fulwell, Ulpian
    Like Will to Like 159

Geoffrey of Monmouth
    Historia regum Britanniae 96–9,
        199, 202
George, Earl of Shrewsbury 152
ghosts 17, 31, 61, chapter six, 172–3,
        205
giants 59, 106
Gildon, Charles 2
Gillespie, Stuart 116
Globe Theatre 26–7, 83
goblins 147
Good Friday 137
Gosson, Stephen 3
Greenblatt, Stephen 136, 138–9
Greene, Robert 9, 112–13, 122, 129,
        131, 133–5
    The Defence of Conny-Catching 115,
        131
    Greene's Vision 129
    James IV 15
    Mamillia 131
    Never Too Late 114
    Pandosto 112, 116, 119–21, 131–4
    Perimedes the Blacke smith 131
    A Quip for an Upstart Courtier 179
Grettir's Saga 151
groundlings 67–8, 70
guilds 18, 23, 81
Guy of Warwick 32, 93–6, 108–9, 111

Halloween 64
Harrison, William 6

Harris, Tim 70, 139
Helgerson, Richard 84
Herod 24, 34, 39
Heywood, John
    Dialogue of Proverbs 157–161,
        163, 167, 171, 173
Hibbard, G.R. 153
Hill, Christopher 49–5
Holinshed, Raphael 96, 98, 104
    Chronicles 100, 109
Homer 1, 198, 200
    Odyssey 13–14
Horace 25, 69
Howell, James 156
humanism 33–4, 54, 78, 143, 201,
    156
humanist drama 19–20, 36, 39, 80
Huon of Bordeaux 94–5

Inns of Court 52

Jackson, Henry 195
James I, King of England (King James
        VI of Scotland) 23, 56–8
    Basilikon Doron 49
    Book of Sports 49
Jenkins, Harold 37
jest books 8, 74
    Scoggin's Jests 8
    A Hundred Merry Tales 8, 74
jesters 70, 72, 85
jests 9, 68, 74, 77, 82, 169, 208
Jesus Christ 18–21, 28, 30, 33, 35–6,
        38, 149
jigs 4–5, 9, 68, 83–4, 187
Johnson, Richard 122
    The Golden Garland 202, 207, 215
    The Nine Worthies of London 122
    *The Seven Champions of
        Christendom* 122–5
    Tom a Lincoln 116, 122–7

Johnson, Samuel 95, 202–3, 215–16
jokes *see* jests
Jones, Emrys 24–5, 35
Jones, James H. 197
Jones, Robert
    First Booke of Songes and Ayres 181
Jonson, Ben 6, 34, 50, 183
    Bartholomew Fair 16
    The Devil is an Ass 32
Jungen, Gil 217

Kastan, David Scott 110
Kemp, Will 67, 72–3, 76, 83–5, 90
Kenilworth 94
King Arthur 95
King Leir 214
King's Men 49
Kirkman, Francis 95
Kittredge, George Lyman 188
Kyd, Thomas
    The Spanish Tragedy 32, 164

Lamb, Mary Ellen 16, 80, 139
laments 33
Langham, Richard 94
Laroque, François 3, 7, 15
Last Judgement 18, 27–8, 40
Latin language 148, 156, 159
Lavater, Lewes
    *Of Ghostes and Spirites Walking by
        Night* 137
Lent 47
Lévi-Strauss, Claude 16
Liebler, Naomi 54, 57
Lodge, Thomas 9, 121, 125
    Rosalynde 116–19, 128, 132
Lollards 21
Lord, Albert B. 197
Lord of Misrule 43, 47–8, 56
Lucian
    Dialogue of Timon 14

Lucifer 18, 32, 35
Lupton, Thomas
    All For Money 159
Luther, Martin 150
Lyly, John
    Euphues 113, 129, 131

Magi 28
Maid Marion 43
Malory, Thomas 8
Manningham, John 195
Marcus, Leah S. 15
Mardi Gras *see* Shrove Tuesday
Marlowe, Christopher 6, 50, 133, 136
    Doctor Faustus 30, 32, 115, 150
    Edward II 32
    'The Passionate Shepherd' 203
    Tamburlaine 5, 20, 29, 100, 115
Marston, John
    Antonio's Revenge 138
Mary I, Queen of England 23
Massacre of the Innocents *see*
    Slaughter of the Innocents
May Day and Maying 42–8, 50, 57,
    59– 64
May dew 60
Maypoles 43, 48
Merlin 98–100
Midsummer 43, 58–64
Milton, John 136
    Comus 150
    L'Allegro 45
misrule 47, 51, 53, 60, 64
morality plays 20, 32
morris dancing 7, 23, 42, 57, 59,
    72–3
Mucedorus 15
mumming and mummers' plays 7–8,
    43, 50, 95
Munday, Anthony 102
Muir, Kenneth 116

A Myrroure for Magistrates 96, 98,
    205
mystery plays 7, 10, chapter one
    individual plays:
        Chester *Shepherds' Play* 34
        Coventry Doomsday play 40
        Crucifixion plays 38
        Digby *Burial of Christ* 35
        Digby *Mary Magdalen* 29
        Towneley *Buffeting* 35
        Towneley *Second Shepherds Play* 33
    cycles:
        Corpus Christi cycles 21
        Coventry Cycle 81
        Kendall Cycle 23
        Midland Cycle 23
        Northern Cycle 23
        N-town Cycle 29, 31, 35
    groups of plays:
        Chester plays 23
        Passion plays 23

Nashe, Thomas 94, 113, 131
Neville, Alexander
    Oedipus tr. 37–8
New Historicism 3, 10, 25, 139
Northbrooke, John 21–2
Nosworthy, J.M. 180

old wives' tales 80
Ovid 34, 78, 169
    Metamorphoses 12, 14

pageants 47, 59
pageant wagons 23, 26
Palmerin 102–3
Palmer, Samuel 162
pamphlets 136, 138, 140–1, 143
Parker, Patricia 12
parody 184
Parrot, Henry 94

Parry, Milman 197
Passion of Christ 28, 35, 36
Past and Present 3
Patterson, Annabel 3
Peele, George
    Battle of Alcazar 100
    Old Wives Tale 30–1
    Titus Andronicus 164
Pepys, Samuel 207–8, 213
Percy, Thomas
    Reliques of Ancient English Poetry
        195, 200–1, 207, 213–14
The Pilgrimage to Parnassus 69
Pity, Our Lady of 35
Plato 150
Plautus 24, 34
play within a play 39, 77, 79, 81,
    89–90
Plutarch 12, 104, 122
    Lives 14
popular fiction 8–9, chapter 5
popular song 68, 156, chapter 8
    individual songs:
    Coventry Carol 33
    'Farewell, dear heart' 180–2
    'Hold thy peace, thou knave'
        180–1, 196
    'O mistress mine' 180–1, 196
    'O' the twelfth day of December'
        180–2, 196
    'Robin Hood and the jolly pinder of
        Wakefield' 197
    'Take thy old cloak about thee'
        203
    'There dwelt a man in Babylon,
        lady, lady' 196, 203
    'Three blind mice' 175
    'Three merry men be we' 180–1,
        196
private theatres 4–5
prodigal son 159

Protestantism 21, 25, 48–50, 137–8,
    148, 150
proverbs *see* sayings
Purgatory 138
Puritanism and the Puritans 20, 41,
    45, 48–54, 57, 62, 137, 183
Purkiss, Diane 17
Puttenham, George 4
    The Arte of English Poesie 93–4

Queen's Players 72
Quintilian 156

Ralegh, Sir Walter 187
    'The Nymph's Reply' 203
    Walsingham ballad 187–8
Reay, Barry 10–11, 142
Reformation, the 20–1, 23, 25, 41,
    136, 141, 144–5
revenants 147, 150–1
Revesby Play 7
rhyme 9, 156, 160–1
Ritson, Joseph 204
Robert the Devil 93
Robin Hood 15, 43, 62, 186, 197
Robin Hood plays 7
Rogation Sunday 43
rogue literature 8
Roman new comedy 69
romance 8–9, 17, chapter 4
Rowley, William
rough music *see* Skimmington
Rubin, Miri 139

St George 7–8
St Stephen's Day 55–6
Saker, Austin
    Narbonus 133
sayings 1, 9–10, 56, 101–2,
    chapter 7
Scandinavian ideas about death 151

Seneca, Lucius Annaeus, the Younger
          12, 19, 24, 34, 37–9, 137–9,
          146–7
     Epistles 159
Seng, Peter 182, 186, 188, 197
Southworth, John 74
Shakespeare, William
     songs in:
     'And will a' not come again?' (*Ham*)
          185
     'By Gis and by Saint Charity'
          (*Ham*) 185–6
     'Childe Rowlande to the dark
          tower came' (*KL*) 106, 199
     'Come away, death' (*TN*) 174,
          180
     'Crabbed age and youth / Cannot
          live together' (*Passionate
          Pilgrim*) 203
     'For bonny sweet Robin' (*Ham*)
          185–6
     'The god of love / That sits above'
          (*MA*) 197
     Gravedigger's song (*Ham*) 203
     'How should I your true love
          know' (*Ham*) 185, 187–9
     'Sigh no more, ladies' (*MA*) 175
     'Take, oh take, those lips away'
          (*MM*) 203
     'They bore him barefac'd on the
          bier' (*Ham*) 185
     'When Arthur first in court' (*2H4*)
          196
     'When daisies pied and violets
          blue' (*LLL*) 177
     'Where griping griefs the hart
          would wound' (*RJ*) 203
     'The Willow Song' (*Oth*) 190–2,
          203–4
     'The wind and the rain' (*TN*)
          182

     works:
     All's Well that Ends Well 75, 129,
          167–8
     Antony and Cleopatra 12
     As You Like It 15, 33, 60, 62–3,
          65, 83, 116, 128, 129, 133,
          162, 166–7, 177
     The Comedy of Errors 34, 69
     Coriolanus 6, 166
     Cymbeline 116, 124, 138, 145–6,
          154
     Hamlet 11, 24, 32, 36–7, 39,
          67–8, 70, 74, 91, 116, 122,
          125–7, 136–9, 143, 146–54,
          157, 161, 175, 180, 183–90,
          199, 203, 205
     1 Henry IV 27, 47, 87–90, 95,
          97–100, 103, 162, 164–6,
          175
     2 Henry IV 27, 47, 87–8, 95, 100,
          106, 175, 196–7, 203
     Henry V 27, 35, 39–40, 95,
          109–10
     1 Henry VI 27, 30, 96–7, 100,
          105, 111
     2 Henry VI 27, 30, 42, 51
     3 Henry VI 27, 30, 36, 157
     Henry VIII 32, 95, 106–8, 110
     Julius Caesar 104, 138, 144–5
     King Lear 35, 38–9, 54–6, 58, 85,
          95–6, 98–100, 104–6, 113,
          168, 175, 184–5, 194,
          199–200, 202–5, 214–17
     Love's Labours Lost 77, 85, 95,
          101–4, 177–9, 203
     Macbeth 32, 35, 60, 63–4, 137,
          143–4, 146, 161–2, 171–3,
          195
     Measure for Measure 129, 167, 203
     The Merchant of Venice 15, 134–5,
          166, 194, 203–5, 208–13

The Merry Wives of Windsor 64–5, 159, 203

A Midsummer Night's Dream 12, 32, 59–62, 78–82

Much Ado About Nothing 74, 76, 129, 163, 175, 197, 203

Othello 30, 33, 36, 65–6, 163–4, 166, 184, 190–2, 203–4

Pericles 29–30, 34, 125, 129

The Rape of Lucrece 159

Richard II 30–1, 35

Richard III 28, 35–6, 128, 143–4, 146

Romeo and Juliet 175, 203

Sonnets 161

The Taming of the Shrew 76–7, 129–31, 162, 168–71, 194, 203–5, 207–8, 215–17

The Tempest 15, 33, 40

Timon of Athens 14–15

Titus Andronicus 31, 34–6, 164, 193–4, 203–7, 217

Troilus and Cressida 30

Twelfth Night 42, 49, 52–5, 59, 62, 75, 86–7, 174–6, 180–3, 185, 196, 203

The Two Gentlemen of Verona 128–30

The Winter's Tale 12–5, 45–6, 58, 86, 112, 116, 119–21, 131–2, 184, 195, 204

shaming rituals 43–5, 64

Shaw, John 18, 23

sheep-shearing festivals 43, 45, 58, 121

Shrewsbury, George, Earl of 152

Shrove Tuesday 47, 64

Sidney, Sir Philip 4, 121
    godfather to Tarlton's child 72
    An Apology for Poetry 28–30
    Arcadia 92, 113

A Defence of Poesie 69–70, 197–8, 200

Sir Eglamour 93

Sir Orfeo 151

Skimmington 43–4, 64–6

Slaughter of the Innocents 28, 32–3, 35

Smith, Bruce R. 10, 181–2, 198

Smith, Sir Thomas 6

Spanish chivalric romance 95, 102

speech act theory 9

Spenser, Edmund
    The Faerie Queene 15–6, 92
    The Shepherd's Calendar 179

Spufford, Margaret 93

The Squire of Low Degree 94, 110

Stafford, Symon 190

States, Bert O. 205

storytelling 9, 138, 140–1

Stow, John
    Summarie of the Chronicles of Englande 109

Strange, Ferdinando, Lord 33

Stratford-upon-Avon 45

Strohm, Paul 92

Stubbes, Philip 48, 50, 53, 59

table-books 9, 74

The Taming of a Shrew

Tarlton, Richard 67, 70–2, 74–5, 85

Tate, Nahum 215–16

Taymor, Julie 217

Ten Things I Hate About You 217

Thistelton-Dyer, Thomas F. 151

Tilley, Morris Palmer 167

Twelfth Night 52

Tyburn executions 32

Ur-Hamlet 125

Uther Pendragon 95

Vergil, Polydore
    Anglicae Historiae 100
Vice, the 87, 128

Wager, William
    Enough is as Good as a Feast
    159
    The Longer Thou Livest the More
    Fool Thou Art 159
Wallace, David 81
Warton, Thomas 216–17
Watt, Tessa 93
Webster, John
    The Displaying of Supposed
    Witchcraft 153
Weimann, Robert 3, 5
West, Robert 137

Whetstone, George 69
Whiting, Helen Wescott 167
Whitsuntide 43
'Wildman in the forest' 15
Wiles, David 68
Wilson, John Dover 137–8, 148
witchcraft trials 147
witches 61, 63, 149, 151–2
wodewose 15
Woudhuysen, Henry 102
Wright, Thomas
    The Passions of the Mind in Generall
    198
Wyatt, Sir Thomas 23
Wydeville, Anthony
    The Dictes or Sayengis of the
    Philosophres 157